A Biblical Theology of Hebrews

A Biblical Theology of Hebrews

DOUGLAS W. KENNARD

WIPF & STOCK · Eugene, Oregon

A BIBLICAL THEOLOGY OF HEBREWS

Copyright © 2018 Douglas W. Kennard. All rights reserved. Except for brief quotations in critical publications or reviews, no part of this book may be reproduced in any manner without prior written permission from the publisher. Write: Permissions, Wipf and Stock Publishers, 199 W. 8th Ave., Suite 3, Eugene, OR 97401.

Wipf & Stock
An Imprint of Wipf and Stock Publishers
199 W. 8th Ave., Suite 3
Eugene, OR 97401

www.wipfandstock.com

PAPERBACK ISBN: 978-1-5326-6456-4
HARDCOVER ISBN: 978-1-5326-6457-1
EBOOK ISBN: 978-1-5326-6458-8

Manufactured in the U.S.A.   11/26/18

This book is dedicated to
My students from diverse Christian traditions.

Contents

1. Introduction | 1

2. God | 5

3. Spokesman for God | 9

4. Hebrews's Epistemology of Prophecy as Rhetorical Proclamation that Christ is Supreme | 12

5. Christ as God-King, Superior to Angels | 20

6. Apostle Jesus, More Glorious than Moses | 29

7. Melchizedek Priest | 36

8. The Law and the New Covenant | 52

9. Christ's New Covenant Atonement | 66

10. The Narrow Exodus Way of Faith to Salvation | 106

11. Warnings in Hebrews | 120

12. Final Letter Features | 136

   Bibliography | 143

1

Introduction

THE AUTHOR OF THE book of Hebrews is unknown. The book does not identify the author. The early church is familiar with the book and is encouraged by its spiritual content and high Christology.[1] Pauline authorship was claimed by early patristics.[2] For example, the author knows Timothy as a mature and equal minister, perhaps after Paul's death, and plans to travel with him (Heb 13:23[3]). However, it was recognized early on that the vocabulary and style do not fit Paul's other writings.[4] Others authors have been suggested, including Barnabus,[5] Apollos,[6] Silas,[7] Luke,[8] Aquila,[9] and Priscilla.[10] Origin claimed that it was not written by Paul, and that only God knows the author.[11]

---

1. Clement of Rome, *Cor.* 12 with Heb 1:3–4; Herm. Vis. 2.3.2 with Heb 3:12; Herm. Sim. 1.1–2 with Heb 11:13–15 and 13:14; Justin, *1 Apol.* 12.63 with Heb 3:1 and *Dial.* 96.113 with Heb 1:13; 5:6; 7:17, 21.

2. Clement of Alexandria claimed by Eusebius, *Hist. eccl.* 6.14.4; Athanasius, *Apol. sec.* 1.4.12; 1.36; 2.48; Gregory of Nazianzus, *Or. Bas.* 38.1; Cyril Jerusalem, *Cat. Lect.* 12.17.

3. Unless otherwise noted, all Scripture citations are from the author's translation.

4. Eusebius, *Hist. eccl.* 6.14.2; Jerome, *Epist.* 129.

5. Tertulian and those around him, *Pud.* 20.

6. Luther, *Hebrews*, 35.

7. Mynster, "Unstersuchung," in *Kleine theologische Schriften*, 91–140.

8. Allen, "Lukan Authorship," 1–22.

9. Bleek, *Der Brief an die Hebräer*, 1:420–22.

10. D'Angelo, *Letter to the Hebrews*, 364–65.

11. Origen quoted by Eusebius, *Hist. eccl.* 6.25.11–14.

With Hebrews likely composed by a unique and unknown author, a biblical theology of the book will best stand on its own without connecting it as from other NT authors.[12]

The book is written to Jewish Christians. The title "to the Hebrews" was affixed to the book before the end of the second century, much like several NT letters had titles added.[13] Hartwig Thyen maintained that Hebrews was similarly positioned as a Jewish-Christian homily with several other volumes of its era.[14] Old Testament citations and allusions permeate the book, implying that the readership has familiarity with them, but with a high Christology of Jesus' deity. The temptation for the readers in the book is to depart from Christ and return to disobedience under the Mosaic law and Judaism (Heb 2:2–4; 3:7—4:13; 10:26–31). This temptation is not what gentile Christians were dealing with in the first century so they do not seem to be the primary audience.

The closing of Hebrews expressed the standard features for letter form,[15] namely, final exhortations (Heb 13:1–19, 22–23), benedictions or blessings (Heb 13:20–21, 25), the plan to visit recipients (Heb 13:23), and greetings (Heb 13:24). The plan to visit might localize the intended original audience to a particular location familiar to Timothy (but not Ephesus, where Timothy had a prolonged ministry). The greetings identify that the author is with a group who had exited *from* (ἀπὸ) Italy,[16] and they greet the readers, probably indicating that the author writes from somewhere other than Italy (Heb 13:24). Might this hint that the author writes to somewhere in Italy? One cannot say definitely. None of the standard letter form features were found in the introduction to the book.

It is difficult to determine the intended location and time of the Jewish-Christian readership of the book. The fact that the author develops a tabernacle instead of the Jerusalem temple (Heb 9:1–10) probably indicates that the book is composed to dispersion Jews. The fact that the LXX

---

12. Lindars, *Letter to the Hebrews*; MacLeod, "Epistle to the Hebrews"; Milligan, *Epistle to the Hebrews*.

13. Romans and the Corinthians epistles also have the same superscription phenomena occur; Lane, *Hebrews 1–8*, lxix; Koester, *Hebrews*, 46.

14. Thyen, *Der Stil des jüdish-hellenistischen Homile*; similar to: 1 Clem.; parts of 1 Macc; parts of 3 Macc; 4 Macc; Did.; Barn.; Herm. Sim.; parts of Tob.; Wis.

15. O'Brien, "Letters, Letter Forms," 551; Deismann, *Light from the Ancient East*; Francis, "Form and Function," 117; Klauck, *Ancient Letters*.

16. ἀπὸ usually indicates "from," as in no longer there (Matt 21:11; Mark 15:43; John 1:44; 21:2; Acts 6:9; 21:27; 24:18).

is amply utilized and modified for quoting the OT further supports that the original readers are among dispersion Jews. The fact that there is no mention of the temple having been destroyed probably also indicates that the book is composed before the destruction of the Jerusalem temple in 70 AD, because to mention such a destruction would have aided the argument in the book for the obsolescence of the Mosaic covenant and the initiation of the new covenant with Christ's atonement.

Many take the dominant theme of the book to be the superiority of Christ.[17] The word κρείττων ("much better") occurs thirteen times in the book, but the *superiority* is more diversified than Christ, so it is better to see its use as part of the method of argument through the book than as a center.[18] That is, Christ is superior to angels (Heb 1:4), the believer has a better salvation than damnation (Heb 6:9), Melchizedek is spiritually superior to Abraham (Heb 7:7), and Christ as a Melchizedek priest obtains better covenant access and atonement with God than the law (Heb 7:19, 22; 8:6; 9:23; 12:24), enabling the believer to obtain a better inheritance (Heb 10:34; 11:16) and better resurrection (Heb 11:35, 40).

Instead of developing a logical order for analysis, the themes that the book focuses on will set the order of development for a summary of Hebrews' biblical theology. Hebrews assumes a Jewish monotheistic idea of God with the addition of Jesus Christ as a second divine power within the Godhead. Prophets spoke for God, but that era had ended. Extending Qumran covenanters' view, a new Messianic prophet, Jesus Christ—who is the exact radiance of God—speaks for God, but oddly Christ doesn't speak much in Hebrews.

OT passages are appropriated from corporate memory through a *pesher* for Jesus' superior roles and to establish a *midrash* of a new exodus journey. Hillel's hermeneutical rules provide guidelines for this exodus *midrash*. Lockean empirical confirmation of the gospel is provided by miraculous supernatural verification providing experiential ownership and filial knowledge of God. Hebrews does not work within Platonism, but within a Jewish *merkabah* mysticism of both earth and heaven as real. Christ's

---

17. Hagen, *Theology of Testament*, 31–55; MacLeod, "Epistle to the Hebrews," 225–53; MacLeod, "Doctrinal Center of Hebrews," 291–300.

18. Watson, "Rhetorical Criticism of Hebrews," 184–87; Koester (*Hebrews*, 181) appeals to similarities among Philippians 2:9–10, Colossians 1:15–18, Ephesians 1:21, and 1 Peter 3:22. Kennard's biblical theology methodology argues for each theme to be developed (Kennard, "Reef of the O.T.," 227–57; Kennard, *Critical Realist's Theological Method*, 249–76).

atonement further provides a Peircian pragmatic verification principle through an Edwardsian religious affection of a cleansed conscience.

Christ is superior to Jewish imagery. In contrast to Jewish development of angels as actors under God, Hebrews presents Jesus as the exact representation of God in a Jewish two-powers configuration as Creator, Sovereign, and Davidic King ruling in a phase of the present kingdom with a greater era of the kingdom to come, to be brought about by the Father. Additionally, Jesus as an apostle over the house of Israel on a new exodus is a more glorious focus for believers than Moses, who serves within the house during the exodus from Egypt. Furthermore, extending beyond the deficiencies of Levitical priesthood, Jesus becomes a Melchizedek king-priest through God's choice. This choice is demonstrated as appropriate based on examining Jesus' unimpeachable life, and effective prayers for his resurrection and believers' salvation. Jesus' new covenant atonement provides cleansing to the heavenly temple and forgiveness to all believers.

The Mosaic law given through angels is superseded by the new covenant because internal transformation to believe and obey with a cleansed conscience was not accomplished by the obsolete law, but is accomplished through Jesus Christ and the new covenant. Christ's communal atonement, as in the Day of Atonement, cleanses and ransoms the heavenly sanctuary and forgives the people. Through Isaiah 53, Jeremiah 31, and Qumran, hope for atonement is accomplished by the Messiah in a manner that internally transforms the believer to have a cleansed conscience and everlasting forgiveness.

God sets Jewish Christians on an exodus with Christ, as apostle and king, leading the way. Continuing the narrow exodus, Jewish Christians need to cultivate faithfulness unto kingdom salvation. Psalms 95:7–10 provides a *midrash* to exhort Jewish Christians not to rebel as Israel had done, and instead by faith enter sacred rest, which primarily conveys an eschatological kingdom, but also encroaches into present time as well. Witnesses testify by their persistent faith that the believer can follow them and Christ into God's heavenly city. Allowing Hebrews' use of terms to determine meaning presents the warnings within a two-way salvation framework in which the narrow exodus way must be continued in faith with Christ and the new covenant.

2

God

BARNABUS LINDARS IDENTIFIES THAT "Hebrews takes for granted the monotheistic idea of God common to Judaism and earliest Christianity."[1]

Hebrews primarily utilized θεὸς to refer to the divine presence (68 times, Heb 1:1, 9; 8:10; 10:7, 31). This is the normal LXX translation of *Elohim* (Heb 1:9), conveying "power" (Heb 1:3 as in all power to uphold the creation) and heavenly "preeminence" (Heb 1:3 as the majesty on high on the divine throne, Heb 8:1; 12:2).[2] As such, God is described as the great "Majesty on high" (Heb 1:3; 8:3) or the "Most High God" (Heb 7:1, which connects with the Melchizedek narrative; Gen 14:22). The title of θεὸς is mentioned four times as the "living God," half of which emphasize God's severity to judge the disobedient, and the other references include God's active cleansing of believer's conscience and vibrant residence within the new Jerusalem (Heb 3:12; 9:14; 10:31; 12:22). Such roles for the living God reflect the prophets' use of the term in contexts where they identify him as challenged and able to judge (Isa 37:4, 17; Jer 10:10; 23:36) and the sovereign creative sustainer of all life, especially his people (Jer 17:13; Dan 6:20, 26; Hos 1:10). The transcendence of God also develops his role as judge by the use of the phrase "Father of the spirits" (Heb 12:9).[3]

With such an OT emphasis in Hebrews, the dominant Hebrew name for God, *Yahweh*, gets only a brief cover by the LXX translation κύριος (Heb

---

1. Lindars, *Letter to the Hebrews*, xi.
2. Quell, "B. El and Elohim in the OT," 84–86.
3. 1QS 3.25; 2 Macc 3:24–25; 1 En. 37–71.

7:21; 8:8, 10; 10:30). This shift is odd since "Yahweh" occurs five times as often as "Elohim" in the OT, and it only makes up about six percent of divine instances in the book of Hebrews, with most of these references referring to Christ. Furthermore, the memorial name "Yahweh" sets up the dominant theme of the presence of the LORD traveling with Israel to facilitate the exodus and bring them into the promised land (Exod 3:14–15). Such an exodus theme is strongly developed in Hebrews, but the meaning of "*Yahweh* as the present one to help"[4] is absent, leaving κύριος to largely emphasize Jesus' kingship (Heb 1:10; 2:3; 7:14; 13:20) and God as covenant facilitator and obligator (Heb 7:14; 8:8, 10; 10:30).

When God is referenced in relationship to the Son Jesus Christ, the title of "Father" appears as describing God Who ordains the Son (Heb 1:5) and rules over the spirits (Heb 12:7; possibly 1:6).

More technically, with Jewish divinity assumed, the author for Hebrews puts his emphasis on the supremacy of Christ over all other aspects of Judaism, consistent with the Jewish two-powers heresy.[5] So, the Trinity is rather undeveloped in Hebrews, but the divinity of the Son is one theme to support the supremacy of Christ. This subject will be developed further within the chapter discussing that and Christ's kingship.

God created the world, including his stopping and establishing sacred time of Sabbath rest as a kingdom metaphor (Heb 11:3; 4:3–4; Gen 2:1–3). Such creation is accomplished by the "word" (ῥήματι) of God, which may be more reminiscent of revelation in divine speech, as in Genesis 1:6, 9, 14, 20, 24, 26, 29, than a Johannine conception of the "Word" (λόγος) as the incarnate Christ (John 1:1–14; 1 John 1:1). This idea of divine speech is further supported by Christ sustaining and possibly creating the universe by using his spoken "word" (ῥήματι, Heb 1:3). The methodology of both divine persons using the spoken word is the same, even if what each accomplished may not be (Heb 1:3; 11:3).

God speaks beyond creation to cultivate his people and his Son (Heb 1:1, 5, 13). This speech provides an avenue of divine engagement, including promising and establishing a blessing through an oath to Abraham that provides everlasting security (Heb 6:13–19). Divine speech was carried

---

4. That is, if one understands the "Yahweh" in Exodus 3:14–15 as a *qal* Hebrew verb, though it could also grammatically be a *hiphil* verb, promising Yahweh's presence to deliver from any future need.

5. Segal, *Two Powers in Heaven*.

through angels into the Mosaic law (Heb 2:2; Acts 7:38, 53; Gal 3:19).[6] This statement of law further develops as divine speech through the prophets (Heb 1:1). Such a venue of divine speech expressed the will of God (Heb 10:7, 9–10, 36; 13:21).

God called out and cultivated his people Israel (Heb 3:4; 11:25). God led Israel's exodus out of Egypt (Heb 3:16). The exodus theme in Hebrews reiterates God's involvement in history. Attridge identifies three events of God interacting with Israel from the exodus story that Hebrews relates:

> (a) That God revealed to Moses a model or "type" of earthly sanctuary (Heb 8:5; citing Exod 25:40), (b) that Moses inaugurated the covenant with sprinkling of blood (Heb 9:18–22, citing Exod 24:8), and (c) that at Sinai a fearsome theophany accompanied the delivery of the Law (Heb 12:18–21).[7]

Ultimately, God develops a kingdom city, to which the congregation charts their exodus course (Heb 11:10, 40; 12:22; 13:14).

The prophetic role presents God as angry to all disobedience and unbelief that stand in the way of the community entering kingdom rest (Heb 3:17—4:3, 5–6; 10:30–31; 12:29). So God as judge holds humans accountable for their work and love (Heb 4:13; 6:10; 12:23). For example, Enoch is mentioned as an illustration of God's pleasure with a man of faith (Heb 11:5). So, there are repeat exhortations to draw near to God in hope and worship (Heb 7:19; 13:15).

This whole narrative history is seen through the lens of early Jewish Pharisaic development of resurrection.[8] As such, Abraham is viewed as potentially trusting God to resurrect his son Isaac if he kills him in sacrifice as God demanded (Hebrews 11:19 reflects the confidence that the Lord will provide in Genesis 22:8, similar to Lazarus' resurrection in John 11:43).

God speaks through the Son in the process of incarnation and ordination (Heb 1:6). God called Jesus Christ into a priesthood within the things of God (Heb 2:17; 5:1, 4, 12). With Jesus' new leadership, God cultivates a new congregation affiliated with Jesus, mirroring Israel in the exodus (Heb 2:13). God provides gracious atonement before God, identifying God as

---

6. Jub. 2.17–19; CD 5.18; Josephus, *Ant.* 15.136; Sifre Num 102; Mek. Exod 20.18; Pesiq. Rab. 21.

7. Attridge, "God in Hebrews," 101.

8. Pesiq. Rab Kah. 9.4; 1 En. 62.14–15 identify that when the Son of Man resurrects, the elect will resurrect also.

the God of peace (Heb 2:9; 9:14; 13:20). After this reconciliation and atonement, Jesus is elevated in honor to the right hand of God (Heb 10:12).

The development of the Holy Spirit is brief in the book. The first issue is that the Holy Spirit reveals OT Scripture (Heb 3:7–11; 9:1–8 recounting of Exod 25–40; Heb 10:15–17, probably 10:29; probably 6:4).[9] In Hebrews 8:8 and 10:16, "the Lord" reveals the Jeremiah 31 quote, whereas in Hebrews 10:16–17 a subsection of this quote is revealed by "the Holy Spirit" (Heb 10:15). This comparison likely indicates an undeveloped Trinitarianism, in which the Holy Spirit is also God (Heb 8:8; 10:15–16). The Holy Spirit also provides divine sign gifts to evidentially support the gospel message communicated (Heb 2:4; probably 6:4). Furthermore, the Holy Spirit provides new covenant cleansing of the Christian's conscience (Heb 9:14). This last ministry begins with the death of Christ, but it is facilitated by the Holy Spirit, who is described as everlasting (Heb 9:14), and thus continues to fund the cleansing without end. All three of these ministries of the Spirit are gracious giving of either Scripture, evidence, or cleansing (Heb 10:29). To deny either of these ministries is to insult the Spirit of grace (Heb 10:29).[10] So, Hebrews has a rather limited development of Holy Spirit ministries when compared to John, Paul, or Luke. In Hebrews, the Holy Spirit is a supportive divine person providing revelation, confirming evidential signs, and cleansing conscience.

Ultimately, God is revealed as "judge of all" (Heb 12:23), and to fall into God's judgment is a fearsome thing (Heb 10:31). The severity of divine judgment is funded by the ominous citation "Vengeance is mine, I will repay" (Heb 10:30, citing Deut 32:35[11]). No one will be excluded from divine judgment when God "will shake the earth and the heaven" (Heb 12:26, citing Hag 2:6,[12] 21). The warnings in Hebrews are founded in this perspective.

---

9. These patristics also support the same epistemic diligence that the prophets operated under inspiration (Ign. *Magn.* 8.2; Barn. 5.6; Herm. Sim. 9.12.1–2; 2 Clem. 17.4; Justin, *1 Apol.* 31–53; 62.4; Justin, *Dial.* 56–7; Irenaeus, *Haer.* 4.20.4; Origen, *Princ.* 3.12).

10. Similar to Josephus' identifying God's command being insulted through practical denial (*Ant.* 20.117).

11. Howard ("Hebrews and the Old Testament Quotations," 210) identified that the quote was neither similar to MT (Masoretic Text) nor LXX, but with one possible LXX influence.

12. Howard, ("Hebrews and the Old Testament Quotations," 210) identified that the quote was neither similar to MT nor LXX but with some LXX influence.

3

Spokesman for God

DEUTERONOMY 18 IDENTIFIED THAT, following Moses, there will be a prophetic lineage. So, Moses becomes a witness of both the pattern and the prophesying concerning a messiah to come (Heb 3:5; John 5:39–47). Instead of the illegitimate ways of divining the future, God promised to raise up a Jewish prophet like Moses as a mediator between God and Israel (Deut 18:15–22).[1] The prophetic pattern shows that this prophet will: 1) speak the divine message (Heb 1:1), 2) be consistent with Moses' teaching, 3) teach in Yahweh's name, and 4) be fully accurate with predictive comments and corroboration in real events that come to pass. Prophecy must then include prediction of future events along with Mosaic consistency, corroborative evidence, and exhortation. The fact that there is discussion about presumptuous prophets shows that the expectation of Deuteronomy 18:15–22 was a series of prophets in Moses' and likely Samuel's lineage (Heb 11:32). Based on the quotes in the book of Hebrews, this lineage especially includes David and Jeremiah. God spoke to the fathers of Israel in many ways through the prophets (Heb 1:1; five words in Greek that begin with a "p" sound emphasize the variety of prophetic speech). The following discussion concerning the epistemology and use of *pesher* in Hebrews showcases part of these many ways.

Isaiah spoke of a prophetic "servant of Yahweh" who would be Spirit-empowered to bring justice through the law and proclamation of God's message of release from bondage through Jubilee (Isa 42:1–4; 61:1–3).

---

1. Echoed in 4Q175 1.5–8.

Jewish tradition includes a ministry of miracle-working and healing as within this role that goes beyond previous prophets (Isa 53:4; 61:1–3; Matt 8:17; Luke 4:18).[2] This empowered servant would not be overly boisterous, but will gently accomplish this goal. He will be called by God from the womb as a chosen and effective weapon from God's quiver, trusting that God would provide justice (Isa 49:1–4). One of the chosen roles of this servant of the Lord is to gather Israel back into the land with a new exodus and national redemption (Isa 40:1–11; 49:5–13; similar to Yahweh's use of Cyrus in Isa 44:24—45:6). Part of the Servant's tools would be effective listening to God and speaking that which brings real comfort (Isa 50:4–5). Isaiah also describes the unfortunate rejection and abuse that this prophet would undergo (Isa 50:6–11; 53:1–12). Yet God guarantees his effectiveness and honor.

With the closure of Malachi and Daniel, there was no continuing writing prophet lineage. Hebrews joins the Maccabees in considering that prophecy had ceased and that they were in a different era of God's work (Heb 1:1).[3] This lack of prophecy was evident, in 1 Maccabees 4.46, where Judas and his companions stored the stones of the defiled altar "until a prophet should come to tell them what to do with them." Likewise, Simon was appointed leader and high priest "until a trustworthy prophet should arise."[4] So the closure of the prophetic movement meant that there was no longer a prophet to speak for God.

Some early Jewish groups believed that there would be the arrival of a messianic prophet like Moses, who would lead a new exodus out of bondage and reestablish the Mosaic covenant with a more accurate interpretation of the law.[5] For example, the Qumran community saw Moses as the premiere historical figure and showed their allegiance by obeying the Torah stringently, which they perceived that the rest of Israel had failed to do.[6] The Qumran community expected an eschatological prophet like Moses, as the *Rule of the Community* 9:9–11 makes clear, and so the primary role of the

---

2. Josephus, *Ant.* 20.167–72; b. Yebam. 121b.

3. 1 Macc 9.27; Ps 74:9; 2 Bar. 81.1, 3; 85.3; Pr Azar 15; m. 'Abot. 1.1; b. Yoma. 9b.

4. 1 Macc 14.41.

5. 1 Macc 14.41; 44.4–46; 1QS 8:13–16; 9:11; 4Q175 5–8; CD 1:4–11; 6:2–11; 4Q394 92–93; Philo, *Spec. Laws* 1.65; Josephus, *Ant.* 20.5.1; Scott, *Customs and Controversies*, 318n35–36; Volz, *Die Eschatologie*.

6. 1QS 1:1–11; 6:6–8; 4Q175 93–118; CD 15:7–15.

Spokesman for God

Qumran covenanters was to maintain this teaching until this final spokesman should arise to speak for God.

Hebrews identified in these last days of present eschatological[7] living that God has spoken again through his Son, as divine creator and ruler of the world (Heb 1:2). Such speaking for God confirms that Jesus Christ is consistent in role and climactic beyond the prophets who spoke for God previously because Jesus is also God (Heb 1:1–2). This definitively[8] introduces the next section of the book in which Jesus is developed as Divine and thus greater than angels.

Oddly, the book of Hebrews does not develop much speaking role for Jesus, except that Jesus as Melchizedek priest continues to pray on Christian's behalf (Heb 7:25; and perhaps 5:7). Instead, Christ's prophetic speaking role is conveyed through those who heard him and testify concerning him (Heb 2:3). In Hebrews' record of testimony, perhaps the *pesher* use of the OT reflects Jesus speaking for God, as on the Emmaus road or other resurrection appearances.

Hebrews introduced Jesus Christ as the radiance of God's glory, identifying the Son with divine majesty (Deut 32:3; Pss 79:11; 145:3, 6; Jude 25).[9] Christ's nature is the exact representation[10] of substance (ὑποστάσεως)[11] of the divine nature (Heb 1:3), the very commitment that the Nicene Creed affirmed of God being both the Father and the Son. This very substance is described by the Wisdom of Solomon as the *shekinah* presence of God provided for Israel in the wilderness.[12]

---

7. Eschatologically (Deut 4:30; Isa 2:2; Mic 4:1; Dan 10:14; Sir 48:24–25) and messianically last days (Gen 49:1, 10; Num 24:14, 17; Hos 3:5; Acts 2:17; 2 Tim 3:1; 1 Pet 1:5, 20; 1QpHab 2.5; 1Q28a 1 1; 4Q174 1 12).

8. Part of the argument of the book is that multiplicity is replaced by singularity (Heb 1:1; 7:23–24; 9:25–26; 10:11–12).

9. 1 En. 5.4; 12.3; 14.16.

10. The exact representation can refer to a coin (Liddell et al., *Greek-English Lexicon*, 1977) or seal (Philo, *Drunkenness* 133) or character of parent (4 Macc 15:4) or distinguishing traits between persons (Philo, *Posterity* 110; Philo, *Spec. Laws* 4.110).

11. Philo, *Worse* 160; Philo, *Dreams* 1.188; Philo, *Eternity* 88, 92; Ps.-Aristotle, *On the Cosmos* 4.395a.

12. Wis 16:21.

4

Hebrews' Epistemology of Prophecy as Rhetorical Proclamation that Christ is Supreme[1]

HEBREWS IS FRAMED BY repeated quotations[2] and allusions to the Old Testament. These prophecies present themselves as revealed by the testimony from the Holy Spirit (Heb 2:4; 3:7; probably 6:4; 9:8; 10:15, probably 29).[3] Such OT quotes are free citations, sometimes showing more similarity to LXX and at other times more similar to MT.[4] These quotes engaged through a *pesher* application to a new contextual agenda within a Christian Pharisaic appreciation of the authoritative books of the OT.[5] For example,

---

1. Much of this chapter is a reworking of Kennard, "Hebrews Epistemology of Prophecy," 215–21.

2. The quotations are close to LXX and MT, but two-thirds have slight differences from both documents, showing that the author is operating within the canons of rabbinic *pesher*; Howard, "Hebrews," 211.

3. These patristics also support the same epistemic diligence that the prophets operated under inspiration (Ign. *Magn.* 8.2; Barn. 5.6; Herm. Sim. 9.12.1–2; 2 Clem. 17.4; Justin, *1 Apol.* 31–53; 62.4; Justin, *Dial.* 56–7; Irenaeus, *Haer.* 4.20.4; Origen, *Princ.* 3.12).

4. Howard, "Hebrews," 208–16.

5. Josephus, *Ant.* 13.171–73, 297; 18.12–15; Josephus, *J.W.* 2.119, 162–63; 4 Macc 5:16–27; Philo, *Dreams* 1.124–25; m. Yad. 4.6–8; b. Qidd. 66a; Resurrection: 2 Macc 7.9–14, 22–23; 14.43–46; 1 En. 22; 58.3; 62.14–16; 91.10; 92.2; 104; 108.11–14; Jub. 5.10; 10.17; 22.22; LAB; CD 3.11–16, 20–21; 7.5, 9; 13.11; 20.17–20, 25–27; 1QH^a 11.19–23 [3.18–22]; 19.10–14 [11.7–11]; 1QS 3.7–12; 4.7; 4Q228, frag. 1 1.9; 4Q266, frag. 11; 4Q385 2; 4Q386 1–2; 4Q396; 4Q521 2.2.12; 5.2.5–6; 2 Bar.[Syriac] 30.1–5; 49–51; 4

Psalms 95:7–10 combines with a *midrash* or retelling of the exodus journey toward the promised land to provide a call to join a persistent faith toward kingdom rest (Heb 3:7—4:13).[6] Such rabbinic use of example also adds rhetorical persuasion beyond a Jewish audience.[7] Even the author's reappropriation of Psalms 110 fits within *midrash* patterns to support the grand theme of Christ's supremacy (Heb 1:13; 5:6; 7:17, 21).[8] George Buchanan explains the *midrash* process for this rabbinic analogy concerning a text such as Psalms 110 applying what originally referenced the lesser Davidic king to the Messiah (an appropriation of the first Hillel logical rule).[9]

> Midrashic composers were resourceful apologists with amazing skill in manipulating words, phrases, and passages to suit their own needs in ways that were far removed from the original meaning of the text. The reason such a method was necessary was the official interpreter had to relate an ancient text that was considered sacred to the needs of a worshiping community in a different period of time and under situations that differed from those that prompted the writing of the scripture on which they depended. Authors of midrashim were not free to ignore the text and present their ideas on the basis of contemporary need and normal logic. The scripture gave them their authority to speak. Their use of scripture represents their skill in presenting their own views on the basis of the sacred text. Rabbis had numerous, well-established rules for doing this and some of them were employed by the author of Hebrews.[10]

Macc 7.19; 16.25; 4 Ezra 7.26–44; Sib. Or. 4.180; T. Benj. 10.6–8; T. Levi 18; T. Jud. 24; Lim, *Pesharim*, 44–53.

6. Buchanan (*To the Hebrews*, xxiii–xxiv) explains Hebrews' discussion of the exodus within Hillel's first rule as a strong *a fortiori* argument: what applies in a minor case also applies in a major case; Josephus, *Ag. Ap.* 2.175–81; Jerusalem synagogue Theodotus inscription; Philo, *Embassy* 311–13; Meg. Taʿan.; y. Hor. 3.5 (48c); b. Tem. 14b; b. B. Meṣ. 59a-b; Sipra Deut. 351; Sipra 193.1.1–11; Gaon, *Iggeret Rav Sherira Gaon*, 1–2; Zeitlin, "Midrash: A Historical Study," 21–36; Wright, *Midrash*, 52–59, 64–67; Ellis, "Midrash, Targum," 61–69; Le Déaut, "Apropos a Definition of Midrash," 259–82; Miller, "Targum, Midrash," 29–82; Bloch, "Midrash," 29–50; Porton, "Defining Midrash," 55–95; McNamara, "Some Issues and Recent Writings," 136–49.

7. Aristotle, *Rhet.* 1.2.8, esp. vivid examples 4.49.62; Quintilian, *Inst.* 5.11.9; Lausberg, *Handbook of Literary Rhetoric*, sec. 410–26; Koester, *Hebrews*, 93.

8. Buchanan, *To the Hebrews*, xxi.

9. Hillel hermeneutical rule: What applies in a minor case also applies in a major case; *Sipra* intr. 1; 'Abot R. Nat. 37; Gen. Rab. 92.7; Pesaḥ. 18b; Yoma 43a; Pool, *Traditional Prayer Book*, 128–30.

10. Buchanan, *To the Hebrews*, xxi–xxii.

The author quoting these authoritative testimonies of revelation fitted them into his agenda for the supremacy of Christ (Heb 2:6; 10:15).[11] Peter O'Brien considers that this biblical foundation for the argument frames the book after a pattern of a synagogue homily.[12] Furthermore, the combining of OT quotes within the textual agenda is a common strategy of early Jewish literature. For example, Herbert Bateman developed that the Midrash on Eschatology, 4Q174 1.1–13 strings together Deuteronomy 23:3–4; Exodus 15:17–18; 2 Samuel 7:10–14; Psalms 1:1 and 2:1–2; Isaiah 8:11; Ezekiel 37:23; and Amos 9:11 in a similar manner to the way Hebrews 1:5–13 strings together Psalms 2:7; 2 Samuel 7:14; Deuteronomy 32:43; Psalms 97:7; 104:4; 45:6–7; 102:25–27; and 110:1.[13] These abutted texts initiate a cross-pollination of multiple texts addressing the same issue from different angles. However, the particular configuration in Hebrews does not so much fuse the meaning across the whole textual family (Hillel's *Binyan av mikatuv eḥad*[14]) but showcases its ideas in pairs of related texts (Hillel's hermeneutical rule, *Binyan av mi-shenei khetuvim*[15]): Psalms 2:7 with 2 Samuel 7:14, Deuteronomy 32:43 with Psalms 97:7,[16] and Psalms 45: 6–7 with 110:1. However, because the author of Hebrews cannot be definitively identified, there is no way to know whether this interpretive stringing of texts is indebted to Hillel or his school or is just part of the environment of early Judaism.

Occasional quotes introduced by "someone has testified somewhere" do not indicate ignorance on the part of the author, but rather that of high

---

11. Buchanan, *To the Hebrews*, xxi; Bock, *Proclamation from Prophecy and Pattern*; Ricoeur, "Hermeneutics of Testimony" cited in Ford, "Paul Ricoeur," 190; Bruce, *Epistle to the Hebrews*, xix–xxii.

12. O'Brien, *Letter to the Hebrews*, 20.

13. Bateman, *Early Jewish Hermeneutics*, 56–75, 149–206.

14. Sipra intr. 3; 'Abot R. Nat. 37; t. Šabb. 7.11; Pool, *Traditional Prayer Book*, 128–30; claimed by Bateman, *Early Jewish Hermeneutics*, 14–17; and responded to by Kennard, "Epistemology and Logic," 146.

15. Sipra intr. 4; 'Abot R. Nat. 37; t. Šabb. 7.11; Pool, *Traditional Prayer Book*, 128–30; Kennard, "Epistemology and Logic," 147.

16. The LXX Psalms 96:7 modifies the MT 97:7 "*Elohim*" to read "his angels," and Hebrews 1:6 recovers the context of both as "God's angels." Also, the verb is changed from the second-person address of "idolaters" in the psalm to the third-person "angels of God." Similar modification occurs in LXX Deuteronomy 32:43a when compared to 4QDeutq 32:43b, though Deuteronomy 32:43b MT lacks these phrases. These changes in Hebrews 1:6 are also reflected in Odes Sol. 2.43; Gheorghita, *Role of the Septuagint*, 41–42.

style in introducing a statement (Heb 2:6; 4:4).[17] The use of "testify" identifies that it is a publically accessible statement with further evidence that could be assessed in a legal setting as valid or corroborated by evidence (Heb 2:6 with "valid" 2:2; "validate" 2:3; "corroborate testimony" 2:4).[18]

Rhetorical critics identify the book of Hebrews as mostly within the Hellenistic category of deliberative rhetoric[19] by offering the readers future rewards for considering to remain within the new covenant and with Jesus (Heb 4:11; 6:18; 10:36; 12:1–2). So evidence of high style is incorporated within the book to increase the readiness of the listeners.[20]

The author of Hebrews also utilized transitional warnings to refocus and regain the attention of his readers (Heb 2:1–4; 3:12–4:13; 6:1–20; 10:26–39; 12:1–13), as is common enough in ancient prolonged arguments of *epideictic* rhetoric.[21] Within this form of rhetoric there are often appeals to hold fast to a goal within one's previous commitments (Heb 3:6; 4:14; 10:23, 35–39; 11:11). This is balanced by warnings of impending shame to threatened damnation if the readers leave Christ and the new covenant to return to the Mosaic covenant. The last of the warnings (Heb 12:1–13) is relaxed a bit, to encourage the readers to consider that damnation is unlikely in their faithfulness, but discipline might still be utilized to make them stronger.

Several interpreters wish to position themselves rhetorically as advocates for a hybrid rhetoric. O'Brien summarized this position as follows: "for those who remain committed to God and Christ, Hebrews is epideictic. But for those tending to drift away from the faith, it is deliberative."[22] Such analysis connects with classical Greek patterns, but may not be that

---

17. Acts 13:35; Philo, *Unchangeable* 74; Philo, *Planting* 90; Philo, *Drunkenness* 61; Barn. 15.2; 1 Clem. 8.4; 29.3; 46.3.

18. Koester, *Hebrews*, 214.

19. Aristotle, *Rhet.* 1.2.8; 3.7.1–2; Quintilian, *Inst.* 8.3.5.

20. Quintilian, *Inst.* 8.3.5; Garuti, *Alle origini*, 33–184; Attridge, *Epistle to the Hebrews*, 20–21; Cosby, "Rhetorical Composition of Hebrews 11," 257–73; Cosby, *Rhetorical Composition and Function*; Koester, *Hebrews*, 92–96; deSilva, *Despising Shame*, 30, 33.

21. Quintilian, *Inst.* 4.3.12–17; Cicero, *De or.* 3.53., section 203; deSilva, *Despising Shame*, 42–46; Eisenbaum, *Jewish Heroes of Christian History*, 136–37; Koester, *Hebrews*, 89.

22. O'Brien, *Letter to the Hebrews*, 26; Koester, *Hebrews*, 82; Lane, *Hebrews 1–8*, lxxix; deSilva, *Perseverance in Gratitude*, 46; Johnson, *Defilement and Purgation*, 13.

helpful, since the book fits into both categories, and subsequent analysis of the book leaves a number of parts of rhetoric absent.[23]

The author of Hebrews considered that the character of those described in the book, who have lived faithfully without making it to the final goal, served as embodied testimony for both author and readers to continue in faith (Heb 11:1–3 [first-person present plural verbs "we understand" νοοῦμεν]; 12:1).[24] The statement and lives of the great cloud of witnesses testify so that believers would continue to endure the race by focusing our attention on the example of Christ as the goal (Heb 12:1–2). So, ultimately, these previous believers point to Jesus' life lived in suffering as providing an example of suffering faith for the believer to live. So there are several levels of testimony occurring in the book. These testimonies press the reader through content to life implications facilitating imitation of Christ and fellow believers who have gone before the readers.

The author joins Christ and the previous speakers, heard by his audience, by pointing to Christ. In this manner, all these testifiers confirm Christ's message (Heb 1:2; 2:3).[25] Such corporate voice reflects a corporate memory of the accounts of the past (Heb 12:17). These spokesmen join together as authoritative confirmation over time within a Pharisaic world view, and thus increase the reader's confidence in the message.[26]

This approach is an externalism of a practical realistic non-foundational empiricism similar to Thomas Reid's common sense realism.[27] Though, when miracles are involved as divine miraculous testimonies, then the epistemic framework is better understood as Lockean supernatural evidence of God vindicating the speaker (Heb 2:4, "signs," "wonders,"

---

23. Koester, *Hebrews*, 82; deSilva, *Perseverance in Gratitude*, 46; Lane, *Hebrews 1–8*, lxxix–lxxx; Westfall, *Discourse Analysis*, 6–7; O'Brien, *Letter to the Hebrews*, 26.

24. Character is an important facet in increasing persuasion of a witness (Origen, *Princ.* 3.12; Aristotle, *Rhet.* 1.2.3–4, 13; Quintilian, *Inst.* 4.1.7; 5.14.24–25; Lausberg, *Handbook of Literary Rhetoric*, sec. 371) and interpreters recognize our author utilized this aspect in his argument (Mitchel, "Use of πρεπειν," 681–701; Eisenbaum, "Heroes and History in Hebrews 11," 380–96; Koester, *Hebrews*, 91–92, 94).

25. Examples of such claims include: Papius recounted in Eusebius, *Hist. eccl.* 5.20.4–7; Irenaeus, *Letter to Florinus*; Clement of Alexandria, *Strom.* 7.106.4; Eusebius, *Hist. eccl.* 2.1.4; Kelber, "Case of the Gospels," 65; Dunn, *Jesus Remembered*, 239–43; Ricoeur, *Memory, History, Forgetting*; Bauckham, *Jesus and the Eyewitnesses*, 295–96, 310–57.

26. Seneca, *Controversiae*, preface 3–4; Bauckham, *Jesus and the Eyewitnesses*, 295–96.

27. Reid, *Thomas Reid*; Abraham, "Epistemology of Jesus," 158–9; Brueggeman, *Pathway of Interpretation*, 115.

and "gifts"; probably 6:4).[28] Thus the confirming divine miracle provides a greater confidence to those who experienced them in the context of receiving the message. Gottlieb Lünemann and Wilhelm Linss claim that experiential ownership of these signs prompts the author to utilize terms of logical conclusion that reflect "inner necessity."[29]

Jesus obtaining answered prayer also supports a Lockean argument for why the readers should affiliate with Jesus as their high priest (Heb 5:7). That is, unlike the Jewish priests who are frail and sin, Jesus is pious and is "heard," with an answer of "yes" to his Gethsemane prayer that death would pass from him so that resurrection would occur (Heb 5:7; Pss 4:2 LXX; 6:8–9; 10:17; 18:6; 19:3; 22:24; 28:6; 31:22; 34:6; 40:1; 61:5; 66:19; 78:21, 59; 106:44; 1 John 5:14–15).[30] There is a real appeal to associate with Jesus as our high priest who, in his piety, can source the believer's everlasting salvation (Heb 5:9).

In the new covenant relationship, the believer obtains a filial knowledge of the Lord, who is the eschatological Judge (Heb 8:11; 10:30, 34).[31] This family relationship reassures the believer that she is authentically God's child rather than illegitimate (Heb 12:8). Thus, any discipline from God is designed to mature the believer, rather than to destroy under his wrath.

Christians also have a once-for-all corporate atonement that is provided by Jesus Christ's sacrificial death after the pattern of a Day of Atonement (Heb 9:1–10:12). This framework was especially understood to operate within a Platonic metaphysic by the philosophical side of early Judaism, the church, and the classical commentators of the nineteenth century (with similar Platonic phrases present within Heb 8:5; 9:23–24; 10:1; 12:27–28).[32] For example, the author of Hebrews identified that Jesus *transcended* a *shadow* existence of *lower dualistic* earthly tabernacle in order to

---

28. Locke, *Essay Concerning Human Understanding* 1.1.15; 2.11.8–9; 2.32.6; 3.3.6–8; Locke, "Discourse of Miracles," 9:256–65; Locke, "Reasonableness of Christianity," 1–158; pre-modern empiricism is apparent in Lactanius, *Opif.* 9–10; Keener, *Miracles*, 1:35–208.

29. Lünemann, *Critical and Exegetical Hand-Book*, 422; Linss, "Logical Terminology," 365–66.

30. Kennard, *Messiah Jesus*, 360–62; Blaising, "Gethsemane a Prayer of Faith," 333–43: this view is not sufficiently countered by the disjunction (contra Gundry, *Mark*, 870).

31. Origen, *Princ.* 3.12; Moser, *Elusive God*, 46–47, 98, 113–23.

32. Philo, *Alleg. Interp.* 3.102, 94–96; Philo, *Moses* 2.74; Origen, *Princ.* 4.2.4, 6, 9; *Biblia Patristica*, 3:453–55; Clement of Alexandria, *Strom.* 1.5, 9; 6.7–11; 7.16; Cody, *Heavenly Sanctuary and Liturgy*, 78–84.

enter the *heavenly*, drawing the believer toward *perfection*, where she can *perceive things unseen*.³³ If such a view were Platonic, it would have implications toward an anti-realist epistemology that would denigrate faith and knowledge below intuition and discursive reasoning.³⁴ However, more recent comparisons with religious Platonism and Jewish-Christian mysticism denies this claimed Platonic heritage for the book of Hebrews. For example, Ronald Williamson concludes that Hebrews and Philo belonged "to two entirely different schools of exegesis."³⁵ For example, in Platonism, only the heavenly realm of the forms is unchangeable truth, and the goal is to perceive this truth, while earthly expressions are derivative shadows reflecting the forms. However, in Hebrews and in *merkabah* ("throne"/"chariot") mysticism, both the heavenly and the earthly realms are real changeable creations by the personal God Who occupies both realms and is perceived through the biblical text, faith, and occasional mystical experiences, all prompting the believer toward a future kingdom goal (Exod 40:34–38; Isa 6:1–8; Ezek 1:24–28; 10:4, 18–20; Heb 1:3, 6; 4:16; 8:1; 9:19–24; 12:2).³⁶ The framework, goals, and methodology of Hebrews and Platonism are very different. In fact, Hebrews is much closer to that of *merkabah* mysticism, which occupies a place within sectarian early Judaism, Paul, and Johannine theology.

Christ's atonement accomplished in the heavenly temple is a superior atonement to that which the high priest would perform in the earthly

---

33. Each of the italicized words were taken by some in a Platonic sense (Plato, *Resp.* 514A–15D; Plotinus, *Enn.* 5.3.6.17; Clement of Alexandria, *Strom.* 1.6, 11; 2.2, 4, 13; 4.20; 7.1; Origen, *Princ.* 2.11.6–7; Origen, *Commentary on the Gospel*, 319; Berlin-Brandenburgische Akademie der Wissenschaften, *Die griechische Schriftsteller der ersten Jahrhunderte*, 38.238–390; Gordon, "Better Promises," 448.

34. Plato, *Resp.* 5.511d–e; Plato, *Tim.* 29c; Philo permits a larger role for faith (*Rewards* 28).

35. Williamson, *Epistle to the Hebrews*, 576–79; Lane, *Hebrews 1–8*, cvii–cviii; Hurst, *Epistle to the Hebrews*, 7–42; in "How 'Platonic' Are Heb. viii.5 and ix.23f?", 156–68, Hurst identifies that Hebrews is not really Platonic.

36. Gal 4:26; Heb 12:22; Rev 3:12; 21:2, 10; Josephus, *Ant.* 3.123, 181; 18.85–88; 2 Macc 2.4–8; 1 En. 14; 37–71; 2 En. 15–17; 4 Ezra 9.26—10.59; 13.35–36; *Life of Jeremiah* 11–19; 2 Bar. 4.2–7; 6.5–9; 32.4; 4 Bar. 3.1–9; LAB 26.12–15; Ascen. Isa. 9; LAE 37; Apoc. Ab. 29; Exod. Rab. 43.8; m. Ḥag. 2.1; b. Ḥag. 14a; 15a; t. Yoma 1.8; Hec. Ab. Rab. 20.1; b. Sanh. 38b; Pate and Kennard, *Deliverance Now and Not Yet*, 98–103; Sholem, *Jewish Gnosticism*; Lincoln, *Paradise Now and Not Yet*, 9–32, 169–95; Dean-Otting, *Heavenly Journeys*; Gruenwald, *Apocalyptic and Merkavah Mysticism*, 29–72; Schafer, *Kehhalot-Studien*; Chernus, "Visions of God," 123–46; Hurst, *Epistle to the Hebrews*, 82–85; Isaacs, *Sacred Space*, 59–61; Koester, *Hebrews*, 97–100.

tabernacle. Not only is Christ's atonement accomplished by a superior priest in a superior place, but it accomplishes everlasting forgiveness for all who believe. This finished everlasting forgiveness is superior over the repeated year by year forgiveness available for Jews during the Day of Atonement. However, this truth of everlasting forgiveness is not itself evidentially noticeable as another aspect of the new covenant, namely, an internal evidential aspect confirming a believer's authenticity as participating within the new covenant (Heb 8:10, 12; 9:13–14, 23, 28; 10:3–4, 14–18). That is, the internal transformation of a believer's conscience toward responsiveness to God's laws and maturely obeying God provides internal atonement-driven Lockean evidence within an epistemic dualism to confirm a new covenant believer with everlasting forgiveness, much like Edwards's sixth sense does in his construct of the Spirit's religious affections.[37] Furthermore, if one was looking for this evidence to reassure whether those who identify with Christ are authentic Christians, as the author of Hebrews does, then this transformed conscience and consistency of life reflecting such a responsive conscience operates as a Peircian pragmatic verification principle of the fact that his readers are authentic believers in Christ unto kingdom (Heb 6:9–12; 10:32–39).[38]

The primary epistemology that the book of Hebrews demonstrates is that prophecy is utilized as *midrashic* rhetoric to support the theme of the book, that the real Christ is supreme over all other options. Multigenerational communal testimony and confirming miracles support this theme within a Lockean epistemic dualism. However, the Lockean evidence is extended into Edwardsian empirical evidence of a cleansed conscience demonstrating authentic, transformed new-covenant nature. Furthermore, the author occasionally utilized this Edwardsian cleansed conscience as a Peircian pragmatic verifying principle to reassure himself that his readers were believers in Christ. This reassurance funds confidence in filial knowledge that the believer is part of God's family, so discipline matures the believer.

---

37. Edwards, *Treatise Concerning Religious Affections*; Edwards, *Freedom of the Will*, 6:342–43 (for the international designation, see sec. 4:1, 337–42); Edwards, *Miscellanies*, number 267; Jenson, *America's Theologian*, 30; Locke, *Essay Concerning Human Understanding*, 1.1.15; 2.11.8–9; 2.32.6; 3.3.6–8.

38. Peirce, *Collected Papers*, para. 9; Peirce, "Fixation of Belief," 1–15; Peirce, "How to Make Our Ideas Clear," 286–302.

5

Christ as God-King, Superior to Angels

IN CONTRAST TO THE diminishing ministry of the prophets, early Jewish angelology supplies the background for the divine giving of the Mosaic covenant by angels (Heb 2:2; Acts 7:38, 53; Gal 3:19).[1] Some angels were called "sons of God" and occupied the heavenly court (Gen 6:2, 4; Job 1:6; 2:1; 38:7; Pss 29:1; 82:6; 89:7; Dan 3:25 = LXX 3:92).[2] These angels were agents of God in early Jewish rewritten biblical tradition, accomplishing what the biblical text ascribed to God.[3] Additionally, early Judaism developed seven intermediary "archangels" between the righteous and God (Dan 9:21; 10:13).[4] In certain early Jewish texts, these archangels were identified as "angels of the divine presence."[5] Furthermore, in early Judaism, angels were considered to have a governance role for orchestrating and influencing the nations (Job 2:1; Pss 29:1; 82:6; 89:7; Dan 3:25 = LXX 3:92; LXX Deut

---

1. Jub. 2.17–19; 2:1; CD 5.18; Josephus, *Ant.* 15.5.3, 136; Sipre Num. 102; Mek. Exod. 20.18; *Pesikta rabbati* 21.

2. LXX Deut 32:8; 4Q44; 1 En. 6.2; Philo, *Giants* 6; Philo, *Unchangeable* 1–2; Josephus, *Ant.* 1.73; LAB, 3.1.

3. Biblical text identifies what God accomplished, while the liturgical rewrite ascribed the action to angels (Gen 11:6 and Jub. 10.22–23; Gen 15:17 and Jub. 14.20; Gen 22 and Jub. 17.15–18; Num 14:10–12, 20 and LAB, 38.359.4; 3 Macc 6:18).

4. Tob 12.15; 1 En. 9.1; 20.1; 21.10; 4 Ezra 4.1; Sib. Or. 2.215; 1QM 9.15–16; 4Q285 frag. 1.

5. Tob 12.15; Jub. 1.27; 1 En. 9.1; 1QM 9.15–16; 1Q28b 4.25; 1QH^a 6.13; T. Levi 8.2.

32:8).⁶ Earthly political conflict mirrors the struggle among the angelic domain (Dan 10:13, 20–21; 11:1; 12:1).⁷ Unfortunately, sometimes these angels lead nations astray in rebellion against God.⁸ This is unreasonable, since angels are *created* by God among his creation (Heb 1:6; ὁ ποιῶν τοὺς ἀγγέλους αὐτοῦ, "created," compared with "created things" in Heb 12:27), and thus they should tremble before God as though they were mutable natural elements of wind and fire (Ps 104:4; Heb 1:7).⁹ Angels are spirits who function under God to aid humans (Heb 1:7, 14). So Hebrews 1 identifies that the Son is superior to angels in divinity, regal role, and honor¹⁰ (Heb 1:4—2:10). This argument could be seen as joining the early Jewish polemic against the worship of angels as pagan deities.¹¹ The text may also polemic the Ebionite conception that Jesus was an angel and not God.¹²

In contrast to this developing angelology, Jesus Christ is presented as divine. Hebrews introduced Jesus Christ as the radiance of God's glory, identifying the Son with divine majesty (Heb 1:3; Deut 32:3; Pss 79:11; 145:3, 6; Jude 25).¹³ Christ's nature is the exact representation¹⁴ of substance (ὑποστάσεως)¹⁵ of the divine nature (Heb 1:3). The LXX identifies the meaning of ὑποστάσεως as "the reality behind the phenomena" (Ezek

---

6. 4Q44; Sir 17:17; Tob 3:17; 11:14–15; 12:11–22; 2 Macc 10:29–30; Jub. 35.17; 1 En. 20.5; Philo, *Posterity* 89, 91–92; T. Naph. 9.4; Tg. Onq. to Gen 11:8.

7. Jub. 35.17; 1 En. 56.5–6; 1QM 13.9–13; 17.5–8; 1QS 3.20–25.

8. Jub. 15.30–32; 48.9, 12, 16–17.

9. 4 Ezra 8:21–22; 1QH 1.10–11; Philo, *Alleg. Interp.* 160, 224, 235; Philo, *Migration* 100; Philo, *Moses* 1.70; Philo, *Decalogue* 49, 173; Yal. Shim'oni 2.11.3; Tg. Ps.-J. also modifies Ps 104:4 from "winds" to "angels"; Howard ("Hebrews and the Old Testament," 211) identified that the quote was neither similar to MT nor LXX but with some LXX influence; Combrink, "Some Thoughts," 27–28.

10. A name conveys honor (Gen 12:12; 2 Sam 7:9; Sir 37:26; 46:12; 1 Macc 2:51; Koester, *Hebrews*, 182).

11. Exod. Rab. 32.4; Mek. Rab. Ishmael, Ba Hodes 6 to Exod 20:4–5; t. Ḥul 40a; y. Ber. 9.13 a–b; b. Sanh. 38b.

12. Epiphanius, *Pan.* 30.16.4; Dunn, *Unity and Diversity*, 242; Lindars, *Letter to the Hebrews*, 38.

13. 1 En. 5.4; 12.3; 14.16; also similar language in Wis 7:25–26.

14. The exact representation can refer to a coin (Liddell et al., *Greek-English Lexicon*, 1977) or seal (Philo, *Drunkenness*, 133) or character of parent (4 Macc 15:4) or distinguishing traits between persons (Philo, *Posterity* 110; Philo, *Spec. Laws* 4.110).

15. Philo, *Worse* 160; Philo, *Dreams* 1.188; Philo, *Eternity* 88, 92; Ps.-Aristotle, *On the Cosmos* 4.395a; Tatian, *Or. Graec.* 5.1; Origen, *Princ.* 4.4.1; Athanasius, *C. Ar.* 1.9; 3; Athanasius, *Ep. Serap.* 1.18; Gregory of Nazianzus and Gregory of Nyssa, as cited by Greer, *Captain of Our Salvation*, 74, 99–101.

19:5; Pss 38:6; 88:48).[16] This underlying reality that funds the appearance is the very commitment of "being" that the Nicene Creed affirmed for God being both the Father and the Son.[17] This very substance is described by the Wisdom of Solomon as the *shekinah* presence of God provided for Israel in the wilderness.[18] By extension, the word also identifies steadfastness of character,[19] which funds the other instances in which the word is used in referring to human "confident assurance" (Heb 3:14; 11:1).

Jesus is the Appointed Son, Heir of all things and thus King (Heb 1:2, 5–13). God begetting the Son is sometimes traditionally identified as eternal generation,[20] but in this context "son" is best identified as initiating the missional role of the Messianic Davidic King (Heb 1:5, use of similar word "son" in Ps 2:7 with[21] 2 Sam 7:14). The royal Psalms 2:7 identifies the Father begetting of the Son as the Davidic King covenanted in the 2 Samuel 7:14 promise, especially through the lens of a climactic Messianic king (1 Chr 17:13).[22] Hebrews does not develop when this covenanting occurs for Christ, simply that it has already declared him the Messianic Davidic King. No angel has ever had the divine declarations which Jesus Christ has already had declared of him. That is, the royal Psalms 2:7 identifies that "Thou art my son, today I have begotten thee" (Heb 1:5). This "today" announcement of the Davidic covenantal authority has already been realized for Jesus Christ. This pronouncement identifies Jesus as the divinely authorized Davidic King, or the Son. This begetting includes the adoption (and possibly incarnation) right by which Jesus reigns already.

The title "firstborn" designates the "inheritor" (Heb 1:6; 12:16; Deut 21:17), not an adoption view in Arius's perspective. In this Messianic king context, "firstborn" climactically means Messianic, as the greatest king

---

16. Koster, "ὑπόστασις," 581–82.

17. Koster, "ὑπόστασις," 575; Koester, *Hebrews*, 180–81.

18. Wis 16:21.

19. Polybius, *Hist.* 4.50.10; 6.55.2; Josephus, *Ant.* 18.24.

20. Augustine, *Enarrat. Ps.* 2.6; Aquinas, *Ad Heb.* 49.

21. Hebrews use of "again" connects multiple citations together (Heb 1:5; 2:13; 4:5, 7; 10:30) similar to John 12:39; 19:37; Rom 15:10–12; 1 Cor 3:20; Philo, *Alleg. Interp.* 3.4; Philo, *Sobriety* 8; Philo, *Heir* 22; Philo, *Dreams* 1.166; 2.19; 1 Clem. 10.4, 6; 14.5; 15.3–5; Barn. 6.2, 4. Additionally, in Hebrews 1:5 the rabbinic hermeneutic of *gezerah shavah* use of "Son" connects these verses. Howard ("Hebrews and the Old Testament," 210–11) identified that both quotes were similar to both MT and LXX.

22. 4Q174 1.10–11 links Ps 2 with a messianic interpretation of 2 Sam 7:14 in 4Q174 1.18–19; Juel, *Messianic Exegesis*, 62–66.

(Heb 1:6, consistent with the royal Ps 89:27).[23] The concept underscores the king inheriting his kingdom (Heb 1:6; 2 Chr 21:3). Such a divine Messianic title warrants the angels to worship Christ (Heb 1:6, citing the Deut 32:43 LXX "ἄγγελοι θεοῦ" reflective of 4Q41 32:43, *elohim*, rather than standard LXX text "υἱοὶ θεοῦ").[24] Jesus has the right to reign, and he reigns as God to be worshipped (Heb 1:6, 8).

In this divine role, Jesus also joined God in creating the world (Heb 1:2; 11:3). As God, the Son governs and bears all things by the word of his power (Heb 1:3). Such "bearing all things" likely indicates that Jesus sustains and guides the universe (Heb 1:3; though it could be a synonymous parallel statement that the Son and Father create the universe by his spoken "word" [ῥήματι] as in Heb 1:2 and 11:3; Gen 1:6–26).[25] Within these roles, the book will develop his priestly ministry of purifying for sins (Heb 1:3).

No OT text or early Jewish tradition develops a definitive statement of a divine Messiah or of the Messiah's preexistence before incarnation. Hints occur from a range of texts. For example, Micah 5:2–5 predicts that there will be a child whose goings are from everlasting, but that he would be born in Bethlehem as king of Israel. The "everlasting goings" hint at preexistence and raise the possibility of divinity. Of course, the rest of the prophecy speaks to the birth and reign of the Davidic Messianic king.

23. In Psalms 89:27, "firstborn" is defined as the highest king, consistent with the Ancient Near East pattern. For example, Marduk is called firstborn of gods to identify his supreme kingship (Pritchard, *Ancient Near Eastern Texts*, Babylonian Creation Epic 4:20). In the same manner, 4Q458 frag. 15 refers to the messianic Davidic King apocalyptically as God's firstborn into the kingdom.

24. The LXX Psalms 96:7 modifies the MT 97:7 "*Elohim*" to read "ἄγγελοι αὐτοῦ," and Hebrews 1:6 recovers the context of both as "God's angels." Also the verb is changed from the second person address to "idolaters" in the psalm to the third person "angels of God" should worship Christ as Lord. Similar modification occurs in LXX Deuteronomy 32:43a, when compared to 4Q44 32:43b, though Deuteronomy 32:43b MT lacks these phrases. These changes in Hebrews 1:6 are also reflected in Odes Sol. 2.43b; an excerpt after the psalter in LXXA; Justin, *Dial.* 130.1; Westcott, *Epistle to the Hebrews*, 25; Koester, *Hebrews*, 193; Cockerill, "Hebrews 1:6: Source and Significance," 51–64; Gheorghita, *Role of the Septuagint*, 41–42. Additional polemics against angel worship: Exod. Rab. 32.4; Mek. Rabbi Ishmael, *Ba Hodes* 6 to Exod 20:4–5; t. Ḥul 40a; y. Ber. 9.13 a–b; b. Sanh. 38b.

25. Φέρων means "carry," usually in *sustaining* the universe (Col 1:17; Wis 7:24; 8:1; Philo, *Dreams* 1.241; Ps.-Aristotle, *On the Cosmos* 6.397b), but can mean "enduringly identify with" (Heb 12:20; 13:13; possibly 9:16), which both would be forms of "guidance" (Heb 6:1; Philo, *Heir* 7; Philo, *Migration* 6), and more ultimately could mean "bringing into existence" (Heb 1:2, "made," parallel with 1:3, "upholds," and 11:3 "creation by word"; Philo, *Heir* 36; Philo, *Names* 192).

However, the greatest possibilities of a divine messiah emerge from Isaiah 9:6 (the Messianic name of "Mighty God") and Daniel 7:13–14 ("Son of Man" as the cloud rider).[26] Some fringe Jews developed this view into the heavenly Jewish two-powers heresy.[27]

In Isaiah 9, the Messianic child will have throne names[28] that declare his glory as king, and maybe even "Immanuel" ("God with us" in more than providence, Isa 7:14; 8:8, 10). This child is named as "Wonderful Counselor," a quality of the ideal wise statesman, which Isaiah develops of the Messianic branch and of God (Isa 9:6; 11:2; 28:29). However, the name that might imply deity the most is "Mighty God"; he is the champion who can carry out those plans under a title used elsewhere only of Yahweh (Isa 9:6; 10:21). Does this hint at "Immanuel" meaning "God incarnate among us"? As "Everlasting Father," he is the enduring benefactor for his people, as is God—possibly referring to deity, as elsewhere in Isaiah, "Father" refers to Yahweh (Isa 9:6; 63:16). As "Prince of Peace," he is the provider of universal peace (Isa 9:5–7; which also points toward "Yahweh," Judg 6:24).

Jesus identifies Daniel's Son of Man (which hints at divinity) with the Davidic king image of Psalms 110:1 at his trial (Matt 26:64; Mark 14:62; Luke 22:69). Daniel 7 concludes the vision of four beasts with the divine Ancient of Days in his throne room, to conquer all the gentile nations which have stood against God. Entering into the midst of this throne room is the Son of Man riding on the clouds (Dan 7:13–14). Some take this title to refer to the primordial man who will rule as mentioned in Psalms 8:4, but most recognize that the cloud-riding identifies the Son of Man as the king of the Gods,[29] similar in pattern to Marduk or Baal, but within

---

26. The cloud-riding Son of Man is a second Sovereign Divine within Jewish monotheism (1 En. 47.3; 60.2; cloud riding as Divine King: Deut 33:26; Judg 5:4; Isa 19:1; Pss 18:11–15; 68:4; 104:3; *Enuma Elish* tablet 4; *KTU* 1.2.4; Jub. 1.28; 1 En. 62.3; T. Mos. 10.7). Some in early Judaism expect this cloud rider to be Messiah (1 En. 46.1; 47.3; 4 Ezra 7.28–29; 12.11; 13.1–9, 25–26, 32, 35–36; b. Sanh. 96b–97a, 98a; Tg. 1 Chr 3:24; Pirqe Masiah, BhM 3.70).

27. Segal, *Two Powers in Heaven*.

28. There is some conjecture that these are also theophanic names to describe God, and grammatically they could be, but the focus in Isaiah 9:5–7 is on the child "called by his own name" (Isa 9:5 [Eng v. 6], καλεῖται τὸ ὄνομα αὐτοῦ; וַיִּקְרָא שְׁמוֹ), not the power behind him. So, throne names are preferred by most exegetes. The concept of throne names identifies qualities which are describing the child king, and not primarily the God behind the child king, as would be the case if they were theophanic names.

29. 1 En. 47.3; 60.2; cloud riding as Divine King: Deut 33:26; Judg 5:4; Isa 19:1; Pss 18:11–15; 68:4; 104:3; *Enuma Elish* tablet 4; *KTU* 1.2.4; Jub. 1.28; 1 En. 62.3; T. Mos. 10.7;

Jewish monotheism. That is, in Judaism's monotheism, the Ancient of Days is clearly the presentation of God. Thus, in Second Temple and rabbinic Judaism, this cloud rider is reinterpreted as the Messiah.[30] Therefore, this quasi-divine Messiah comes up to God and receives his dominion to rule the kingdom. This Danielic Son of Man is explicitly called "Messiah" in the Similitudes of Enoch 46.1; 47.3 and in 4 Ezra 7.28–29; 12.11; 13.32. In fact, 1 Enoch 62:7–9 describes the Son of Man as preexistent from the beginning,[31] ready to come to judge and rule. Furthermore, the Dead Sea Scroll (DSS) manuscript 4Q246 refers to "the Son of God" (namely, the messianic king) in profoundly Danielic language as before the throne of God, and then coming to earth to conquer his enemies and establish his everlasting kingdom. Drawing upon the insights of John Collins (from 4Q246) and N. T. Wright (from Mark 13), Marv Pate argues that the Danielic Son of Man is portrayed as fighting on behalf of the righteous (Essenes or the disciples of Jesus, respectively), whose enemies include the nation of Israel.[32] However, the Jewish tradition generally regarded Daniel's Son of Man to be the messiah beneficial for Israel unto kingdom.[33] Additionally, this Son of Man title was tied by Jesus to refer to the Melchizedek king-priest of Psalms 110 (Matt 26:64; Mark 14:62; Luke 2:69). This Melchizedek figure is described in the Qumran as *elohim* in his role as eschatological judge.[34] This might hint at divinity, or indicate that he holds a place among the court of divinity, including angels. This king's reign will be an everlasting dominion (Dan 7:14; Ps 110:4; Heb 1:11–13).

So, the OT and early Judaism hint toward a divine messianic king, but such lofty language is inconclusive and could be explained by honoring vocabulary. Likewise, in the Graeco-Roman world, human kings such as

---

Sabourin, "Biblical Cloud," 290–311, esp. 304.

30. 1 En. 46.1; 47.3; 4 Ezra 13.1–9, 25–26, 35–36; b. Sanh. 96b–97a, 98a; Tg. 1 Chr. 3:24; Pirqe Mashiah, BhM 3.70; Marmorstein, " Les Signes du Messie," 184.

31. Rabbinic works also speak of the Messiah emerging in the mind of God in the beginning before creation: b. Pesaḥ 54a; b. Ned. 39a; Gen. Rab. 1.4; 2.4; Pesaḥ Rab. ch. 35.

32. Pate, *Communities of the Last Days*, 127–32.

33. 1 En. 37–71; 4 Ezra 13; Tg. 1 Chr. 3.24; b. Sanh. 38b; Rabbi Akiva sees it as a messiah reference while Rabbi Jose does not.

34. 11Q13 10–11, 13–14. This *elohim* view was interpreted late in the fourth century by Eliphanius of Salamis as indicative of divinity (*Pan.* 55.7.3) and some others have followed his view, esp. a fifth-century AD gnostic sect referred to as the Melchizedekians (Horton, *Melchizedek Tradition*, 89–113; Pearson, "Figure of Melchizedek." In *Gnosticism, Judaism, and Egyptian Christianity*, 108–23).

the Caesars were referred to as "god" (θεός), "lord" (κύριος), "son of god," and "savior of the world."[35]

Psalms 45:6–7 leaves the marriage feast context to declare some of the extent to which Christ reigns already as Davidic King. He has the throne, which should be seen as the Davidic throne following this Davidic covenant statement by a mere three verses (Heb 1:5, 8). Jesus is addressed as God on that Davidic throne, in contrast to what is said in the address to angels (Heb 1:7–8). In the MT, the vocative address calls the King to be God (based on the second-person pronominal suffixes leading up to אֱלֹהִים/ĕlōhîm, Ps 45:7 MT, verse 6 in English; Heb 1:8, πρὸς δὲ τὸν υἱόν . . . ὁ θεός).[36] However, the King as God is also co-regent with God over his reign as well (אֱלֹהִים אֱלֹהֶיךָ, Ps 45:8, verse 7 in English: "God, thy God"; Heb 1:9, ὁ θεὸς ὁ θεός σου). In this second instance, אֱלֹהֶיךָ אֱלֹהִים ("God, thy God") should be taken as a nominative subject of the sentence rather than vocatively addressed, because the vocative is rarely found between the subject and the verb. In translation, the LXX Psalms 44 is consistent with the MT Psalms 45, handling the verse 7 address of the king as God in a vocative (ὁ θεός) and verse 8 as a nominative subject, "God, Thy God" (ὁ θεὸς ὁ θεός σου; additionally parallel to LXX Ps 44:3c, which is also in the nominative), to anoint the king. This is one of the rare LXX texts cited in the NT applying ὁ θεός (God) to refer to Christ (LXX Ps 44:7–8; MT Ps 45:8–9; Heb 1:8–9).[37] Hebrews 1:8b adds καί to the LXX text, which could join quotations, as in Hebrews 1:10a, but here it marks a division within a single quotation, as in 2:13, as well as 10:30 and vv. 37–38. Then Hebrews moves the article from the second to the first ῥάβδος (scepter), inverting the subject and predicate to make two parallel lines. Throughout these changes, it is best to keep the first ὁ θεός (God), as a vocative address of Christ, parallel to the address of angels in verse 7, in which the πρός before both clauses is interpreted as "to" the angels and "to" the Son respectively, indicating "to" whom the following

---

35. On kings as god and savior of world, see Deismann, *Light from the Ancient East*, 344–69. On kings as lord, see Bietenhard, "Lord, Master," 511; Cullmann, *Christology of the New Testament*, 197–99; Suetonius, *De Vita Caesarum* 13.2; the title was also used to describe gods (1 Cor 8:5). Ancient Near East examples of kings as sons of god include the Egyptian Pharaoh as son of Re; Ugarit and Mesopotamia's Keret as son of El; and the Roman Caesar as son of God; see von Martitz, "υἱός, υἱοθεσία," 336–40; Hengel, *Son of God*, 24; Dunn, *Christology in the Making*, 14–16; Deismann, *Light from the Ancient East*, 346.

36. Harris, *Jesus as God*, 187–204; אֱלֹהִים/ĕlōhîm as a vocative does not normally take an article, even though vocatives generally do.

37. Harris, *Jesus as God*, 205–28.

is said by the Father. This is consistent in identifying the Son as the Jewish monotheistic God, since Christ has an everlasting reign (Heb 1:5, 8–9) and is the creator (Heb 1:10–12). The extraordinary feature of this vocative address is that God the Father addresses the Son as God. It is with divine authority that the Father calls all his angels to worship the Son (Heb 1:6).[38]

The Son's throne will last forever, so the everlasting continuance of his reign has already begun. He has the Davidic covenant kingship motifs, which began at his coronation (Heb 1:8–9). He is anointed ("Christed" or ἔχρισέν) by God to be king. The anointing includes the oil of gladness, identifying his reign as being above his co-sharers. Along with having the Davidic throne already, he has the Davidic scepter of his own righteous kingdom. This imagery of the scepter is even a messianic title in Qumran.[39] These motifs, already possessed, identify that Christ has already begun to reign. And, of course, Christ has the perfect right to reign since he created everything (Heb 1:10–12). Psalms 110:1 already declares from God that Christ is to "sit at my right hand until I make thine enemies a footstool for thy feet" (Heb 1:13). The footstool metaphor is the Ancient Near East way of indicating that, although Jesus is already the Davidic King, there will be an era in the future when he will put his foot on the necks of his enemies as evidence of their utter defeat. So, the kingdom has begun already, but there will be a greater era of an eschatological kingdom. The place of seating in this context is the Davidic throne, which Christ already has (Heb 1:5, 8). Christ is already sitting on this throne at the right hand of God (Heb 1:3), showing that he has already begun to reign. The fact that Christ awaits God's climactic judgment to subdue his enemies shows that there is a grander phase of Christ's kingdom yet to occur when no opponent will try to thwart his reign. This Davidic kingly reign realizes the aspirations of God for all humankind ruling over the creation, for Christ as king (appointed by God) rules over all the creation already (Ps 8:4–6; Heb 2:6–8). So Christ as a new Adamic king accomplishes God's original design that humans would rule the creation (Gen 1:26; Ps 8:4–6; Heb 2:6–8). God has subjected everything to Christ in his reign. Part of the effectiveness in his kingly reign identifies him in the fused king-priest role (Pss 2:7; 110:1–4; Heb 1:5, 13; 5:5–6; 7:17, 21). That is, in the begetting Christ as king, he is simultaneously begotten as priest. The extensive priestly ministry developed in Hebrews as before,

---

38. While προσκυνησάτωσαν can be honoring, the term is best taken as "worship" elsewhere in Hebrews (Heb 1:6; 11:21), and in this context, the Son is identified as God.

39. CD 7.19–20 = 4Q266 frag. 3.iv.9; 1Q28b 5.27–28; 4Q161 frags. 2–6.ii.17.

during, and after his death shows him to be king as well. And since the kingly and priestly ministries are fused into one begetting and role, he has effectively functioned as king-priest in an extended Davidic covenant manner to provide atonement for his brethren.

In contrast to such a divine Christ, angels are to render service under him to those who will inherit salvation (Heb 1:14). With salvation conceived as the future eschatological goal, the readers are warned to keep believing in this sign-attested salvation message of Christ (Heb 2:1–4).

This message includes[40] that Jesus is the human to whom the future world will be subjected (Heb 2:5). Extrapolating Psalms 8:4–6 beyond collective humanity as a miniature sovereign role ("rule" in Gen 1:26, 28),[41] Hebrews uses this text to affirm a *pesher* for Christ's kingship; in Daniel 7:13, the "Son of Man" is envisioned as the human Davidic king, who for this ministry role[42] is made lower than the angels for a little while (Heb 2:6–9 follows the LXX Ps 8:6 ἀγγέλους, replacing the MT Ps 8:7 *elohim*, "heavenly beings").[43] This human role of being lower than angels shows itself especially in Christ experiencing death for everyone (Heb 2:9). However, even in his suffering, the passage identified him as "crowned with glory and honor." That is, Christ does not diminish his deity, while Jesus experiences the most servile experience of his human suffering. Everything is for Christ, and he created all things (Heb 2:10). His death experience is used by him to bring many sons to glory, in being the author of their salvation. As such, God subjected all things to Christ, even though we do not yet see all things subjected to him (Heb 2:8[44]). There will be a future moment in which God will visibly subject all under Jesus' feet in submission (Heb 1:13, "until"; 2:8, "not yet").

---

40. The γὰρ does not introduce a new section, but returns to and carries a previous argument forward as in Hebrews 4:12, 7:1, and 10:1, contra to Koester, *Hebrews*, 213.

41. 3 En. 5:10; Pesiq. Rab. 34a.

42. 1 En. 62.7–9, and perhaps 4Q246, "Son of God," with Daniel 7 activity.

43. Syriac, Targums, and Vulgate follow "a little lower than the angels of God," whereas Aquila, Symmachus, and Theodotion translate this reference to be "a little lower than God"; Cragie, *Psalms 1–50*, 108; Gheorghita, *Role of the Septuagint*, 45.

44. Most manuscripts include that the subjection is "to him" (dative singular), underscoring that Christ (the continuing focus of the discussion, in contrast to angels and not corporate humanity) is supreme over creation.

6

Apostle Jesus, More Glorious than Moses

THE THEME OF JESUS' temptation and suffering mostly demonstrates Jesus' character as priest, but it is woven into another theme for showing the greater glory that Jesus has over Moses (Heb 3:1–6, with logical conjunction Ὅθεν). Instead of driving this discussion by OT quotes, the author utilizes indirect discourse to fund a hortatory call to consider Jesus as an apostle (Heb 3:1).[1]

Jesus is the apostle of the believer's confession (Heb 3:1 ἀπόστολον). In the LXX, the term ἀπόστολον was used to refer to the spies *sent* to spy out the land of Canaan, or Nehemiah *sent* to build the city of Jerusalem (LXX Num 13:2; Neh 2:9). The *Samaritan Targum* on Exodus 23:20 and 23 identifies that God will send "my apostle" (שׁלחי) for Israel to bring them into the Promised land.[2] Jesus is sent by God as the apostle and pioneer to lead the new exodus toward the heavenly city which he is building (Heb 3:1, 7, 13–16; 4:7; 11:10; 13:14).

Jesus is the pioneer sent to establish the new exodus (Heb 2:10; 3:1, 16). He is the *pioneer who authors* the salvation of the new exodus (Heb 2:10, ἀρχηγὸν; 5:9, αἴτιος). The term αἴτιος was used of "author" or "source"

---

1. The use of the participle in the predicate after verbs of knowing expresses indirect discourse (Heb 2:8–9; 3:1; 10:25; 13:23; Turner, *Grammar of New Testament Greek*, 3:161; Wikgren, "Some Greek Idioms," 149; Lane, *Hebrews 1–8*, 71).

2. Echoed by Justin, *1 Apol.* 12.9; 63.5, 10, 14.

or "cause as the responsible agent" of their salvation (Heb 5:9).³ The term ἀρχηγὸν was used to describe the "leader" of the tribes during the exodus (Num 10:4; 13:2–3) and in battle (Judg 5:15; 9:44; 11:6, 11; 1 Chr 5:24; 8:28; 26:26; 2 Chr 23:14; Neh 2:9; Jdt 14:2). As such, Jesus authors and leads the new exodus out toward the promised goal, the city he founds (Heb 2:10; 3:1, 16).⁴ With the same meaning, Jesus is the *forerunner* who leads the group of heralds or in war or a race (Heb 6:20, πρόδρομος).⁵ In Hebrews 12:2, Jesus has completed the race that his followers continue to run. His completion gives believers hope and direction for continuing to run the race toward kingdom. Simply put, follow Jesus.

Jesus is greater than Moses because Jesus is the builder of the house of Israel, while Moses contributed within the house of Israel (Heb 3:3–6). This activity reflects the divine role of Yahweh building Israel and all things (Heb 3:4; LXX Isa 40:28; 45:7).⁶ Likewise, Yahweh established Moses as faithful within his house of Israel (Heb 3:2, 5; Num 12:7).⁷ Such orchestrations by God are advocated by Lane to fund a priest-king messianic role within God's holy house of Israel (1 Sam 2:35 MT; 1 Chr 17:14 MT, Tg., and LXX).⁸ The author of Hebrews stressed the continuity of faithfulness of Jesus with Moses, but also developed a discontinuity in that Moses was within the house and Jesus was over the house (Heb 3:2–6). As such, Moses is faithful within Israel as a servant (Heb 3:5; Num 12:7)⁹ and a witness (Heb 3:5; John 5:39–47; Rom 3:21). In this role, Moses received glory because he repeatedly saw the glory of the Lord and his face shone with diminishing radiance over time (Num 12:8 LXX; Exod 34:29–30; 2 Cor 3:12–18). However, Jesus as Son is King of the household of faith (Heb 3:6). In such valuing, honor is to be proportionally granted to the person's merits and contribution.¹⁰

---

3. 2 Macc 4:47; 13:4; Philo, *Agriculture* 96; Philo, *Spec. Laws* 1; Josephus, *Ant.* 14.136; Josephus, *J.W.* 42; *Let. Arist.* 205.

4. ἀρχηγὸν is sometimes used as the author or founder of a city (Dio Chrysostom, *Cor.* 33.47), which is analogous to Peter's claim in Acts 3:15 that Jesus is the author of salvation.

5. Wis 12.8; Josephus, *Ant.* 7.345; 12.314; 12.372; Herodotus, *Hist.* 1.60; 4.121–22; 7.203; 9.14; Aeschylus, *Sept.* 80; Sophocles, *Ant.* 108.

6. Wis 9.2; 13.4; Philo, *Eternity* 39, 41; Josephus, *J.W.* 6.191; *P. Oxy* 892.8.

7. Tg. Neof. Num 12:7.

8. Lane, *Hebrews 1–8*, 76.

9. Exod 4:10; 14:31; Num 11:11; Deut 3:24; Josh 1:2; 8:31, 33 [9:2 LXX]; 1 Chr 16:40 LXX; Wis 10:16.

10. Sir 10.30–31; Aristotle, *Eth. nic.* 4.3; 5.6.

Therefore, Jesus, who is the divine glory (Heb 1:3) and will bring his people into the glory of the divine presence (Heb 2:10), has received greater glory as builder of his people than Moses' service within Israel (Heb 3:3). Jesus' glory surpasses Moses in the same manner as the redeemer surpasses the redeemed.

The community has been called by God *from*[11] heaven to become a new people on a new exodus *toward*[12] heaven (Heb 3:1; both heaven options are permitted by the genitive, plus the extended exodus imagery of Heb 3–4). Additionally, the new community has begun as holy brethren because priest Jesus has sanctified them (Heb 2:11; 3:1). This new community becomes the household of faith, provided that we hold fast to our boldness of hope (Heb 3:6). The author of Hebrews at this point does not explain how this boldness is obtained; rather, his concern is that we continue to boldly and firmly hope with Jesus until the end.

This exodus approach that the community is to firmly pursue until the end sets up a two-way soteriology unto an eschatological judgment (Heb 2:10; 3:1, 6, 16). Jesus' narrow way within a two-way orientation heads toward an eschatological justification, which assesses every human at an eschatological forensic judgment according to her deeds.[13] This approach

---

11. It is possible that the genitive identifies the origin of the call as is done with "heavenly gifts" in Hebrews 6:4.

12. It is possible that the genitive takes heaven as the destination of the call: Heb 11:16; 12:22; Philo, *Planter* 26–27; Philo, *Alleg. Interp.* 3.101–3; Philo, *QE* 2.46; Dey, *Intermediary World and Patterns*, 161–64; Koester, *Hebrews*, 242.

13. Nairne, *Epistle of Priesthood*, 205, 226–28; Käsemann, *Wandering People of God*, 86; Spicq, *L'Epître aux Hébreux*, 1:243–46, 269–80; Johnston, "Pilgrimage Motif," 239–51; This judgment according to deeds is continued in the two-way teaching of the church: Did. 1.1.1–4; 4.14b; 1 Clem. 34–35; 2 Clem. 6.8; 8.4; Polycarp, *Phil.* 10; Ign. *Phil.* 5.1; Ign. *Eph.* 3.1; Barn. 16.7–8; 18.1–2; 19; Justin, *Dial.* 3.4; Justin, *1 Apol.* 16.8–9; Justin, *2 Apol.* 9; Irenaeus (*Haer.* 3.1.10) maintained this as the universal teaching all Christians held at the time; Herm. Mand. 2.7; Herm. Sim. 3.8.6–11; Clement of Alexandria, *Strom.* 4.6; Clement of Alexandria, *Quis div.*, esp. 1.6–7; 16.5; Commodianus, *Instr.* 28; Origen, *Comm. Matt.* 14.10–13; Origen, *Fr. Prin.* 2.9.7–8; 3.1.12; Cyprian, *Fort.* 12–13; Dionysius of Alexandria, *Exegetical Fragments* 7, "Reception of Lapsed"; Methodius of Olympus, *Banquet of the Ten Virgins* 9.3; Methodius of Olympus, *Oration Concerning Simeon and Anna* 8; Lactantius, *Inst.* 3.12; 6.3–7; 7.10; Lactantius, *Epit.* 73; Lactantius, *Constitutions of the Holy Apostles* 7.1.1–2; Lactantius, *Clementine Homilies* 18.17; Eusebius, *Hist. eccl.* 2.19; 3.20.6–7; 5.1.10, 48; 5.8.5; 5.13.5; Eusebius, *Council of Sardica Lengthy Creed*: Socrates Scholasticus, *Hist. eccl.* 2.19 = Athanasius, *Syn.* 26; 351 = Hilary of Pointers, *On the Councils* 34 and 359 AD *Sirmium Creed*: Socrates Scholasticus, *Hist. eccl.* 2.30 = Athanasius, *Syn.* 27 = Hilary of Pointers, *On the Councils* 38; *Synod at Ariminum Creed*: Socrates Scholasticus, *Hist. eccl.* 2.37; 359 AD *Seleucia Creed*: Socrates

fits within Judaism's two-way perspective of the Mosaic covenant as a Suzerainty treaty binding Israel in a relationship that offers blessing or curse dependent upon her obedience.[14] For example, Israel is already blessed in a covenant relationship with *Yahweh*. This relationship is expressed as coming from the exodus and heading toward the promised land and the kingdom. Furthermore, if Israel obeyed all the law, then they would be wonderfully blessed, enabling kingdom to come (Deut 28:1–14; 30:8–20). However, if Israel disobeyed then they will be horribly cursed (Deut 28:15–30:20). This sets up a narrow way of blessing and a broad way of wrath. The prophets call Israel back from their wandering ways to the narrow way of covenant faithfulness (1 Kgs 19:10; Jer 21:8; Ezek 9:8–10). However, these two ways (one of blessing and the other of curse) are also evident in the wisdom tradition, for wisdom calls the wise to follow in a narrow way, fitting into the patterns of creation, in contrast to the many broad ways of the fool that lead to destruction. In this approach, wisdom is vindicated in one showing a consistency to the narrow way of the wise, in contrast to the broad way

---

Scholasticus, *Hist. eccl.* 2.40 = Athanasius, *Syn.* 8; 359 AD *Confession at Niké* and 360 AD *Constantinople Creed*: Athanasius, *Syn.* 30; 359 AD *Ariminum Creed* and modified for the 381 AD Council at Constantinople: Socrates Scholasticus, *Hist. eccl.* 2.41; Athanasius, *Inc.* 57; Cyril, *Catechetical Lectures* 15.1, 24–25, 33; Gregory of Nyssa, *On Pilgrimages*, paragraph 1; Gregory of Nyssa, *Great Catechism* 40; Gregory of Nazianzus, *Or. Bas.* 4; Ambrose, *Off.* 1.16.59; Augustine, *Conf.* 1.11.17; Augustine, *Civ.* 13.8; 14.25; 19.11; 20.1–8, 12, 14, 22; 21.1; Augustine, *Trin.* 8.7–8; Augustine, *Enchir.* 15; 31–32; 55; 107; 113; Augustine, *Doctr. chr.* 1.12.10; Augustine, *Perf.* 42–44; Augustine, *Ennarat. Ps.* 31.25; 112.5; Augustine, *Tract. Ev. Jo.* 124.5; Hilary of Poitiers, *On the Trinity* 12.45; Leo the Great, *Sermons* 46.3; 49.2, 5; 63.2, 7; 67.5–6; 72.1; 95.1–9; Vincent of Lérins, *Commonitory* 23.57–59, which he claims is the teaching everyone held at that time: 23.4–6; John Cassian, *Cassian's Conferences* 1.1.5; 1.6.3, 8; 1.40.9; 2.13.13, 18; 2.14.3, 9; John Cassian, *Seven Books of John Cassian* 3.13–14; Leo the Great, *Sermons* 23.5; 24.1–5; 26.2; 66.7; 90.2; 95.1–9; Saint John Climacus, *Ladder of Divine Ascent*, 9.1; summary on step 30; Thomas à Kempis, *Of the Imitation of Christ*, esp. 1.23; 2.7; 3.44, 56; Bunyan, *Pilgrim's Progress*, esp. 18, 187; Reiche, "New Testament Concept of Reward," 195–206; Jeremias, *Neotestamentliche Theologie*, 209; Willard, *Divine Conspiracy*; Yinger, *Paul, Judaism, and Judgment*, 285—summary, but argued through the book; Grindheim, "Ignorance is Bliss," 313–31; Kim, *God Will Judge Each One*; Dunn, *New Perspective on Paul*, 72–73; Dunn, "If Paul Could Believe," 135, and Dunn, "Response to Thomas Schreiner," 106–8. However, this view can be granted from outside the two-way tradition, such as from the Reformed tradition: Calvin, *Institutes of the Christian Religion*, 3.15.8; 3.16.1; "we are justified not without works, and not by works, since in the participation in Christ, by which we are justified, is contained not less sanctification than justification" (16.3); 18.1; Schreiner, "Justification," 78–79.

14. Mendenhall, "Covenant Forms in Israelite Tradition," 50–76; Baltzer, *Das Bundesformular*; Kline, *Treaty of the Great King*.

of the fool (Prov 28:6; Matt 7:24–27; 11:19; Luke 7:35). These revelational approaches, covenant and wisdom, have come together through a two-way expression in the wisdom and torah psalms (Pss 1:6; 119:29–32; 139:24). This two-way orientation is embraced even more in sectarian purifying within early Judaism, like Qumran and the Essenes.[15] The continuation of the domination of Israel by gentile powers indicated in this Deuteronomist approach that Israel had repeatedly chosen the way of disobedience (Deut 9:7; 28:15—30:20; 2 Kgs 17:23; Neh 9:32; Isa 9:1–2; Ezek 21:3; 20:31; Mic 5:3–4).[16] Their precarious condition before wrathful *Yahweh* was confessed by *Baruch* 1.18–19.

> We have disobeyed Him, and have not heeded the voice of the Lord our God, to walk in the statutes of the Lord that he set before us. From the time when the Lord brought our ancestors out of the land of Egypt to this day.

So while Judaism hoped for the kingdom, their domination by gentiles reminded them that they were disobedient, repeatedly choosing the broad way of rebellion.

However, God promised that he would transform Israel into a kingdom (Deut 30:1–6; Jer 31:33–34). Within early Judaism, the hope of the messianic kingdom coming was strong, and included the desire that the tribes of Israel be regathered in covenant blessing (Isa 40; Jer 31:27–28; 32:6—33:26).[17] It also included the expectation that gentiles would be converted, destroyed, or subjugated (Isa 60:10–14; Dan 2:44–45; 7:14).[18] The Jewish hope for Jerusalem was that it will be made glorious, with the temple

---

15. Sir 2.12; 15.11–17; 21:10–14; Wis 5.6–7; 2 Esd 7:6–14; 30.15; 42.10; Pss. Sol. 9.5; 14.10; 3 Macc 5.51; 2 Bar. 59.10; 85.13; 4 Ezra 7.3–9, 48, 82, 129, 137; Sib. Or. 2.150; b. Ber. 28b; m. 'Abot 2.9; Philo, *Sacrifices* 2; Philo, *Agriculture* 103–4; 'Abot R. Nat. 14, 18, 25; T. Ash. 1:3, 5; 6.3; T. Jac. 2.17; Pesiq. Rab. 179b; t. Soṭah 7.11; t. Sanh. 14.4; b. Ber. 28b; b. Ḥag. 3b; b. 'Erub. 19a; Mek. Exod. 14:28; Sipre Deut. 11:26; 1QS 3:13—4.26; Apoc. Zeph. 3.9. The early church continued in this two-way teaching: Did. 1–6; Barn. 18–20; Herm. Mand. 6; Herm. Sim. 9.12.5; Ps.-Clem. Hom. 3.52.2; 5.7; T. Ab. 10–11; Const. Ap. 1–5; Kennard, "Two Ways Christian Life View," 313–14.

16. 1 Esd 8.73–74; 2 Esd 9.7; Bar 1.13, 18–19; 2.6.

17. Sir 35.11; 48.10; Bar 4.37; 5.5; 2 Macc 1.27; 2.18; Jub. 1.15; Pss. Sol. 11.2; 8.34; 17.50; 17.28–31; 1QM 2.2, 7; 3.13; 5.1; 11QT 8.14–16; 57.5; Philo, *Rewards* 164.

18. Sir 36.1–9; Jub. 24.29; 1 En. 90.19; Pss. Sol. 17.24, 31; T. Mos. 10.7; 1QM; CD 14.6; Sib. Or. 3; Philo, *Rewards* 93–97, 164.

rebuilt and purified (Ezek 40–47; Jer 33:18–22).[19] In this time of the kingdom, worship would be pure, and the people would be righteous.[20]

Such a narrow way framed virtues like faith, hope, and perseverance, which imitate Christ and identify a person in a love relationship with God and Christ. Jesus' narrow way is still a gracious salvation because the virtues identify one's loyalty unto either God and salvation, or idolatry and damnation. For example, in this framework, Augustine recognized that God's justification was graciously grounded upon Christ's death transformed into the inherent condition of the elect so that the believer might journey the narrow way (unhindered by previous legal debt), accruing virtue unto eschatological justification and kingdom.[21] Roman Catholic salvation portrays God's gracious placing of those who encounter Christ into a mystical relationship in Christ so that his supernatural love would synergistically render Christians sufficiently mature so as to have meritorious works to vindicate us upon death (Heb 12:23; 2 Cor 5:8; Phil 1:23) and before the eschatological judgment undertaken by Christ (Heb 12:23; Matt 25:31–46; John 5:28–29).[22] Protestant models tend to develop this narrow way as a pilgrimage or race in the wake of Christ's efficacious death for our sins.[23] A gracious patristic and charismatic Lutheranism results through the Holy Spirit fruiting lifestyle transformation, fulfilling the virtues of the law that presently demonstrate a living justification in the life of the believer in Christ,[24] but Hebrews does not develop this role of the Spirit.

19. Tob 13.16–18; 14.5; 1 En. 90.28; 91.13; Jub. 1.17, 27, 29; 25.21; 11QT 29.8–10; Pss. Sol. 8.12; 17.30; Sib. Or. 3.657–709; 5.420–25; Philo, *Rewards* 168.

20. Jub. 33.11, 20; Josephus, *J.W.* 2.7; 1QSa 2.3–10; 1QM 7.5; 11QT 45.11–17; Pss. Sol. 17.26; Sib. Or. 3.756–81.

21. Augustine on past justification: *Grat.* 17.33; 19; 21; Henninger, *Sanctus Augustinus et doctrina de duplici iustitia*, 79; McGrath, *Iustitia Dei*, 409; narrow way to future justification: Augustine, *Civ.* 13.8; 14.25; 19.11; 20.1–8, 12, 14, 22; 21.1; Augustine, *Enchir.* 15; 31–32; 55; 107; 113; Augustine, *Perf.* 42–44; Augustine, *Ennarat. Ps.* 31.25; 112.5; Augustine, *Tract. Ev. Jo.* 124.5.

22. *Catechism of the Catholic Church*, 487, no. 2011; *Council of Trent*, Session 6, ch 5; Session 6, ch. 8 cited from Schroeder, *Canons and Decrees*, 31, 35; Barber, "Catholic Perspective," 161–84.

23. Bunyan, *Pilgrim's Progress*; Schreiner and Caneday, *Race Set before Us*.

24. Augustine, *Spir. et litt.* 26–29, and esp. 46; Luther, *Luther's Works*, 25:243–44; 9:179; Melanchthon, *Loci Communes of Philip Melanchthon*, 123; Oecolampadius, *In Hieremiam prophetam commentariorum*, 2.162a; *The Thirty Nine Articles of the Church of England* (1571), art. 7; Augustine, Ambroisiater, and Pelagius held this Christian worldview (Bray, *Romans*, 205–6); Godet, *Commentary on Romans*, 302; Murray, *Epistle to the Romans*, 283; Cranfield, *Critical and Exegetical Commentary*, 383–84; Keck, "Law,"

This Spirit fruiting virtues could also be understood as an Edwardsian Reformed demonstration of religious affections vindicating one's regeneration, and thus indicating who the justified elect are.[25] This Edwardsian approach would subsume the two-way as a vindication of Christ's vicarious atonement for the elect. Thus in a Reformed model, such Spirit-guaranteed vindication through virtues identifies those who are authentically the elect of God. However, Hebrews does not develop an elaborate election theme as do Paul, Peter or John. It is better to leave Hebrews' exodus-perseverance theme within a two-way salvation strategy.

As apostle, Jesus pioneers the narrow exodus way toward the kingdom. Jesus' believers should follow him in his narrow way of faith and perseverance toward his kingdom because he is already king there.

52–53; Sanders, *Paul, the Law*, 93–4; Räisänen, *Paul and the Law*, 65–67; Hübner, *Law in Paul's Thought*, 146–47; Schnabel, *Law and Wisdom*, 288–90; Dunn, *Romans 1–8*, 423–24; Wright, *Climax of the Covenant*, 212; Stuhlmacher, *Paul's Letter to the Romans*, 120; Schreiner, *Law and Its Fulfillment*, 71–73; Schreiner, *Romans*, 404–8; Thielman, *Paul & the Law*, 242–43; Dabney, "Justified by the Spirit," 50; Seifrid, *Christ, Our Righteousness*; Das, *Paul, the Law and the Covenant*, 226; McFadden, "Fulfillment of the Law's DIKAIŌMA," 483–97.

25. Edwards, *Treatise Concerning Religious Affections*.

7

Melchizedek Priest

THE PRACTICE OF ANOINTING a priest is evident in Leviticus 4:3, 5, 16 and 6:20, thus placing priesthood within the bounds of the anointed (messiah). Four Jewish strands weave together to inform a priestly messiah idea: a Mosaic-Davidic-Hasmonean pattern, Qumran's "the messiah of Aaron," Joshua (the priest of Zechariah 4), and Melchizedek. Hebrews especially develops the Melchizedek high priest concept.

THE JEWISH HERITAGE OF KING-PRIEST

The Mosaic pattern presented a leader of the people who also did priestly roles as well. For example, Moses fulfilled the priestly role by cleansing the tabernacle as well as Aaron, the high priest, and his sons (Exod 39:43; 40:17–35; Lev 8–9). In early Judaism, Philo considered Moses to be both king[1] and high priest,[2] though Hebrews never presents Moses as an exemplar of kingship under God as king or of this priesthood.[3] Furthermore, when David moved the tabernacle into Jerusalem, he sacrificed oxen and danced in the parade, which tends to merge the royal and priestly roles (2

---

1. Philo, *Heir* 301; Philo, *Confusion* 1; Meeks, *Prophet-King*, 100–163; Williamson, *Epistle to the Hebrews*, 449–91; Williamson, "Philo and New Testament Christology," 439–45; Holladay, *Theios Aner in Hellenistic Judaism*, 104–67.

2. Philo, *Moses* 2.66–186; Philo, *Rewards* 52–55; Philo, *Giants* 52–54.

3. Isaacs, *Sacred Space*, 137–38; contra Dey (*Intermediary World and Patterns*, 157–63), who maintains "high priest" as one of Moses' titles following Philo.

Sam 6:13–15). David also showed a priestly concern in trying to construct the temple, which Solomon actually constructed (2 Sam 7:2, 13). David also contributed to the worship in the temple with his composition of psalms, which helped to express the prayers of the people. Once the monarchy had disappeared during the Babylonian captivity, the high priest appropriated the royal paraphernalia, such as the crown, indicating that he was the head of the nation (Zech 6:9–14; cf. 2 Sam 12:30; Jer 13:18; Ezek 21:31). Under Seleucid domination of Israel, the high priesthood was vacant, for sale to the highest bidder. With the resolution of the Maccabean revolt, Jonathan—of an obscure priestly lineage of Yehoyarib—was elevated by the Seleucid emperor to high priest for the Feast of Booths in 152 BC and then promoted to be military and civil governor of Judea.[4] Under the Hasmoneans, the eight high priests (from Jonathan to Antigonus) were also kings, and took the title as well. Antigonus Mattathias, the last king-priest of this line (40–37 BC) was replaced by Herod the Great. Thereafter, the high priest was at the disposal of the sovereign, who could appoint and dismiss nominees at his caprice.

The Qumran community had an eschatological hope of "the messiah of Aaron" to bring a stable reign and era of peace. The Damascus Document occasioned considerable interest, with a repeated hope of the rise of "the messiah of Aaron and Israel."[5] The singular noun in these texts left only the possibility that there would be one messiah, who would be priest and king for Israel. When the plural noun "messiahs" turned up in other texts,[6] indicating the Qumran expectation of "messiahs of Aaron and Israel," the majority of Qumran interpreters concluded that Qumran expected two messiahs: a priestly one and a royal one. Marvin Pate conjectures that the reason for the bifurcation of the messiah into two personages was due to the Essenes objection to the Hasmonaean combination of the two roles into a unified king-priest.[7]

---

4. 1 Macc 2.1; 10.65.

5. CD 12:23—13:1; 14:19; 19:10–11; 20:1; *Charter of a Jewish Sectarian Association* 9.11; text 7, 19; 4Q171 3.15; 4Q175 1.14; 4Q521 frags. 8, 9. Some also argue that 4Q174's "interpreter of the Law" should be identified as the priestly messiah because of its close proximity to the blessing of Levi of Deuteronomy 33 in this text, a blessing that in the earlier 4Q175 probably refers to the eschatological priest. A priestly messiah is also supported by 1QS 9.11 and T. Levi 4.2; 17.2; 18.6–7.

6. 1QS 9:16; 19:11; *Rule of the Congregation* 2:11–22; and 4Q175.

7. Pate, *Communities of the Last Days*, 120.

In Zechariah 4, there are two anointed figures envisioned: the royal figure Zerubbabel and the anointed righteous high priest Joshua.[8] During the Babylonian exile, Zerubbabel and Joshua share the leadership of the Jewish community. This eschatological priest pattern developed further in ben Sir 45–50, and especially 49:11–12.[9] For example, ben Sir 45:6–24 describes Aaron at greater length than David (47:2–11). However, the priestly messiah comes to full fruition in the Testaments of the Twelve Patriarchs, where Levi (the priest) is superior to Judah (the king).[10] The Testament of Levi 18.3–4 predicts that a new priest will come to replace the judged wicked ones, described as "his star shall rise in heaven like a king" and he "will shine forth like the sun in the earth." Also, in the Qumran scrolls, the priestly messiah (the messiah of Aaron) is greater than the messiah of Israel.[11] The rabbis connected this priestly image with Melchizedek and Elijah.[12]

THE MELCHIZEDEK TRADITION[13]

The Melchizedek tradition begins with an enigmatic appearance of Melchizedek in Genesis 14:18–24. The name of Melchizedek in Hebrew means "king of righteousness" (Gen 14:18; Heb 7:2).[14] He is also king of Salem or peace (*shalom*), the city that would eventually be known as Jeru-

---

8. Similar allusions to two messiahs: a king and priest in Jer 33:15–18; Hag 2:1–7; Zech 6:12–13; and 4Q254 frag. 4.

9. 1QS 9.11; 1QSa 2.11–17; 4Q174 3.11–12; T. Reu. 6.8; T. Jud. 21.1–5 where the priest is above the royal figure; T. Sim. 5.5 with 1QM; 2 Macc 1.10.

10. In Testament of Judah 21:2–4, the Lord "set the kingship beneath the priesthood . . . as heaven is higher than the earth, so is the priesthood of God higher than the kingship on the earth" (Hollander and de Jonge, *Testaments of the Twelve Patriarchs*, 222). Additionally, a small fragment of Testament of Levi reads, "the kingdom of priesthood is greater than the kingdom" (1Q21, frag. 1).

11. The Messiah of Aaron takes precedence over the Messiah of Israel (1QS 9.11); the Messiah of Aaron stretches out his hand to the bread before the Messiah of Israel (1QSa 2.17–21); and the blessing of the high priest precedes that of the prince of the congregation (1QSb); Collins, *Scepter and Star*, 74–77, 83–95.

12. Comparing t. b. Sukkah 52b with Song of Songs Rab. 2.13–14; Horton, *Melchizedek Tradition*, 125–30.

13. This is a subject that the author of Hebrews indicates is difficult, and thus becomes one indication of an individual's maturity in spiritual matters (Heb 5:11—6:1).

14. Josephus (*J.W.* 6.438 and *Ant.* 1.179–81) describes Titus's destruction of Jerusalem and the temple reports that the founder of the city was a Canaanite chieftain known as the "king of righteousness" (Philo, *Alleg. Interp.* 79).

salem[15] (Gen 14:18; Heb 7:2). In early Judaism, Melchizedek's rule becomes identified as over all the forces of light.[16]

No genealogy in Genesis or Hebrews identifies who Melchizedek is;[17] he just appears as a priest of the Most High God in the narrative (Gen 14:18; Heb 7:3). Sectarian Jewish literalists would likely consider such an individual without a genealogy to be an angel,[18] and this is why Hebrews discusses Jesus' superiority over angels. Similarly, many Christian literalists consider Melchizedek to be a pre-incarnate visitation of Jesus.[19] However, Hebrews identified that Jesus follows after Melchizedek's pattern, so Melchizedek is someone different than Jesus for Jesus to be compared to him (Heb 5:5–6, 10; 7:17).[20] Furthermore, the author of Hebrews engages this topic, admitting that he is viewing the subject metaphorically (Heb 7:9, καὶ ὡς ἔπος εἰπεῖν) without recording a genealogy,[21] so these two literalist groups are forcing an identification beyond what the text supplies. Mainstream Judaism views Melchizedek as a faithful human initiating worship at Jerusalem.[22] Without a genealogy mentioned in Genesis, the individual priest becomes the focus, rather than a lineage of high priests. Additionally,

---

15. Salem is traditionally identified as Jerusalem (Ps 76:2; Josephus, *Ant.* 1.180; 1QapGen ar 22.13–14; Tg. Neof. on Gen 14:18; Vincent, "Abraham à Jérusalem," 360–71; Winter, "Note on Salem-Jerusalem," 151–52).

16. 4Q545 frags. 2, 3.15–16.

17. Beginning with the second century AD, rabbis identify Melchizedek as Noah's son Shem late in his life (Gen. Rab. [Lech Lecha] 44.7; Tg. Neof. 1; Tg. Ps.-Jon.; Midr. Teh. on Ps. 76.3; Fitzmyer, *Genesis Apocryphon*, 31–32; Hayward, "Shem, Melchizedek, and Concern," 67–80). This view is countered by the Davidic perspective of Ps 110 and the Qumran eschatological Melchizedek in 11Q13.

18. 4Q545 frag. 2, 3.15–16; 11Q13 2.10–11, 13–14, 22, 24–25.

19. Philo, *Dreams* 1.215; Philo, *Alleg Interp.* 3.82; Philo, *Giants* 52; Philo, *Migration* 102; Dunn, *Christology in the Making*, 53–54.

20. John Chrysostom, *Hom.* 12.3; Epiphanius, *Panarion* 55.1.7.

21. Lane, *Hebrews 1–8*, 158; Plutarch utilized ἀπάτωρ to refer to a "genealogy as unknown" and the Syriac Peshitta utilized the phrase "without father and mother" as indicating that the genealogy was not recorded (Liddell et al., *Greek-English Lexicon*, 181; MM 54–55; Cockerill, *Melchizedek Christology in Heb. 7:1–28*, 42–50).

22. 1QapGen ar 22, 12–25; Philo, *Prelim. Studies* 99; Philo, *Abraham* 235; Josephus, *Ant.* 1.179–82; J.W. 6.438; Charlesworth, *Old Testament Pseudepigrapha*, 2:880; Jub 13.25. Rabbinic sources regularly identify Melchizedek as Noah's son Shem late in his life (see footnote 9). Rabbinic tradition further identified that Melchizedek turned over this human priesthood to Abraham (b. Ned 32b; Lev. Rab. 25.6).

the lack of a genealogy sets up a meme of a perpetual priesthood within which Jesus operates (Heb 7:24–25).[23]

Abram heard that the forces of Chedorlaomer had taken his relative Lot captive, so he went after them with three hundred and eighteen men, defeating the rear guard and freeing the captives. As he returned with these rescued captives and spoil from the battle, Melchizedek, the king of Salem, came out to meet Abram with provisions of bread and wine (Gen 14:18; Heb 7:2, 4).[24] Melchizedek blessed Abram with prayer[25] to the name of God Most High, "El Elyon," to which Abram could relate (Gen 14:19–20; Heb 7:1, 6–7). Abram responded by giving God's priest, Melchizedek, a tenth of the spoil,[26] and thereby indicating that both recognized that the victory was from God. Apart from this tithe of gratitude to God and the spoils consumed by his fellow warriors, Abram insisted on returning the people and the spoils to their rightful kings (Gen 14:21–24).

The enigmatic pictureof Melchizedek continues in the Davidic[27] royal Psalms 110. Here the Davidic king (or a king greater than David) is seen as having a willing and strong conquering army. However, Yahweh swore by an oath that this king was a priest forever[28] "after the pattern of" (עַל־דִּבְרָתִי; κατὰ τὴν τάξιν) Melchizedek (Ps 110[LXX109]:4). The phrase עַל־דִּבְרָתִי/'ldbrt or κατὰ τὴν τάξιν ("after the pattern") does not indicate that a new priestly order is being established, but rather the comparison that

---

23. Syriac Peshitta Heb 7:3 identified that "the priesthood remains forever," not that Melchizedek "remains as priest forever" (Koester, *Hebrews*, 349).

24. 1QapGen ar 22.15 presents the Genesis text literally in Aramaic, but adds that Melchizedek's generosity of food and wine was for all the men with Abraham. Josephus (*Ant.* 1.181) describes that these gifts and provisions foster a festival honoring the conquerors with Abram.

25. Philo (*Alleg. Interp.* 3.79–82; *Prelim. Studies* 99; and especially the fuller *Abraham* 235) adds to the Genesis account, that Melchizedek lifts his hands in prayer and then offers victory sacrifices. According to Philo, this mutual generosity begins a lasting friendship between Abram and Melchizedek.

26. Howard ("Hebrews and the Old Testament Quotations," 211) identified that the quote was similar in both MT and LXX. Josephus, *Ant.* 1.181; 1QapGen ar 22.17 presents the Genesis text literally in Aramaic, but adds that the spoils came from the flocks of the king of Elam and his allies.

27. Most commentators see this as a Davidic psalm based on the superscription in the first verse, and the similarity of this kind of oath with the Davidic covenant (Allen, *Psalms 101–150*, 81). However, a few see this as a Hasmonean composition perhaps justifying Simon Maccabeus royal priesthood (ca. 142–143 BC) on the basis of a tenuous acrostic (Simeon) beginning each verse.

28. "Forever" (עוֹלָם) indicates perpetuity in time (Pss 106:1, 31, 48; 107:1; 111:5, 8–9).

this king-priest is "after the pattern" or "in the manner of" Melchizedek in role.[29] That is, there are only two, Melchizedek (the original) and Jesus, who fits within that pattern (Heb 5:5–6). The psalm is an oath promising that Yahweh will destroy kings and nations in judgment in order to establish this king-priest as triumphant in his kingdom of refreshment (Ps 110:5–7).

In Qumran, an eschatological priest was to be associated, if not equated with Melchizedek. Marvin Pate summarizes the primary document for this view, 11Q13 as interpreting the Year of Jubilee (Lev 25:13)[30] and the return from the Babylonian exile[31] (Isa 61:1–3)[32] as ultimately fulfilled in the Qumran community.

> Three points dominate the work:
>
> 1. The DSS people are the true inheritors of the land of Israel (11Q13 2:1–4).
>
> 2. They have followed the true interpretation of the law (11Q13 2:20–24); therefore Melchizedek, the heavenly priest, has made atonement for their sins (11Q13 2:6–9).
>
> 3. When Melchizedek, the heavenly priest, wages eschatological war against those who follow Belial, which have departed from the true Torah (11Q13 2–5; 11–13; 25), the Essenes will be vindicated and rule with him (11Q13 2:10–11, 14–24; cf. 1QM 17:1–9, where Michael most likely is to be equated with Melchizedek).
>
> The purpose of the Essenes' aligning themselves with Melchizedek was as the true descendants of Aaron (see CD 6:2–6; 1Qsa 2), to legitimate their interpretation of the Law of Moses over against the Jerusalem leadership's reading of the Torah.[33]

---

29. The other Biblical instances of this word indicate a comparison meaning "manner," "likeness," or "concern" (Eccl 3:18; 7:14; 8:2). The words could indicate "because" or "in the case of," as in Job 5:8, but this meaning would not fit this Psalms context. Likewise, the LXX Ps 109:4 statement of κατὰ τὴν τάξιν indicates the "quality," "manner," or "condition of likeness" so that if it had been preceded by the preposition ἐν, the possibility of a fixed order of priests would be more likely (Bauer et al., *Greek-English Lexicon*, 811).

30. 11Q13 7; for text and analysis of this document, Kobelski, *Melchizedek and Melchireša'*.

31. 11Q13 6.

32. Parts of Isaiah 61:1–3 are quoted or alluded to in 11Q13 15–18.

33. Pate, *Communities of the Last Days*, 123; Yadin, "Dead Sea Scrolls," 36–55.

Melchizedek is described in Qumran as *elohim* in his role as eschatological judge.³⁴ However, the *elohim* are plural here, for he is standing among the *elohim* and exacting the vengeance for our God (*elohenu*). However, the Qumran interpreter takes the *elohenu* to refer to Melchizedek, and cites passages which he takes to be angels judging fallen angels.³⁵ In this role of judging angels and the saints, Melchizedek is also "the Messiah of the Spirit" who cultivates a people for himself.³⁶ This identifies Melchizedek with the Messiah of Daniel 9:26: "After sixty-two weeks the Anointed One shall be cut off."³⁷ After this undeveloped death, Melchizedek announces Jubilee comfort and rules over "all the sons of righteousness who uphold the covenant."³⁸ There is no Second-Temple Jewish echo of who this Melchizedek might be and when he comes.

It is broadly acknowledged that there is similarity between Melchizedek here and the archangel Michael of the *War Scroll,* though the two are never equated in any Qumran document.³⁹ F. Garcia Martinez has even suggested that Melchizedek may be identified with "the Son of God" from another Qumran document, the *Aramaic Apocalypse.*⁴⁰

William Schniedewind suggests that the Melchizedek tradition at Qumran should be read as a dualism with a rival figure, the chief evil angel *Melchiresha* (king of wickedness) in 4Q543–48 and 4Q280.⁴¹ This *Melchiresha* leads an angelic rebellion from God, so that these Melchizedek texts describe the climactic demise of this rebellion at the judgment meted out by Melchizedek.

Second Enoch 71–72 described a Melchizedek tradition that may be later than Hebrews.⁴² In 2 Enoch, "Melchizedek" is a title, with several "according to the order of Melchizedek," after the pattern of the greatest

---

34. 11Q13 10–11, 13–14. This *elohim* view was interpreted late in the fourth century by Eliphanius of Salamis as indicative of divinity (*Panarion* 55.7.3) and some others have followed his view, esp. a fifth century AD gnostic sect referred to as the Melchizedekians (Horton, *Melchizedek Tradition,* 89–113; Pearson, "Figure of Melchizedek," 108–23).

35. 11Q13 24–25, citing Pss 82:1; 7:8–9; 82:2; and Isa 52:7.

36. 11Q13 18.

37. 11Q13 18.

38. 11Q13 19–25.

39. 1QM 9:14–16.

40. 4Q246; Schniedewind, "Melchizedek, Traditions of," 694.

41. Schniedewind, "Melchizedek, Traditions of," 694; Rainbow, "Melchizedek as a Messiah," 186.

42. 2 En. 71–72 manuscripts A and J; Gieschen, "Different Functions," 364–79.

Melchizedek described in Genesis. This one great original Melchizedek in 2 Enoch was born "fully developed" as a three-year-old with the birthmark of the high priest upon him, and thus he must have been protectively hidden in the Garden of Eden for seven years by the agency of Michael, the archangel. The great Melchizedek of 2 Enoch is then established at the center of the creation as the high priest and head of the order of Melchizedek.[43] As in Genesis, Abraham comes upon him and is honored by him.

Mainstream Judaism marginalizes the Qumran and Enochian constructs of Melchizedek, reducing him back to a human king-priest. For example, Josephus and Philo describe Melchizedek simply as a righteous human king of Jerusalem after the Genesis pattern.[44] The second-century Aramaic Targum Neofiti and the Fragment Targum (and later Targum Pseudo-Jonathan) identified Melchizedek as Noah's son Shem, who they say served as high priest before God. All the Ethiopic copies of the manuscript Jubilees 13:25–29 recount Abraham having a conversation with the king of Sodom, without Melchizedek even entering the story, and only that the Levitical priests have the right to receive tithes in Israel. Latter rabbinic traditions identify that this Shem-Melchizedek high priesthood was transferred to Aaron through Abraham. For example, b. Zebaḥ. 62a read Psalms 110:4 as "You [Abraham] are a priest forever." This might be a Jewish reaction to Christian Melchizedek teaching about Jesus Christ. However, even within mainstream Judaism, b. Sukkah 52b identifies Melchizedek as a human priest who translated into heaven (as occurred to Enoch in Hebrews 11:5) and would reappear in the messianic age.

Likewise, in mainstream Judaism, the Levitical priests took on the role of priest for Israel without an oath because they are born into a genetic lineage of priests, which was initiated by an oath. They can operate as priests because God called Aaron and his lineage to this ministry (Heb 5:4; Exod 28:1; Num 3:10; 18:1).[45] Obviously, there were a lot of these priests to carry out the sacrifices offered in the court as proscribed by the law because the task was large and they would eventually die (Heb 7:23; 9:6). However, by this time in early Judaism, the high priest had become a political appointment at the caprice of the Herodian king or Roman governor. Under this arrangement, there were twenty-eight high priests from 37 BC to AD 70, so family members within the best endowed priestly families would pass

---

43. 2 En. 71:35 [J].
44. Josephus, *Ant.* 1.10.2; Philo, *Alleg. Interp.* 3.25–26.
45. Sir 45.6–7a; Josephus, *Ant.* 3.188–92.

the role around (Matt 26:3, 57; Luke 3:2; John 11:49; 18:13–14, 24; Acts 4:6; 23:2, 4; 24:1). So, not only was there continual turnover of the Levitical priests, there was fairly rapid turnover of the high priest.

None of the Gospels develop Jesus in a priestly manner. James Dunn suggests that the reasons for this were: 1) Jesus' lineage was known well enough to establish him in the tribe of Judah as Davidic, and to exclude him from that of a priestly lineage of Aaron (Matt 1:1–17; Luke 3:23–33; Heb 7:14), and 2) the Gospel writers considered that it would be inappropriate to create such facts.[46] Such is the case, even though Jesus quotes from Psalms 110:1 to elevate their Jewish understanding, "If David calls him Lord, how can he be his son?" (Matt 22:41–45; Mark 12:35–37; Luke 20:41–44).

Hebrews identifies that Melchizedek appears in Genesis as king of Salem to meet Abraham (Heb 7:1–10). Hebrews identifies that Melchizedek is greater than Abraham, because the lesser is blessed by the greater (Heb 7:7). Additionally, this sentiment is extended to Melchizedek as greater than Aaron through a figurative analogy (Heb 7:9, "so to speak"/καὶ ὡς ἔπος εἰπεῖν). So, this text is not trying to teach a biological and theological seminalism that the subsequent generations are actually within the previous generations, participating in the deeds of the previous generation. However, in a literary analogy ("so to speak"), Levi (who collected tithes from Israel) was metaphorically within Abraham, as he was part of the lineage yet to come. Thus, when Abraham paid tithes to Melchizedek, so did Levi (Heb 7:4–10). Thus, in Hebrews' argument, Melchizedek being greater than Abraham further identifies that Melchizedek priests are greater than Levitical priests.

This literary analogy points out that Levi and his sons are mortal humans in order to carry the literary analogy further into the issue of genealogy, whereas, in contrast, Melchizedek is described as living on (Heb 7:8, ζῇ). Hebrews identifies this Melchizedek in this Genesis narrative as "Without father, without mother, without genealogy, having neither the beginning of days nor end of life" to present the point that "he abides a priest perpetually" (Heb 7:1–3, μένει ἱερεὺς εἰς τὸ διηνεκές). If Melchizedek actually did not have parentage, nor beginning, then he would be divine, or an angelic being. Such a view fosters interpretations of: 1) the Christian

---

46. Josephus, *Ag. Ap.* 1.18, 26; Dionysius, *Thuc.* 8; Diod. Sic. 4.8.3; Livy 6.1.3; Dunn, *Jesus Remembered*, 655.

interpretation of Melchizedek as a pre-incarnate visitation of Jesus Christ,[47] and 2) the angelic dualism of Archangel Michael/Melchizedek[48] with a rival figure, the chief evil angel *Melchiresha* (king of wickedness).[49] However, the emphasized metaphors do not speak of the eternality of Melchizedek, but rather that once on the scene he is a perpetually living and functioning priest (Heb 7:3, μένει ἱερεὺς εἰς τὸ διηνεκές; v. 8, ζῇ). Furthermore, nowhere in this text does our author ever identify that Jesus Christ *is* Melchizedek. Instead, Hebrews repeatedly identifies that Jesus fits into a previous pattern provided by the historical figure of Melchizedek (Heb 7:15, 17, 21–22). Thus Hebrews' emphasis is not that Jesus is Melchizedek, but that Jesus follows Melchizedek's priesthood pattern in certain ways. Thus, the literary analogy is still being developed, and there is no record of Melchizedek's human genealogy in Genesis, so one can think of him as appearing and then disappearing so that he can become a metaphor for perpetually remaining as a high priest (Heb 7:3, 8).[50] Some interpreters conjecture that, with the absence of a genealogy, there is an attempt to establish Jesus as the "Messiah of Aaron" by a mystical manner.[51] Hebrews does not develop it that way, for there is an extended argument developing that the Mosaic covenant and the priesthood of Aaron must be changed because mortal men of Aaronic priesthood could not bring about perfection for the people (Heb 7:8, 11–13, 23; 8:6—10:18). So, Jesus' perpetuity as a Melchizedek priest goes further than the climax of a lineage ("Messiah of Aaron") to that of all priests (a perpetual Melchizedek priest). Hebrews quotes portions of Psalms 110:4 three times, but always includes that Jesus is a priest *forever* (Heb 5:6; 7:17, 21; αἰῶνα indicating perpetuity in time). While the high priests of Aaron were still functioning in series, Jesus became a Melchizedek high priest perpetually.

Jesus is identified as a superior high priest because he did not glorify himself to become high priest, but became a Melchizedek priest with an oath that God initiated: "The Lord has sworn and will not change His mind,

---

47. Thompson argues for this position in "Conceptual Background and Purpose," 209–23.

48. 1QM 9:14–16.

49. 4Q543–48; 4Q280; Schniedewind, "Melchizedek, Traditions of," 694.

50. Demarest develops this position ("Hebrews 7:3," 141–62) and argues additionally that, if Melchizedek was a historical figure other than Christ (not Thompson's view), he would encroach upon the eternal priesthood of Christ.

51. Yadin, "Dead Sea Scrolls," 36–55; Delcor, "Melchizedek from Genesis," 115–35; Gieschen, "Different Functions," 364–79.

Thou art a priest forever like Melchizedek" (Heb 5:5–6; 7:20–21; Ps 110:4). The oath with regard to Jesus' priesthood is fused with his kingship in that Psalms 2:7 is also seen as the divine oath to initiate Jesus into priestly ministry, since it initiates Jesus into kingly ministry and the Melchizedek role is a king-priest: "Thou art my Son, today I have begotten thee" (Heb 1:5; 5:5; Ps 2:7). Within chapter 5, I discussed that the affirmations from the Father at Jesus' baptism and transfiguration are evidence that the Sonship role of Psalms 2 is operative (Matt 3:17; 17:5; Mark 1:11; 9:7; Luke 3:22; 9:35). In both Psalms 2 and 110 there is military conquest imagery, prefiguring the judging role of messianic priest and king within early Judaism, but Hebrews does not develop this of Jesus within the priestly imagery in the same manner as Hebrews does for Jesus as king. Instead, the priestly development comes after a prolonged section of Hebrews warning about the need for entering into faith and rest *today* by following Christ in his exodus way to the kingdom (Heb 3:7, 13, 15; 4:7). In this exodus, the *todayness* is emphasized, showing the perpetual need to be faithful. Likewise, this same *todayness* is emphasized for divine support and authority to Jesus' priesthood role. Not only has God unusually initiated Jesus by an oath into Melchizedek priesthood, but God affirms this distinct role, which Jesus performs on a daily basis of *today*.

Levitical priests offer gifts and sacrifices for sins to purify the flesh of the worshipper, but the benefits from these don't transform the worshipper (Heb 5:1; 9:13). However, such priests "can deal gently with the ignorant and misguided, since he himself also is beset with weakness; and because of it he is obligated to offer for sins, as for the people, so also for himself" (Heb 5:2–3). Through this means, the priest can help the people of the old covenant with the possibility of drawing near to God (Heb 10:1; 11:6). However, Levitical priests are described as weak and useless in their inability to perfect the worshipper within their conscience (Heb 7:11, 18–19, 28; 9:9; 10:2–3). That is, there is no guarantee of internal transformation for the worshipper through the ministry of the Levitical priests. In fact, with the repeated sacrifices, there is repeated reminder of their sins, which can work against a conscience that is cleansed (Heb 10:2–3).

Jesus becomes identified as a Melchizedek priest on the basis of an indestructible life (Heb 7:16). He does not become a priest by some physical requirement, such as a genealogy. Rather, in the same internal manner in which the new covenant transforms our lives, so Jesus' character identifies him to be a priest after the pattern of Melchizedek. Therefore, Jesus' character is critical to his station as high priest.

> For it was fitting that we should have such a high priest, holy, innocent, undefiled, separated from sinners and exalted above the heavens; who does not need daily, like those high priests, to offer up sacrifices, first for his own sins and then for the sins of the people, because this he did once for all when he offered up himself. (Heb 7:26–27).

Jesus is both victorious as high priest and sympathetic to our weakness. The word "sympathize" (συμπαθῆσαι) always includes an element of active help (Heb 4:15; 10:34).[52] Which concept of help goes further in benefiting us than the priests' "gentle" (μετριοπαθεῖν) activity? It is a restraint and moderation of his feelings so that he can gently help the ignorant and misguided (Heb 5:2).[53] In this context, the emphasis is that, as high priest, Jesus helps the helpless, weak, ignorant, misguided, and prone to be judged. Jesus' capacity to provide this significant help comes from the fact that, as human, he "has been tempted (πειρασθείς) in all things as we are, yet without sin" (Heb 2:17–18; 4:15). Jesus negotiated these temptations without sin and remained "undefiled," so that he knows how to live life without sin and has the strength of will to accomplish such sinless life (Heb 2:17–18; 4:15; 7:26). Additionally, the tribulation (πειρασθείς) that Jesus experienced made him unusually able to come to the aid of other humans in temptation (πειραζομένοις, Heb 2:18). In fact, in his humanity, Jesus grew through the process of temptation such that it was instrumental in developing human maturity, especially equipping him to be a merciful (ἐλεήμων) and faithful high priest, so as to accomplish "merciful forgiveness" (ἱλάσκεσθαι)[54] for the sins of the people (Heb 2:17–18). That is, Jesus learned obedience from the things which he suffered (Heb 5:8). This suffering lasted, beyond the initial temptations, all the way through his Gethsemane prayer to his death on a cross (Heb 5:7; Phil 2:7–8). The Gethsemane prayer developed the cup of God's wrath, a metaphor of severe judgment, and in this case of his im-

---

52. 4 Macc 4.25; 13.23; T. Sim. 3.6; T. Benj. 4.4.

53. Yarnold, "*Metriopathein apud* Heb. 5, 2" *VD* 38(1960) 149–55; the fact that this gentleness is extended to the ignorant and misguided may show a further limitation of the Levitical high priest who limited such atoning aid to sins committed in ignorance (Heb 5:2; 9:7; Lev 4:2, 13, 22, 27; 5:2–4; Num 15:30–31), while Jesus sacrifice transforms us in rebellion.

54. Heb 2:17, ἱλάσκεσθαι is similar in meaning to the other NT instance in the sinner's prayer "God be *merciful* to me the sinner" (Luke 18:13, ἱλάσθητί).

pending death (Matt 26:37–38; Mark 14:33–34; Pss 11:6; 75:8; Isa 51:17, 22; Jer 25:15, 17, 27; 49:12; 51:7; Rev 16:1—18:6). In fact, in Hebrews, such suffering (ἔπαθεν) especially indicates Jesus' death (Heb 2:9–10; 9:26; 13:12), though Jesus' followers join him in experiencing suffering while continuing to follow him (Heb 10:32). One aspect of this is that he can come to the aid of those who are tempted (Heb 2:18). This tested perfection remains Jesus' human moral condition, thus extending beyond the grave into his current condition of priest (Heb 5:9; 7:28). It is this condition of an indestructible life that makes Jesus uniquely qualified to be a Melchizedek high priest (Heb 5:8–10; 7:16). From this vantage point, Jesus offers himself to help in our time of need (Heb 4:16). It is thus from this lived basis that Jesus became the source of everlasting salvation for all who obey him.

The exhortation to obey takes a particular priestly direction to prayer.[55] The verb "to draw near" (προσερχώμεθα) is in the present tense, indicating (in this context) the repeated activity to draw near in prayer (Heb 4:16; 7:19; 10:19–22). "Let us *again and again draw near* with bold frankness to the throne of grace" is cultic imagery, through which we followers of Jesus enter into a priestly activity of prayer and God's generosity, so that we may receive this help from him in our time of need. However, the throne imagery speaks of accessing the ark of the covenant and thus alludes to benefits of the Day of Atonement, which are developed in chapter 9 as benefits to meet our needs. Whereas, in the Day of Atonement, only the high priest would draw near to God's throne/ark (which had been gone since the Babylonian captivity), now all followers draw near to God's throne in prayer because Jesus remains at the heavenly throne of God (Heb 4:14; 1:13).

Jesus as priest has become the guarantee of a better covenant (Heb 7:22; 8:6). In Jesus' high priest ministry, he has completed his sacrifice[56] and sits at the right hand of God's throne with continued access to God in the true heavenly tabernacle (Heb 1:3; 8:1–2; 9:11; 10:12). This heavenly tabernacle supersedes the earthly real tabernacle, since the earthly is merely a copy.[57] Furthermore, with the temple still standing before the destruction

---

55. In Peter's writings, the priesthood is primarily a corporate function as the church suffers persecution while declaring God's glory and doing good (1 Pet 2:5—3:17), but Jesus offers up himself as a hint to his priestly ministry (1 Pet 2:23).

56. Cf. chapter 9 for comparisons of Jesus' new covenant sacrifice as superior than the Mosaic Day of Atonement sacrifices.

57. Often the better place of heaven is developed through a Platonic framework, but this is foreign to the text. In Platonism, the heavenly forms are the only reality, with the earthly objects being merely a shadow of this reality imposed upon our senses through

of Jerusalem in 70 AD, Hebrews identifies that the Holy Spirit has not disclosed the way into the holy place while the tabernacle is still standing (Heb 9:8). Presumably this condition changes with the Romans destruction of the temple in 70 AD and Jesus' institution of the new covenant by his death sacrifice offered in the heavenly tabernacle. This sacrifice of himself is better than the Levitical sacrifices because his sacrifice cleanses the conscience from dead works (Heb 9:14; 8:10; 10:16, 22). With this cleansing underway, Jesus only needs to offer himself once for all time (Heb 9:28; 10:10–12); this is the internal transformation of conscience to match our real condition, being forgiven by God, grounded in Jesus' sacrifice (Heb 8:12; 9:28; 10:10, 12, 17–18). Such cleansing of conscience is the act of perfecting accomplished (τετελείωκεν) for those who are set apart (Heb 10:14). With this cleansing accomplished, we can draw near to God with confidence, corporately encouraging each other to do so (Heb 10:22–25). In contrast, Peter identifies this role to be that of our responsibly maintaining a good conscience (1 Pet 3:16, 21). However, the book of Hebrews urges its readers to pray that the author could maintain this good conscience (Heb 13:18).

Jesus as high priest completely saves[58] those who draw near to God through him, since he always lives to make intercession for them (Heb

---

the recollection of our souls' pre-incarnate life among those heavenly forms. If the truth is present in the heavenly, then it is present in the earthly as well, because the earthly is a mere shadow of the heavenly. In Hebrews 9:23–25, both the heavenly tabernacle and the earthly copies of the heavenly tabernacle are real, as evidenced by the Hebraic pattern of *Merkabah* mysticism. That is, both the heavenly and earthly temples are real, and different things may be occurring in these different realities. For example, the heavenly temple is normally thought to be where God's presence dwells (Isa 6:4), but the amazing thing is that God dwells on earth with the cleansed tabernacle, the Ark of the Covenant serving as his throne (Exod 40:34–38). However, the uncleanness of the earthly temple dislodges the divine presence from the earthly temple, while he remains in the heavenly temple (Ezek 1:4–28; 11:22–25). The different conditions of the pure heavenly temple and the occasionally unclean earthly temple show that they are both real in this multidimensional Hebraic framework rather than the idealism of the earthly shadows, which Platonism would portray (1 En. 14; 37–71; 2 En. 15–17; 4 Ezra 9.26—10.59; 13.35–36; 2 Bar. 4.2–7; 6.9; 32.4; Gal 4:26; Heb 12:22; Rev 3:12; 21:2, 10; Ascen. Isa. 9; LAE 37; Apoc. Ab. 29; Exod. Rab. 43.8; m. Ḥag. 2.1; b. Ḥag. 14a; 15a; Hec. Ab. Rab. 20.1; b. Sanh. 38b; Pate and Kennard, *Deliverance Now and Not Yet*, 98–103; Sholem, *Jewish Gnosticism*; Lincoln, *Paradise Now and Not Yet*, 9–32, 169–95; Dean-Otting, *Heavenly Journeys*; Gruenwald, *Apocalyptic and Merkavah Mysticism*, 29–72; Schafer, *Kehhalot-Studien*; Chernus, "Visions of God," 123–46; Isaacs, *Sacred Space*, 59–61; Koester, *Hebrews*, 97–100).

58. The completeness of salvation (Heb 7:25, σῴζειν εἰς τὸ παντελὲς δύναται) shows no lack since it is salvation to the fullness of power, but it is not built upon completed fact or accomplishment of Christ, but rather the continued character of Jesus' life, which

7:25). "Intercession" (ἐντυγχάνειν) in the OT is often praying for recovery from threat (Gen 18:22–33; Exod 32:11–14; Num 14:13–19; 1 Sam 7:5–9).[59] Early Judaism understood such intercession to include the high priest praying for Israel's "forgiveness of sins."[60] Early Christian writings identify that such intercession was accomplished by Jesus to recover the Christian from her sins (1 John 2:1–2).[61] Thus completeness of salvation from Jesus is not accomplished in Jesus' past activity in his death, but in his continued life of praying[62] for those who follow him in drawing near to God. This means that, as high priest, Jesus' effectiveness in prayer is critical in completing our salvation. The Gethsemane prayer (wherein Jesus offered up prayers for God to save him from death) becomes an example of Jesus' piety and priestly effectiveness in prayer (Heb 5:7; Matt 26:37–44; Mark 14:33–41; Luke 22:42–44). Jesus prayed, "If it is possible let this cup pass from me" (Matt 26:39, 42, 44; Mark 14:36, 39, 41; Luke 22:42). Jesus is not trying to get out of his death in a moment of weakness. Rather, he knows his death is imminent. He has been prophesying throughout his ministry, including just a few moments before at the Passover meal, that he was about to die. So, since Jesus is not asking "do not let me die," then his request must be this: "Father, let the wrathful judgment pass on from me after I die." That is, Jesus is praying for his own resurrection on the other side of the judgment.[63] Matthew 26:42 implies that the cup cannot pass away unless he drinks it. This would mean that Jesus' "will" is for release from judgment to obtain resurrection, though he is open to the Father's will if it should run counter and damn him. As understood, Jesus actually received from the Father the passing on of the cup in resurrection after his death, as Jesus had asked for in his prayer. This interpretation best fits the description of the Gethsemane prayer in Hebrews 5:7 as being answered in the affirmative since the word "heard" means a positive answer (1 John 5:14–15 and in the

---

evidences his persistence as high priest, praying for those who follow him in drawing near to God.

59. 2 Macc 7:37–38; 4 Macc 6:27–29.

60. Philo, *Moses* 2.134; m. Yoma 4.2; 6.2; Bauernfeind, "ἐντυγχανω," 8.242–45.

61. 1 Clem. 56.1; Polycarp, *Phil.* 4.3; Hermes, *Sim.* 2.6, 8; Kennard, *Gospel*, 224–36.

62. Heb 7:25, πάντοτε ζῶν εἰς τὸ ἐντυγχάνειν ὑπὲρ αὐτῶν; this identifies that Jesus joins the Holy Spirit in interceding for the saints (Rom 8:26–27).

63. Blaising, "Gethsemane a Prayer of Faith," 333–43; this view is not sufficiently countered by the disjunction (contrary to Gundry, *Mark*, 870) because Jesus is willing to be damned (as the alternative to resurrection) if the Father wills, but he asks for resurrection instead (Kennard, *Messiah Jesus*, 361–62).

Psalms). So, while the cup briefly alludes to the precariousness of Jesus' death, the passage actually emphasizes the effectiveness of Jesus' prayer life to obtain resurrection on the other side of death. So, as a high priest, he is unusually effective in praying because of his piety (Heb 5:7). This is a profound encouragement, for in his priestly ministry it means that Jesus completely saves those who draw near to God through him, since he always lives to make intercession for them (Heb 7:25).

Jesus is the impeccable high priest after the pattern of Melchizedek. He is able to offer a superior sacrifice in the heavenly tabernacle. He is able to bring in the new covenant with transformation and cleansing for the believer's conscience. As priest, he is an effective advocate to propitiate the believer's sin by his ongoing advocacy ministry. In all these ways, Jesus shows himself to excel as messianic priest.

8

The Law and the New Covenant

HEBREWS QUOTES THE CORE of Jeremiah's new covenant promise and applies part of its benefits to the lives of Jewish Christians in the first century to show the superiority of the new covenant over the Mosaic covenant. Such superiority of the new covenant over the Mosaic covenant is a crucial perspective for these Jewish Christians who are tempted to depart from Christ with his new covenant and return to Judaism with its Mosaic covenant. This contrast sets up a two-way salvation framework which identifies that alignment with Christ and the strictured new covenant way is that which accesses eschatological salvation (Heb 2:10; 5:9; 6:9; 9:28).[1]

---

1. Nairne, *Epistle of Priesthood*, 205, 226–28; Käsemann, *Wandering People of God*, 86; Spicq, *L'Epître aux Hébreux*, 1:243–46, 269–80; Johnston, "Pilgrimage Motif," 239–51; This judgment according to deeds is continued in the two-way teaching of the church: Did. 1.1.1–4; 4.14b; 1 Clem. 34–35; 2 Clem. 6.8; 8.4; Polycarp, *Phil.* 10; Ign. *Phil.* 5.1; Ign. *Eph.* 3.1; Barn. 16.7–8; 18.1–2; 19; Justin, *Dial.* 3.4; Justin, *1 Apol.* 16.8–9; Justin, *2 Apol.* 9; Irenaeus (*Haer.* 3.1.10) maintained this as the universal teaching all Christians held at the time; Herm. Mand. 2.7; Herm. Sim. 3.8.6–11; Clement of Alexandria, *Strom.* 4.6; Clement of Alexandria, *Quis div.*, esp. 1.6–7; 16.5; Commodianus, *Instr.* 28; Origen, *Comm. Matt.* 14.10–13; Origen, *Fr. Prin.* 2.9.7–8; 3.1.12; Cyprian, *Fort.* 12–13; Dionysius of Alexandria, *Exegetical Fragments* 7, "Reception of Lapsed"; Methodius of Olympus, *Banquet of the Ten Virgins* 9.3; Methodius of Olympus, *Oration Concerning Simeon and Anna* 8; Lactantius, *Inst.* 3.12; 6.3–7; 7.10; Lactantius, *Epit.* 73; Lactantius, *Constitutions of the Holy Apostles* 7.1.1–2; Lactantius, *Clementine Homilies* 18.17; Eusebius, *Hist. eccl.* 2.19; 3.20.6–7; 5.1.10, 48; 5.8.5; 5.13.5; Eusebius, *Council of Sardica Lengthy Creed*: Socrates Scholasticus, *Hist. eccl.* 2.19 = Athanasius, *Syn.* 26; 351 = Hilary of Pointers, *On the Councils* 34 and 359 AD *Sirmium Creed*: Socrates Scholasticus, *Hist. eccl.* 2.30 = Athanasius, *Syn.* 27 = Hilary of Pointers, *On the Councils* 38; Synod at

The Law and the New Covenant

God made a promise to Abraham about a continued lineage of blessing (Heb 6:13–14).[2] Hebrews especially develops this lineage in the context of an extraordinary priest after the pattern of Melchizedek, showing continuity of Jesus' priestly ministry as extending the Abrahamic promise.

The Mosaic covenant was established with Israel by the divine giving of the Mosaic covenant through angels (Heb 2:2; Acts 7:38, 53; Gal 3:19; in LXX Deut 33:2 angels joined God in giving the law).[3] However, the Mosaic covenant as an external document failed to bring about internal transformation of Israel in their exodus toward the promised land (Heb 3:7–11; 9:14). Thus, the Mosaic covenant extends into a new covenant transformation.[4]

The superiority of the new covenant is grounded in the superior revelation of Jesus himself, as God's Son over God's house (Heb 1:1–4; 3:1–6).

Ariminum Creed: Socrates Scholasticus, *Hist. eccl.* 2.37; 359 AD *Seleucia Creed*: Socrates Scholasticus, *Hist. eccl.* 2.40 = Athanasius, *Syn.* 8; 359 AD *Confession at Niké* and 360 AD *Constantinople Creed*: Athanasius, *Syn.* 30; 359 AD *Ariminum Creed* and modified for the 381 AD Council at Constantinople: Socrates Scholasticus, *Hist. eccl.* 2.41; Athanasius, *Inc.* 57; Cyril, *Catechetical Lectures* 15.1, 24–25, 33; Gregory of Nyssa, *On Pilgrimages*, paragraph 1; Gregory of Nyssa, *Great Catechism* 40; Gregory of Nazianzus, *Or. Bas.* 4; Ambrose, *Off.* 1.16.59; Augustine, *Conf.* 1.11.17; Augustine, *Civ.* 13.8; 14.25; 19.11; 20.1–8, 12, 14, 22; 21.1; Augustine, *Trin.* 8.7–8; Augustine, *Enchir.* 15; 31–32; 55; 107; 113; Augustine, *Doctr. chr.* 1.12.10; Augustine, *Perf.* 42–44; Augustine, *Ennarat. Ps.* 31.25; 112.5; Augustine, *Tract. Ev. Jo.* 124.5; Hilary of Poitiers, *On the Trinity* 12.45; Leo the Great, *Sermons* 46.3; 49.2, 5; 63.2, 7; 67.5–6; 72.1; 95.1–9; Vincent of Lérins, *Commonitory* 23.57–59, which he claims is the teaching everyone held at that time: 23.4–6; John Cassian, *Cassian's Conferences* 1.1.5; 1.6.3, 8; 1.40.9; 2.13.13, 18; 2.14.3, 9; John Cassian, *Seven Books of John Cassian* 3.13–14; Leo the Great, *Sermons* 23.5; 24.1–5; 26.2; 66.7; 90.2; 95.1–9; Saint John Climacus, *Ladder of Divine Ascent*, 9.1; summary on step 30; Thomas à Kempis, *Of the Imitation of Christ*, esp. 1.23; 2.7; 3.44, 56; Bunyan, *Pilgrim's Progress*, esp. 18, 187; Reiche, "New Testament Concept of Reward," 195–206; Jeremias, *Neotestamentliche Theologie*, 209; Willard, *Divine Conspiracy*; Yinger, *Paul, Judaism, and Judgment*, 285—summary, but argued through the book; Grindheim, "Ignorance is Bliss," 313–31; Kim, *God Will Judge Each One*; Dunn, *New Perspective on Paul*, 72–73; Dunn, "If Paul Could Believe," 135, and Dunn, "Response to Thomas Schreiner," 106–8. However, this view can be granted from outside the two-way tradition, such as from the Reformed tradition: Calvin, *Institutes of the Christian Religion*, 3.15.8; 3.16.1; "we are justified not without works, and not by works, since in the participation in Christ, by which we are justified, is contained not less sanctification than justification" (16.3); 18.1; Schreiner, "Justification," 78–79.

2. Kennard, *Biblical Covenantalism*, 1:66–103.

3. Jub. 1.27, 29; 2.1, 17–19; CD 5.18; Josephus, *Ant.* 15.5.3, 136; Sipre Num. 102; Mek. Exod. 20.18; Pesiq Rab. 21; Kennard, *Biblical Covenantalism*, 1:104–243.

4. Kennard, *Biblical Covenantalism*, 2:73–89.

The superior role of God's Son is identified with the Davidic covenant.[5] Psalms 2 as a royal psalm affirms that the king rules by God's authoritative relationship with him. This is explicitly identified as a realization of the Davidic covenant in Hebrews connecting Psalms 2:7 with 2 Samuel 7:14 (Heb 1:5). The pronouncement that Jesus is already the Son indicates that he is already the Davidic King, anointed by God to rule his kingdom forever, on his throne with a righteous scepter (compare Heb 1:8–9 ἔχρισέν with Heb 3:6 Χριστὸς). Psalms 110 speaks of a future expression of the kingdom where all the Davidic King's enemies will be subjected to him indicating a greater era of his reign to come. Hebrews identifies that this future kingdom is Jesus' future (Heb 1:13). So, while Jesus was on earth suffering and dying in his humanity, he was lower than the angels, but now he has been crowned with glory and honor as a Davidic King; he has already inherited a more excellent name than angels (Heb 1:4–5; 2:7–9). Jesus as Davidic King awaits God's subjecting all things to him, which is a greater stage of his kingdom (Heb 1:13; 2:8). This comparison of Jesus' superiority over angels is certainly overturning the order of creation that Psalms 8 speaks about, but it may also be showing the superiority of Jesus over angelic-laden Judaism of the first century (Heb 2:8; Ps 8:7 MT and LXX [Eng v. 6]). Thus, Jesus is a superior revelation over the Mosaic covenant of the fathers, which was believed to come through the mediation of angels (Heb 1:1–2; 2:2; Acts 7:30, 38, 53; Gal 3:19). From this basis, Christ as Son is the Davidic ruler over his house (believers in Christ), thus superior to Moses, a servant within the house (Heb 3:1–6).

Moses and Christ cooperate within God's creation program to bring his house into Sabbath rest. God finished his creation of the world and stopped working on the seventh day (Gen 2:2; Heb 4:3–4). Yahweh identifies within the Mosaic covenant that this creation rest is the basis for the Sabbath rest (Exod 20:8–11). The Sabbath rest, as the sign of the Mosaic covenant and its extensions, like the Day of Atonement and Sabbatical year, speaks about rest from labors to worship Yahweh (Exod 31:13–17; Lev 16:31; 23:32; 25:2–8). Faithful obedience to the Mosaic covenant was to stop harmful beasts, enemies, and warfare from encroaching, permitting blessings of peace to overwhelm them (Lev 26:6; Ps 8:3 MT and LXX [Eng v. 2]; Isa 14:4; 16:10; 17:3; 21:2; Jer 48:33, 35; Ezek 30:10, 13, 18). Unfortunately Israel rebelled and was stopped under covenant curse. Thus, the problem with the Mosaic covenant is Jewish rebellion, and the Mosaic

---

5. Kennard, *Biblical Covenantalism*, 2:25–72.

covenant response to rebellion is covenant curse, which does not resolve Jewish rebellion (Deut 28–29).[6] Hebrews cites Psalms 95 as a reminder that the Mosaic covenant did not bring Israel into rest because they rebelled in unbelief on the way (Heb 3:12, 16–19). They started with the dramatic exodus out of Egypt but Israel's hardening of their hearts to disobey prevented Moses and Joshua from bringing about rest. Through David, the Spirit calls Israel in his day to worship Yahweh and not harden their hearts in disobedience, so that they might enter into the rest that was promised to them (Ps 95; Heb 3:7–11; 4:7). In the same view, the author of Hebrews echoed the same warning to his readers, indicating the precarious place they are in today, so that they would not harden their heart in unbelief to the way of good news (Heb 3:12–15; 4:1–3). We enter into this rest by faith in the goodness of Christ. This faith is a long-standing character trait (a believing heart that holds our assurance firmly from its beginning until the end), even though a person began the new covenant journey by believing the goodness of Christ in the past. To become this kind of believer already renders us as co-sharers (μέτοχοι) with Christ (Heb 3:14). This co-sharing (μετόχους) is in the divine calling of the Davidic kingdom, revealed and evidenced by the Spirit, as legitimate sons disciplined by God for our strength (Heb 1:9; 3:1, 14; 6:4; 12:8). The author of Hebrews is calling his readers to this kind of continuing life of faith so that they might join Christ in the benefits of the kingdom that the Mosaic covenant failed to provide while they were under covenant curse. The Mosaic covenant failed because it did not transform Israel's hearts to believe. So Yahweh vowed to curse them with his wrath, in not forgiving them.

The new covenant provides the framework for understanding the relationship between Israel and the church. Richard Hays earlier understood the new covenant to be a supercessionist claim that Israel is replaced by the church.[7] However, Hays has since re-evaluated this claim to conclude with E. P. Sanders that Hebrews presents a form of "restoration eschatology" with

---

6. Kennard, *Biblical Covenantalism,* 1:151–60, 225–36; Fisher resists annulment of the Mosaic covenant through the lens of Matthew 5, so the problem is with rebellious Jewish people ("Covenant, Fulfilment and Judaism," 184).

7. Hays, *Echoes of Scripture,* 98–99, 177; an early supercessionist attack indicated Christians as true heirs (Barn. 4.8; 6.19; 13.6; 14.45–46), with Israel forfeiting the covenant by idolatry (Barn. 4.8; 16.1–2), disobedience (Barn. 8.7; 9.4; 14.1–4), and ignorance (Barn. 10.2, 9); Tertullian, *Adv. Jud.* 4, 6; Cyprian, *Treatises* 12.1.16–17; Cyprian, *Test.* 12.1.6; Origen, *Comm. ser. Matt.* 11.13–15; 14.19–20.

all the exodus imagery.[8] Others reject supercessionism, instead considering Hebrews to indicate a new covenantalism for the Jewish Christians being addressed.[9] The language of the book of Hebrews better follows this last trajectory, which means that there were Jewish Christian sects that were still committed to practicing the Mosaic covenant within their form of Christianity.[10] Jewish Christians were still on an exodus toward the kingdom, only now they follow Jesus as well as Moses (Heb 3:2; 11:27–29; 12:2–5). In this two-way salvation, the readers view themselves as an extension of their earlier Jewish lineage, even though early Judaism damns the Jewish Christians in their Jewish prayers.[11] In Hebrews, no major appeal was made to leave Judaism as was done by several Patristics,[12] even though there are appeals in the book of Hebrews to not leave Christianity for mere-Judaism (Heb 6:6; 10:26–31).

This new covenant restoration eschatology for Jewish Christians was argued in the second century by Justin Martyr. In *Dialogue with Trypho the Jew*, Justin addressed the possibility of an authentic salvation for Jews, who practice their Judaism, and also believe in Christ and obey Christ's teaching.[13] Justin concedes that Christians who have faith in Christ may keep the law if they wish, but it is not for salvation.[14] Consistent with this, the communities behind the *Kerygmata Petrou* (ca. 200 AD) and the *Ascents of James* were Jewish Christians with a high Christology trying to continue their law-informed faith in Christ.[15] Justin Martyr suggests that, unfortu-

---

8. Hays, "Here We Have No Lasting City," 161; Sanders, *Jesus and Judaism*, 77–119; 1QpHab 2.1–10; 1QS 6.18–19; 8.20–21; 19.34; 20.11–13.

9. Skarsaune, "Does the Letter to the Hebrews," 174–182; Kennard, *Biblical Covenantalism*, 3:162–74.

10. Hayman, "Image of the Jew," 440; Klijn, "Study of Jewish Christianity," 419–31; Taylor, "Phenomenon of Early Jewish Christianity," 313–34; Velasco and Sabourin, "Jewish Christianity," 5–26.

11. Epiphanius, *Pan.* 29.9.2; Jerome, *Epist.* 112.13; *Birkat haMinim*, Twelfth Benediction; Justin, *Dial.* 16, 95–96, 110; Skarsaune and Hvalvik, *Jewish Believers in Jesus*, 482–83.

12. Epiphanius, *Pan.* 30.7.1–7; 30.9.4; Ign. *Magn.* 10; Ign. *Phld.* 6; Barn. 2–4; Irenaeus, *Haer.* 1.26.2; Hippolytus, *Haer.*; Clement of Alexandria, *Strom.* 2.9.45.5; Tertullian, *Marc.* 4.8; Origen, *Princ.* 4.3.8; Ps.-Clem 1.28.1–2; 1.32.4; 1.35.2; 1.37.1–4; John Chrysostom, *Hom. Act.* 1.1 and 8.1 (see Chrysostom, "Hom. Act.," 844, 849, and 927); Murray, *Symbols of Church and Kingdom*, 41; Meeks and Wilken, *Jews and Christians*, 31–32, 86, 105; Klijn and Reinink, *Patristic Evidence*.

13. Justin, *Dial.* 46.1; also Justin, *1 Apol.* 11.

14. Justin, *Dial.* 47.

15. Strecker, "Kerygmata Petrou," 102–27, esp. 210–22 and 270–71; Strecker, *Das*

nately, *diaspora* Jewish synagogues rooted out Christians from their midst by denouncing them and saying that their faith in Christ was incompatible with synagogue participation.[16]

There is no parallel appeal in Hebrews for Jewish Christians to leave the practices of Judaism, as was accomplished by the early church judging[17] the Nazarene community out of existence. For example, *The Canons of the Council in Trullo* attacks Sabbath fasting as a damning practice, for which any in the church who fast in this manner are to be "cut off" from the church and salvation.[18] The *Laodicean Canons* attack Christians who fraternize with Jews or join in the practice of Jewish festival celebrations such as Passover.[19] In Hebrews, features of the Mosaic covenant are superseded only to the extent that they violate the new covenant. A prime example is that, in the new covenant, one's conscience is cleansed so that, if a person reminds his conscience of his sins by continued practice of Jewish sacrifices, then such practice of Mosaic covenant works against the cleansing effect of the new covenant (Heb 10:2–8; 9:14). In such a competing situation, the believer must align with the practice of the new covenant.

Hebrews presents the concept that the Mosaic covenant is deficient, and the new covenant is better in two primary features: 1) transforming a heart to believe and 2) establishing an everlasting relationship with Yahweh in forgiveness. There are other ways in which the new covenant is better than the Mosaic covenant, but they are not described by Hebrews as failures in the Mosaic covenant, so they will be developed elsewhere.

A word study of "perfect" in Hebrews helps to develop the continuity and superiority of the new covenant over the Mosaic covenant. The root word τέλος simply means "end," but in Hebrews it emphasizes a goal that stretches throughout one's whole life (Heb 3:14; 6:11; 7:3). To be "perfect"

Judenchristentum; Schoeps, *Theologie und Geschichte*; Schoeps, *Jewish Christianity*; Van Voorst, *Ascents of James*.

16. Justin, *Dial.* 16, 95–96, 110.

17. Tertullian, *Adv. Jud.* 5; John Chrysostom, *Hom. Phil.* 1.13.

18. "If any cleric shall be found to fast on a Sunday or Saturday (except on one occasion only) he is to be deposed; and if he is a layman he shall be cut off" (*Canons of the Council in Trullo*, canon 55).

19. "It is not lawful to receive portions sent from the feasts of Jews or heretics, nor to feast together with them" (Schaff and Wace, *Nicene and Post-Nicene Fathers*, 150–51); "It is not lawful to receive unleavened bread from the Jews, nor to be partakers of their impiety" (Schaff and Wace, *Nicene and Post-Nicene Fathers*, 151); canon 35 also raises the issue of angelology; Hefele et. al., *Histoire des concilesd'après*, 1.2, 989–1028.

(τέλοις) in Hebrews takes up two different foci: maturity and responsive conscience. The Mosaic earthly tabernacle was constructed following the more perfect heavenly tabernacle identified with new covenant (Heb 9:11). The readers should have perfected to maturity, but instead they remained dull and unable to teach (Heb 5:14). This perfecting process (τελειῶσαι) was something that Jesus went through in his sufferings so that he would be perfected for ministry and become the source of our everlasting salvation (Heb 2:10; 5:9; 7:28).[20] Jesus, the perfecter, offered his body to vicariously perfect our conscience and sanctify us in forgiveness so that the spirits of the righteous will be made perfect (Heb. 10:14; 12:2, τετελειωμένων; 12:23). However, unlike other vicarious offerings accomplished externally on behalf of the sinner, the affect accomplished on behalf of the believer here is an internal transformation of the believer's conscience. Such transformation would entail human involvement under divine orchestration, perhaps as a compatibilism or semi-Augustinianism. This transformation contrasts with what the law provides with its gifts and sacrifices, since the law can't perfect the conscience of the participant (Heb 7:11, τελείωσις; 7:19; 9:9; 10:1). The new covenant is superior over the Mosaic covenant in Jesus' ability to positively transform a conscience, whereas the law cannot do this (Heb 9:9, 14). The perfecting process extends beyond this individual perspective as we complete the faithful by faithfully joining them (Heb 11:40).

After quoting Jeremiah 31:31–34 (LXX 38:31–34; Heb 8:8–12)[21] at length, select parts of the new covenant quote return, emphasizing what aspects of the new covenant are already in place until the Davidic King's enemies are defeated (Heb 10:10–18). The context is set up with Jesus' superior sacrifice of his own body, in contrast to the many offerings of the Levitical priests.[22] Jesus offered sanctification forgiveness and maturation of the readers with lasting perfected conscience (Heb 10:10, 14). The emphasis of sanctification in Hebrews is on a setting apart for the purpose of cleansing (Heb 9:13). This cleansing in the Mosaic covenant is closely identified with relational forgiveness (Heb 9:22; Exod 34:6–7; Ps 103:12; Mic 7:18–20). Jesus' vicarious offering forgives the reader's sins in a lasting way that means that they are set apart to God with no future severing of this

---

20. The emphasis of perfection of Christ is maturity for ministry, and is thus not essentially "resurrection," contrary to Moffitt, "If Another Priest Arises," 68–79.

21. Howard ("Hebrews," 210) identified that the quote was neither similar to MT nor LXX, but with some LXX influence.

22. Kennard, *Messiah Jesus*, 293–332; Joslin, *Hebrews, Christ, and the Law*.

relationship with God (Heb 10:10, 17). Additionally, Heb 8:10 (Jer 31:33 or LXX 38:33), "teaching my laws to their mind and upon their heart," is requoted in Heb 10:16 with phrases left out and the order flipped to more blatantly emphasize that Christ's new covenant transformation is "in their heart and mind." This re-arrangement emphasizes the heart-conscience transformation over one of teaching legal information. In this transformation, Jesus' offering perfected those who are sanctified (Heb 10:14). Such perfecting in Hebrews emphasizes the active divine transformation of the believer's conscience as superior over the possibility of humans working or praying for transformation (Heb 9:9; 10:1–2, 14–16; Deut 10:16; 30:6; Ps 51:10 [MT 12]). The everlasting forgiveness in the new covenant serves as the foundation for transforming the reader's conscience (Heb 9:14; 10:14). Such a claim for internal transformation is broadly similar to that found in early Judaism (Deut 30:6; Jer 31:33; Joel 2:28–29).[23] Extending this claim, Hebrews emphasizes the new covenant as superior over the Mosaic covenant in that the new covenant provides everlasting forgiveness and a transformed conscience (Heb 8:10–12; 10:16–17).

The Mosaic covenant involved the high priest on the Day of Atonement, offering sacrifice for sins committed in ignorance (Heb 9:7). These special sins were forgiven after the Mosaic pattern of cleansing, which usually utilized blood of a sacrifice (Heb 9:22).[24] Hebrews emphasizes the role

23. Pharisaic Judaism described an inner transformation of a new covenant manner: Jub. 1.17–18 and 23–25; 1 Bar. 2.35. Sectarian early Judaism viewed the new covenant as being realized among their new covenant community in Israel: Charter of a Jewish Sectarian Association (1QS, 4Q255–64a and 5Q11) 3.7–12, 26; 4.22–23; 5.5, 21; Damascus Document (CD 4Q268 frag. 1 = 4Q266 frag. 2 col. 1) v. 6; 6.19; 8.21; 14.1–2; B col. 19, v. 12–13—here the new covenant is still clearly law, like Jer 31:33 MT; 19.33; 20.12; 1QpHab 2.3—there is a lacuna where likely בְּרִית stood as referring to new "covenant"; 11.13, "circumcision of heart's foreskin"; 4 Ezra 9.31; Freedman and Miano, "People of the New Covenant," 7–26, and Evans, "Covenant in the Qumran Literature," 55–80; Joslin, "Hebrews 7–10," 100–105—internalizing law but not Christologizing law as Matthew does, contra 102, 111–17. Paul extends the new covenant to gentiles.

24. Hebrews indicates that "almost" (σχεδὸν) all things are cleansed with blood (Heb 9:22). Actually, cleansing in the Mosaic covenant with its forgiveness incorporates other avenues than blood sacrifice. For example, the poor could offer a grain offering for atonement forgiveness (Lev 5:11). Furthermore, during the Day of Atonement, the scapegoat atoned for the people by leading the goat into the wilderness without it dying (Lev 16:10, 21–22). Philo indicates that this bloodless scapegoat is a superior sacrifice (*Ebr.* 7; Stökl Ben Ezra, *Impact of Yom Kippur*, 113). Likewise, offering gold to atone was effective in another occasion (Num 31:50). Furthermore, the voluntary didrachmon or half shekel temple tax for males twenty-to-fifty years of age was considered sacred money to support the temple, and thus atoning, because some of it was used to pay for sacrifices (Exod

of the ark of the covenant in this atonement (Heb 9:4–5), which of course had not been in the temple since the Babylonian captivity.[25] Hebrews states that the daily offerings of the priests can never take away sins in contrast to the once-for-all offering of Jesus' body that forgives for all time (Heb 10:10–12). Instead of taking the Mosaic covenant as unable to forgive through its sacrifices (the Mosaic covenant would contradict this since it claims to forgive, e.g., Lev 4:20, 26, 35; 5:10, 13, 16, 18), and believing that God forgives past sins everlastingly within the Mosaic covenant (Exod 34:6–7; Ps 103:12; Mic 7:18–20), it is better to emphasize the contrast being made in these verses about lasting forgiveness accomplished even for future sins. That is, the Mosaic covenant's past sacrifices forgave past sins forever, but never brought closure to sin with forgiveness because future sins remained unforgiven. Offerings continue to be made, showing that sins are a perpetual problem in the Mosaic covenant. This perpetual sin problem sets up a reminder of sins year by year so that the consciousness of sin prompts further offerings for sins (Heb 10:1–3). The Mosaic sacrifices don't perfect or cleanse the conscience; rather, they remind the conscience of its sins while they cleanse the flesh (Heb 9:13; 10:1–3). While the Mosaic covenant sacrifice does atone for each sin committed, the Mosaic covenant cannot in any effective final atonement remove sins by providing everlasting forgiveness (Heb 10:4). A major reason for this problem is that the Mosaic sacrifices do not penetrate the issue deep enough to please God (Heb 10:5–8). This sin problem is not resolved with hearts and minds being transformed so that they would tend not to sin, nor is there an everlasting forgiveness freeing them from the need to offer for sin (Heb 10:16–18). This Mosaic covenant lack is exactly what Jesus' once-for-all offering accomplishes, showing the superiority of the new covenant over the Mosaic.

The Mosaic covenant is faulted in contrast to the superior new covenant. The blame (ἄμεμπτος) levied at the Mosaic covenant is due to the blame (μεμφόμενος) of the people who didn't live it (Heb 8:7–8). The new covenant is then superior in enabling the people under it to live it. Hebrews

---

30:13; Neh 10:32–3 LXX; Matt 17:24–7; Philo, *Heir* 186; Josephus, *Ant.* 16.6.3; 18.9.1; m. Šeqal. 1.1–3; Tosepta Šegalim 1.6, "they effect atonement"; Garland, "Temple Tax," 69–98, esp. 97). However, when the Jewish temple was destroyed, Vespasian rendered this tax mandatory for men and women up to the age of sixty-two and redirected it for the temple of Jupiter, which put it beyond atonement (Tcherikover and Fuks, *Corpus Papyrorum Judaicarum*, 2:169, 171, 218, 223, 421). Additionally, the Mosaic covenant also utilizes water, fire, and time to cleanse (Num 19:11–19).

25. Josephus, *J.W.* 5.219; b. Yoma 22b.

quotes Jeremiah 31:31–34 (Heb 8:8–12). Some features of the quote are not commented upon, such as God electing a people who know the Lord (Exod 6:7; 19:5–6),[26] because these features continue in the new covenant (Heb 1:9; 3:6; 6:1; 10:30). However, Israel did not continue to practice the Mosaic covenant, showing that the fault of the covenant is the fault of the people (Heb 8:7–9). The new covenant places God's laws within the minds and hearts of the people so that they would continue to live it, knowing their God (Heb 8:10–11). While the Hebrew text of Jeremiah 31:33 uses the singular "law," showing the new covenant to be an internalized extension of the Mosaic law, the plural "laws" in the Septuagint (LXX Jer 38:33) and Hebrews 8:10 is a bit more ambiguous, permitting whatever laws God mandates for these readers. The relationship with God in the new covenant provides the superior everlasting forgiveness that provides the foundation for this internalized commitment to obey in relationship to God (Heb 8:12; 9:14; 10:14).

The Mosaic covenant is weak and useless to affect this internalized transformation to obey (Heb 7:18–19). Such "weakness" (ἀσθενὲς) is clearly an impotence of the Mosaic covenant, but it does not have to reflect poor design, because this same word is used of wives as weaker vessels (1 Pet 3:7), and does not merely refer to the tired and sick. The point is that the law is "useless" (ἀνωφελές) to perfect a person's conscience, and to motivate responsive obedience (Heb 7:18–19; 9:9).

This inability of the law to perfect a person's conscience is the basis for the Mosaic covenant being set aside or annulled (Heb 7:18; ἀθέτησις). Since this perfection is not through the Mosaic covenant and the Levitical priesthood, then the law is "changed" (μετάθεσις) from the Mosaic to the new covenant (Heb 7:12). This change to the new covenant occurs in Jesus' incarnation sacrifice, where he "takes away" (ἀναιρεῖ; present active indicative) the Mosaic covenant for the purpose of "establishing" (στήσῃ; aorist active subjunctive) the new covenant in place (Heb 9:16–17; 10:9). The new covenant realizes its perfecting of the hearts and minds of the readers as they are forgiven (Heb 10:10, 14–18). This move to the new covenant makes the Mosaic covenant obsolete. The Mosaic covenant is already rendered "obsolete" (πεπαλαίωκεν; perfect active indicative) with a lasting condition of obsolescence (Heb 8:13). Such obsolescence is as a wearing out of a garment which is then no longer worn (Heb 1:11). However, this obsolescence takes time to work out in practice, so that the Mosaic covenant is

---

26. Kennard, *Biblical Covenantalism*, 1:104–21.

presently "becoming obsolete" (παλαιούμενον; present passive participle) to reflect its actual "obsolete" (πεπαλαίωκεν; perfect active indicative) condition. This change from the Mosaic to the new covenant is a growing old of the Mosaic (γηράσκον; present active participle) that renders the Mosaic covenant "ready to vanish" (ἀφανισμοῦ). With the new covenant already in place in these effective ways, Hebrews makes strong warnings not to resist the new covenant in one's life (Heb 10:28–29). Under the Mosaic covenant, to set it aside (ἀθέτησις) would bring death by capital punishment as a rebel. However, with the Mosaic covenant annulled (ἀθέτησις), readers' embracing of the new covenant means that they are under a death sentence by the Mosaic covenant, if that is where their trust lies. That is, if they are tempted to return to the Mosaic covenant, then this covenant would sentence them to death. Likewise, if they disregard the new covenant, which provides rest, then they will be under harsher judgment from God.

As the new covenant begins, with such a strong discontinuity and closure to the Mosaic covenant, it is helpful to remind oneself that there is some continuity between these two covenants in Hebrews. Both explore priesthoods and sacrifices, though the new covenant is superior. Both explore a tabernacle pattern. Here the new covenant is superior as the heavenly pattern, but the Mosaic is a close earthly copy of the heavenly tabernacle shown to Moses on the mountain (Heb 8:5; 9:23).[27] The priestly and sacrificial functioning of the Mosaic tabernacle train the Jews in basic concepts that the new covenant completes in the one sacrifice of Jesus Christ. Jesus' once-for-all sacrifice is emphasized in Hebrews (Heb 7:27; 9:12, 14, 25, 28; 10:10, 12, 14, 18), so why, when the heavenly things are cleansed for new covenant effectiveness, does Hebrews say that they are cleansed with "sacrifices" (plural: θυσίαις) instead of Jesus' one sacrifice (Heb 9:23)?

Might these plural sacrifices hint at the burnt offerings and sin offerings which the Levitical priests use to cleanse Ezekiel's altar (Ezek 43:18–27)? With Hebrews' emphasis, the plural cleansing sacrifice should be argued to be the singular sacrifice of Jesus, here rendered plural "sacrifices" (θυσίαις) out of attraction to the plural "with these" (τούτοις),[28] or by a theological appeal of Christ's sacrifice sufficiently replacing all of the Levitical sacrifices (Heb 9:23).

> The plural is used in the sense that the one sacrifice stands as the complete fulfillment of all the different sacrifices in the old order.

---

27. 2 Bar. 4.5; Philo, *Moses* 2.74; Josephus, *Ant.* 3.123, 181; Josephus, *J.W.* 5.213, 218.

28. Lane, *Hebrews 9–13*, 247.

It may be said that the sacrifice of Christ is so many sided that it required a whole range of sacrifices to serve as adequate copies.[29]

Hebrews develops Christ's one sacrifice as the one in the context that was done in the heavenly temple.

Amid the final exhortations of Hebrews, a devotional homily reminds the reader to follow their Christian leader's faith in grace, thereby worshipping God and doing good in the new covenant (Heb 13:7–16). The rationale reminds the reader that we live in grace, so the faith of Christian leadership should be emulated (Heb 13:7–9). Such a gracious life contrasts with that of those diminishing grace with strange teaching that sees real benefit in food. Perhaps this food issue refers to a Jewish liturgical meal with a peace offering because of the Jewish context, in which the Jewish worshippers eat major portions of the sacrifice on the first two days and the priest officiating obtains the right thigh of the sacrifice for his food (Heb 13:9–10; Lev 7:15–17, 32–33).[30] Such eating was festive as an expression of thanks to God, often with the blessing that the food strengthens the heart (Ps 104:14–15).[31] The use of the plural "foods" (βρώμασιν) in Hebrews 13:9 may also indicate the issue of kosher, which was a significant Jewish issue at that time,[32] because the LXX only uses the plural βρῶμα to refer to kosher food in contrast to that which is impure (Lev 11:34),[33] and the other instance of the word in Hebrews is broader than a sacrificial sense (Heb 9:10). However, in either view, the food was merely physical food passing through one's body, polemicizing such food without lasting benefit to the one who partakes of it (Heb 13:9), a theme Philo acknowledged as he saw the value in the heart transformation as far more important than food.[34]

---

29. Guthrie, *Letter to the Hebrews*, 196.

30. m. Pesaḥ. 10.6; Jub. 22.3–9; 32.7; 49.6.

31. m. Ber. 6.1, 3.

32. Dan 1:1–21; Esth 3:28; 4:16; Tob 1.9–12; 4.12–13; Jdt 10.5; 12.1–2, 9–19; 13.8; 2 Macc 7, esp. 7.9 and 8.2; 3 Macc 3.4–7; 7.11; 4 Macc 1.8, 10; Jos. Asen.; Let. Aris. 139–42; Josephus, *Ant.* 14.185–267; Josephus, *Vita* 14, includes Jewish priests, imprisoned in Rome in 61 AD, abstaining from meat on kosher grounds; T. Isaac 4.5; Macrobius, *Sat.* 2.4.11; Riggenbach, "Die Starken und Schwachen," 655–68; Strathmann, *Geschichte der frühchristlichen Askese*, 1:1–13; Rauer, *Die "Schwachen" in Korinth*, 138–69; Behm, "ἐσθίω," 694; Dunn, *Romans 9–16*, 799–802; Elliott, "Asceticism among the 'Weak,'" 231–51, esp. 239–45; Winter, "Roman Law and Society," 90–91; Pucci Ben Zeev, *Jewish Rights*, 381–408; Hellerman, "Purity and Nationalism," 401–21.

33. Lane, *Hebrews 9–13*, 534.

34. Philo, *Spec. Laws* 2.193–94, 198–99.

The polemic continues in that new covenant Christians have an altar, presumably Christ's original heavenly altar, which is aligned with the new covenant, so those Levitical priests of the Mosaic covenant do not have a right to eat from it (Heb 9:23–24; 13:10 in contrast to Lev 7: 32–33).

The Day of Atonement sacrifice from which the high priest took blood into the holy place had its remains burned outside the camp (Heb 13:11; 9:7–8; Lev 16:27).[35] By connecting Jesus' sacrifice with the blood sacrifice at the Day of Atonement, Hebrews identifies Jesus' sacrifice as a vicarious substitution. Since Jesus was excluded and killed outside the Jewish camp, the Jewish Christians could relate to his exclusion. By similarity, Jesus suffered outside the gate in his death so as to sanctify the people (Heb 13:12). Upon this basis, the author exhorts, "let us go outside the camp, bearing His reproach," presumably calling his readership to remove themselves from mainstream Judaism by identifying with Jesus as their Messiah and atonement, with its hope of an everlasting kingdom to come (Heb 13:13–14). Ignatius extends these phrases in his *Letter to Magnesians* to argue for abstinence from kosher and Jewish sacrifices.

> Gather together—all of you—to the one temple of God, as it were, to one altar, to one Jesus Christ . . . Do not be led away through strange teachings and outmoded fables, which are not useful. If we still go on observing Judaism, we acknowledge that we never received grace.[36]

However, the metaphor of "going outside the camp" (ἔξω τῆς παρεμβολῆς) may function on a level of positively identifying with Christ in "bearing his reproach," rather than necessarily leaving Jewish practices, since this metaphor also is used positively in LXX Exodus 33:7–8 three times for the place where the tabernacle is set up and where Moses met Yahweh in this tabernacle.[37]

With our Messianic kingdom hope, the Christian's life should be characterized by worship, doing good and sharing with others "for with such sacrifices God is pleased" (Heb 13:15–16). In aligning with Christ we should continually offer up a sacrifice of praise to God, especially giving thanks to Christ's name. Joining these sacrifices are those that meet

---

35. Rabbinics saw that the Day of Atonement forgave all sin between the worshipper and God (m. Yoma 8.9; y. Yoma 8.9, 45c; b. Yoma 65ab; Sipra Ahere Mot 8.5).

36. Ign. *Magn.* 7.2—8.2.

37. Lane, *Hebrews 9–13*, 542–44.

The Law and the New Covenant

practical needs like doing good and sharing with others. All these forms of worship and doing good are sacrifices that please God.

Hebrews' perspective realizes many factors of the Davidic and new covenants so that its readers see that the Mosaic covenant has been superseded to prompt them to not place their trust in it. Jesus is already the Davidic King over his house of believers in Christ. The new covenant makes believers already partakers of rest if we continue in faith. The new covenant establishes a lasting relationship with Yahweh in forgiveness. The new covenant matures the conscience by internalizing God's laws.

9

Christ's New Covenant Atonement

IN HEBREWS, CHRIST'S ATONEMENT is compared to the corporate atonement pattern of the Jewish Day of Atonement and to Moses' initial cleansing of the people and tabernacle (Heb 9:1–28; Exod 24; Lev 16). Similarly to these events, Christ's sacrifice accomplished corporate atonement for the group in establishing everlasting forgiveness and purifying the heavenly tabernacle (Heb 8:12; 10:17). Additionally, Christ's atonement set in motion a new covenant transformation of the heart and conscience within the believer (Heb 8:10; 10:16) and brought believers to inherit everlasting salvation (Heb 1:14; 6:12; 9:15).

MOSAIC SACRIFICE CONTEXT

In the Mosaic covenant context, sin is divided into unintentional sins where atonement is available (Lev 4:2; 5:1, 15, 20–23; Num 15:27, 29) and high-handed rebellion where covenant exclusion (Lev 18:29; 20:2–5, 18; 23:29–30) and death is the outcome (Lev 8:35; 10:1–2; 20:2–5; 22:9; 23:29–30; Num 4:15–20; 15:30–36; 18:22).[1] Often the death risk is an active divine judgment, but sometimes it is to be meted out in capital punishment (Lev 20:9–16; 24:10–23; Num 15:32–36). The only hope for defiant sinners is if a mediatory figure stands before Yahweh to seek pardon for

---

1. Levine, *Leviticus*, 3; Gane, *Cult and Character*, 233; Sklar, *Sin, Impurity, Sacrifice, Atonement*, 11–43; Sklar, "What the Pentateuch Teaches Us"; "Lessons from the Pentateuch," 472–89; Boda, *Severe Mercy*, 68.

the people (Exod 15:25; 17:4; 32–34; Num 11:2, 11; 12:13; 14:13–19; 16:22; 20:6; 21:7). At times, intentional sin might not be a high-handed rebellion because the sinner repents quickly and brings an appropriate sacrifice (Lev 5:1, 20–26; 6:1–7; Num 5:5–8; 19:21–22).[2] However, sacrificial atonement is a privilege granted by Yahweh alone, not an inalienable right.[3] So any high-handed sin runs the risk of identifying the sinner as a rebel to be killed and excluded from covenant (Num 15:30–36).[4] In these priestly contexts, ritual is never a replacement for righteous acts and reparation; social justice is part of the ritual (Lev 6:5–6; Amos 5:21–24).[5]

Any violation of righteousness infects Israel with ontological uncleanness. For example, Jacob Milgrom developed the concept of uncleanness through the metaphor of the picture of Dorian Gray, which identifies that violation of righteousness affects the ontology of "clean."[6] Ultimately, sins defile Yahweh's holy name and bring covenant curse (Ezek 43:7–8). Israel pollutes itself and the land with ontological uncleanness by a variety of sins, including idolatry (Ezek 14:11; 20:31; 22:3–4; 23:7–38), necromancy (Lev 19:31; 1 Sam 28:8–14), Molech-worship (Ezek 20:26, 30–31), apostasy (Josh 22:17), sexual immorality (Gen 34:5, 13, 27; Lev 18:20, 23–24; Num 5:11–31; Ezek 18:6, 11, 15; 22:11), murder (Deut 19:13; 21:8), and all their sins (Ps 106:39; Ezek 14:11; 20:43).[7] Such sins include the despoiling of the temple by means of idols, idolatrous practices, violation of kosher, adulterous trusting of gentile power rather than Yahweh, and the presence of the dead or unclean within the temple (2 Chr 23:19; 36:14; Ps 79:1; Isa 66:17; Jer 7:30; 32:34; Ezek 5:11; 9:7; 20:7, 18, 30–31; 22:3, 12–17, 24; 23:7, 13, 30, 38; 36:18; 37:23; 43:6–9; Mal 1:11–12).[8] Cleansing from such practices requires the removal of all idols and the avoidance of such practices (Gen 35:2; Josh 22:17; Ezek 24:13). Cleansing the tabernacle requires the communal rituals of the Day of Atonement (Lev 16; Heb 9:23–24). Likewise,

---

2. Sklar, "What the Pentateuch Teaches Us."

3. Gane, *Cult and Character*, 204.

4. Sklar, "What the Pentateuch Teaches Us."

5. Balentine, *Leviticus: Interpretation*, 59; Boda, *Severe Mercy*, 73.

6. Milgrom, "Israel's Sanctuary," 390–99.

7. As. Mos. 5.3; Jub. 33.6–7, 10, 19–20; Pss. Sol. 1.8; 2.3; 8.13; Num. Rab. 7.1; Lev. Rab. 15.4–5; 16.2, 6; 17.2–3, 6; 18.4; m. Šebu. 1.4–5; t. Šebu. 1.3; b. ʿArak. 16a; Tanḥ. Mesoraʿ 15.

8. As. Mos. 5.3; Pss. Sol. 1.8; 2.3; 8.13; m. Šebu. 1.4–5; t. Šebu. 1.3–4; Tos. Kippurim 1.12; y. Yoma 2.2; b. Yoma 23a.

cleansing and atonement includes recovering the person and the nation, as well, as the tabernacle (Lev 16; Heb 9:14, 26–28).

In the novel *The Picture of Dorian Gray*, Oscar Wilde's adventurer does not age or suffer the consequences of his adventures.[9] In a similar manner, Milgrom identifies that Israel's sins infect the tabernacle, much like the picture of Dorian Gray: "Sin may not leave its mark on the face of the sinner but it is certain to mark the face of the sanctuary; and unless it is quickly expunged, God's presence will depart."[10] By the time of the prophets, the people and land of Israel were severely polluted by sin-caused impurity, and is thus precariously perched toward captivity (Ps 106:38–39; Isa 24:5; Jer 2:7; 3:9; Hos 5:3; 6:10). John Gammie affirms Milgrom's construct of Dorian Gray. However, Gammie also notes that the purification offerings atoned for the individual and not only for the tabernacle: "Sanctuary and sancta indeed reflected the state of the people's sinfulness precisely because the uncleanness that the former accrued were not removed at every [purification][11] offering."[12] And again later, rabbinic sources recognized that Israel's disregard for their public promises had brought Israel drought in 66 AD and warned that their noncompliance with the Sabbath, Sabbatical, and Jubilee year rendered them impure, tumbling Israel toward impending exile and dispersion yet again.[13] Unfortunately, Israel was unresponsive about her sin, and suffered captivity and dispersion repeatedly. The answer to sin in Israel is to study and live the law, thereby returning to righteous living (Pss 19:7–14; 119:9–16).[14]

The concept of כִּפֶּר/*kpr* indicates ransom and atonement. For much of the nineteenth and twentieth century, כִּפֶּר/*kpr* was identified with Arabic *kafara*, "to cover" sin;[15] however, meaning is not determined by etymology, but by use.[16] Richard Averbeck claims that such an etymology is confused when compared to other options like the Hebrew piel stem and Akkadian D

9. Wilde, *Picture of Dorian Gray*.

10. Milgrom, "Israel's Sanctuary," 390–99.

11. Technically, Gammie used *hatta't*, which will be explained in this direction momentarily.

12. Gammie, *Holiness in Israel*, 41.

13. 1QH^a 7.29; 12.35; CD 1.3–4; 1QS 2.8; y. Ta'an. 3.3; b. Šabb. 33a.

14. b. Qidd. 30b; b. Soṭah 21a.

15. Kurtz, *Sacrificial Worship*, 67–71; Janowski, *Sühne als Heilsgeschehen*, 20–22; Stamm, *Erlösen und Vergeben*, 61–66; Elliger, *Leviticus*, 71.

16. Saussure, *Cours de linguistique générale*; Barr, *Semantics of Biblical Language*; Feder, "On *kuppuru, kippēr*," 535–45.

stem.¹⁷ For example, in Genesis 32:20, כִּפֶּר/*kpr* does not mean to "cover" the face, since the face of Esau is immediately seen by Jacob. Instead, כִּפֶּר/*kpr* (or *kipper*) is better related to כֹפֶר/*kpr* (or *kopper*), which means "ransom" (Exod 30:12–16; Lev 16:10, 21–22; 17:11; Deut 21:1–9)¹⁸ and also carries the meaning of atonement.¹⁹ Ransom is clearly seen in the use of כִּפֶּר/*kpr* concerning both census and the law of homicide (but not murder), the latter of which permitted a certain amount of money to be paid "to ransom a life" (Exod 21:29–30; 30:12–16; Num 31:50; 35:31–33; while there is a prohibition banning ransoming in response to the sin of adultery, Prov 6:34–35).²⁰ These are payments made as "vicarious atonement," on behalf of the beneficiaries. Milgrom also identifies that the Levite guards "siphon off God's wrath upon themselves when an Israelite encroaches upon the sancta,"²¹ thus being a "vicarious" atonement diffusing the wrath on behalf of Israel (Num 1:53; 8:19; 18:22–23). Extending further, Phineas ransoms Israel through vicarious penal substitution from imminent wrath through capital punishment, killing Baal-worshipping Jews (Num 25:7–12). The sacrifice was "substitutionary" because the sacrifice was in place of all Israel, which as a whole were viewed by God as guilty, even though only those who were killed actually committed the sin. Additionally, Israel is vicariously ransomed by slaying Saul's sons for violating the Gibeonite covenant (2 Sam 21:3–6). In contrast, Babylon could not ransom or avert their fate; it was judged under covenant curse (Isa 47:11; on an individual level, Ps 49:8–9 is similar). Through intercession, Moses vicariously ransomed Israel from the sin before the golden calf without a substitute (Exod 32:30–40). Furthermore, the blood at the altar must be drained away to "ransom your lives" (Lev 17:11). Such a ransom 1) delivers the guilty party, 2) appeases the injured party, 3) avoids penalty, and 4) reestablishes a peaceful

17. Averbeck, "רפכ," 689–710, esp. 692.

18. Hermann, *Die Idee der Sühne*, 99, 101–2; Hermann, "ἱλάσκομαι, ἱλάσμός," 301–10, esp. 303; Brichto, "On Slaughter and Sacrifice," 19–55, esp. 26–27 and 34–35; Levine, *In the Presence*, 67; Schenker, "*kōper* et expiation," 32–46; Milgrom, *Leviticus 1–16*, 1082–83; Sklar, *Sin, Impurity, Sacrifice, Atonement*, 46–72.

19. Janowski, *Sühne als Heilsgeschehen*, 185–276; Gese, "Die Sühne," 85–106 and Gese, *Essays on Biblical Theology*, 93–116.

20. Milgrom, *Numbers*, 370 identifies that atonement prevents Yahweh's wrath. In a similar ransom situation, 11Q19 21.7–9; 22.15–16 has first fruits offering to ransom the rest of the crop for common purposes.

21. Milgrom, *Studies in Levitical Terminology*, 28–31; Milgrom, *Leviticus 1–16*, 1082–83.

relationship between them, 5) including forgiveness, which completely entails atonement. The early church viewed the redemption by Christ's death through this form of Jewish atonement so that it is not an invention of the new perspective in Paul (Heb 9:1—10:18).[22]

Such a ransom could be identified as "penal" (from the Latin *poena*, meaning penalty) only when covenant judgment is being averted onto the representative humans who die in judgment (Num 25:7–12; 2 Sam 21:3–6). That is, in penal atonement, wrath goes upon the guilty or the substitutionary sacrifice. Such a representative ransom is a "substitute" because the representative animal or person atoning takes the place of those under covenantal judgment in death, even though the actual place of death on an altar is not where the sinner would die.[23] So, the term "penal" may not be so helpful because such Jewish sacrifices are only rarely in a legal framework. Usually describing the sacrifice as a covenantal ransom or substitute would clarify the covenantal atonement stipulations better than appeals to legal fines. Only a few of these ransoms are in a forensic framework, such as in a homicide case, but these substitute only monetary penalties, rather than blood sacrifice (Exod 21:29–30). However, all ransom is covenantal, and any that involve blood and sacrifice fit a covenantal atonement substitution better than describing it as a forensic substitute (Lev 1–7; 16). None of these covenantal animal sacrifices are ever described as taking God's wrath upon themselves, so they are not described as "penal." That is, all the blood sacrifices ransoming the believer employ a covenantal sacrifice rather than a forensic framework. The issue is that the emphasis is on covenant rather than law, and atonement sacrifice rather than legal substitute. The atonement is a real covenantal recovery to the appropriate holy, righteous, and clean condition in covenant through the appropriate covenantal means. Justification and atonement are not legal fiction, but restoration of covenantal relationship. Hebrews, John, Paul, and the early church viewed Christ's death through this Jewish covenantal sacrificial model rather than a legal one, so such metaphors are not to be seen as inventions of the new perspective in Paul (Heb 9:7–28; John 1:29, 36; Rom 3:25).[24]

---

22. Origen, *Comm. Rom.* 2:110 cited in Oden, *Justification Reader*, 65.

23. 4 Macc 4.11–12 the heavenly army's wrath is propitiated; contrary to Finlan, *Background and Content*, 102.

24. Barn. 7–8; Jesus' death is paralleled with the Day of Atonement and red heifer cleansing; Justin, *Dial.* 13.1–9, 40.1–4, 72.1, 111.2–3 develop Jesus' death as parallel to the paschal lamb, Day of Atonement, and sacrificial lamb of Isaiah 53 (Markschies, "Jesus Christ," 332–33; Janowski and Stuhlmacher, *Suffering Servant*, 378–79; Cyprian, *Test.*

Christ's New Covenant Atonement

The Mosaic covenant includes atonement as accomplished through purification sacrifice. This means that the concern in the Mosaic covenant is for Israel to be clean; this is appropriate in light of the relationship that Israel already has with Yahweh. Throughout the Ancient Near East, the issue of purity identifies and retains a people with their god. Within the Mosaic covenant, Israel is in a clean ontological condition, grounded in the initial cleansing act of sprinkling the people (Exod 24:5–8; Heb 9:18–22). As such, Israel is not initially trying to obtain this clean condition; rather, they are corporately trying to retain and maintain it. To do so, Yahweh instituted a sacrificial system.

The problem which the sacrificial system addresses is primarily that of the communicable disease of uncleanness. Uncleanness can be transmitted by normal issues of life (like a woman's menstrual period or defecation) or by touching something that has touched an unclean thing (Lev 12:2; 15:2–33; Deut 23:10). So, uncleanness is not primarily sin because uncleanness can be transmitted without sin occurring. However, sin can bring about

---

15—Jesus' death is parallel to Jewish sacrifice, Isaiah 53, and the Passover lamb; *Letter* 63.14.4 in Filium, *Corpus Scriptorum Ecclesiasticorum Latinorum*, 3c:410–11; Origen, *Comm. Jo.* 6.32–38, Augustine, *Trin.* 4.14 and 19, and Augustine, *On Forgiveness of Sins, and Baptism* 54–55 identify Jesus' death parallel to Jewish daily sacrifices; Theodoret of Cyrrhus, *Interpretation of the Letter to the Romans* in *Patrologia Graeca*, 82, and John Chrysostom, *Hom. Rom.* 7, are both mentioned in Oden, *Justification Reader*, 62; Origen, *Comm. Rom.* 2:110, is cited in Oden, *Justification Reader*, 65; Cyril, in *Catechetical Lectures* 13.3, develops Jesus' death as parallel to the Day of Atonement; Eusebius, *Theoph.* 3.59, *Comm. Isa.* 2.42 on Isa 53:5–6 and 11–12, and *Dem. ev.* 3.2.61–62 develop Jesus' death as a Jewish sacrifice and sin offering (Markschies, "Jesus Christ as a Man" 305, 308, 312–13); Nazianzen, *In Defense of His Flight to Pontus* 1.3–4 develops Jesus' atonement as a parallel to Passover; Ambrose, *Fid.* 3.11.67 as a parallel to Melchizedek sacrifice; Leo the Great, *Sermons* 55.3; 56.1; 59.5, 7; 68.3 as a parallel to daily Jewish sacrifice and Passover; Presbyterian Church of England, *The Articles of the Faith, 1890*, Article XIII, "Justification by Faith" in Schaff, *Creeds of Christendom*, 918. See also the abundance of early church iconography presenting Jesus as a sacrificial lamb, and the profusion of Jesus' death conceived through the lens of Jewish sacrifice; as examples, a third-century Roman catacomb lamb image for Christ; Jesus as lamb with a cruciform halo in the apex of a dome in a sixth-century church of Ravenna; the sixth-century basilica of Saints Cosmos and Damian in Rome, showing the Lamb of God on a rock, surrounded by the twelve apostles as lambs, which indicated mimetic atonement; and a seventh-century Roman altar portraying the Lamb of God on the altar with the cross. The eighty-second canon of the 692 AD Council of Trullo affirmed that Jesus was incarnate in human flesh by banning the very common practice of representing Jesus' death as a lamb: "we decree that henceforth Christ our God must be represented in His human form but not in the form of the ancient lamb" (Sanday and Headlam, *Critical and Exegetical Commentary*, 122–24).

uncleanness, and a condition of uncorrected uncleanness is sin.[25] That is, natural defilement could become moral defilement if Israelites did not use the available sanctification means for recovering from uncleanness.

As such, the purification sacrifice articulates the idea of collective responsibility to recover Israelites and the nation from their uncleanness. Uncleanness is overcome, returning the unclean to a metaphysically clean condition through the sacrificial system. For example, a Jewish mother must offer the appropriate sacrifice after the birth of her baby for them to be returned to a condition of cleanness, even if that baby is the sinless Messiah (Lev 12:3–8; Luke 2:22–24). So the Mosaic context involves definite atonement for the group, with the benefits applied to the individual to the extent that their life reflects the covenantal obligation. If the individual Israelite continues to rebel, then the benefits that the group receives are of no effect for the rebel. To the extent that individual Israelites do not purify themselves, the nation needs to purify: 1) itself, 2) the tabernacle, and 3) the land on the Day of Atonement, or God's presence will depart from the nation Israel.

The basic purification offering is the חַטָּאת/*htt't*, which many translate as "sin offering," following the description of sin (Lev 4:3; חַטֹּאתוֹ) and of the sacrifice in the LXX as "sin offering" (ἁμαρτία). As such, most view this sacrifice too restrictively as a sin offering, which then means that their idea of Christ's sacrifice is legally dealing only with their sins. However, Jacob Milgrom takes issue with the conception of "sin offering" compellingly re-identifying it as the "purification offering." Milgrom explains:

> This translation is inaccurate on all grounds: contextually, morphologically, and etymologically.
>
> The very range of the *hatta't* in the cult gainsays the notion of sin. For example, this offering is enjoined upon recovery from childbirth (Lev 12), the completion of the Nazirite vow (Num 6), and the dedication of the newly constructed altar (Lev 8:15; see Exod 29:36–37). In other words, the *hatta't* is prescribed for persons and objects who cannot have sinned.

---

25. Klawans provides an excellent discussion of the full range of this topic in his book entitled *Impurity and Sin in Ancient Judaism*. Additionally, two-fifths of Rabbinic writings develop the issue of uncleanness, purification, and atonement (cf. Šeqal., Tamid, Yoma, Zebaḥ., Menaḥ., ʿArak., Bek., Meʿil., Tem., Makhš., Ṭehar., ʿUq., Kelim, Parah, Miqw., Ṭ. Yom, Yad, and Ḥag.).

Grammatical considerations buttress these contextual observations. Morphologically, it appears as a *pi'el* derivative. More importantly, its corresponding verbal form is not the *qal* "to sin, do wrong" but always the *pi'el* (e.g., Lev 8:15), which carries no other meaning than "to cleanse, expiate, decontaminate" (e.g., Ezek 43:22, 26; Ps. 51:9). Finally, the "waters of *hatta't* (Num 8:7) serve exclusively a purifying function (Num 19:19; see Ezek 26:25). 'Purification offering' is certainly the more accurate translation. Indeed, the terse comment of Rashi (on Num 19:19) is all that needs to be said: *hatta't* is literally the language of purification" (cf. also Barr 1963:874).

It is not my intention to investigate the origin of this mistranslation. It can be traced as far back as the LXX, which consistently renders ἁμαρτία, followed by Philo (*Laws* 1.226) and Josephus (*Ant.* 3.230). It is, however, important to note that if the rabbinic sources had been carefully read, the subsequent translations could have avoided this mistake. True, the sage Rabbi Eliezer states unequivocally that "the *hatta't* is brought on account of sin" (*m. Zebah.* 1.1), but his generalization is directed only to chap. 4 (and its parallel, Num 15:22–31), where the *qal,* meaning "to sin, do wrong," indeed is found. All other *hatta't* sacrifices are prescribed for specific physical impurities, such as the new mother . . . the contaminated Nazirite, and the like; and in these cases, not one sage claims that the afflicted brings this sacrifice because of his sins. Indeed, this idea is vigorously denied (*b. Šebu.* 8a; *Ker.* 26a). Moreover, not only is the *hatta't* unrelated to sin in rabbinic thought, but most authorities deny emphatically that the impurity itself was caused by sin. Even the minority who see a causal connection between sin and affliction argue that the affliction in itself suffices to expiate the sin (*'Arak.* 16a; *b. Nazir* 19a; *Nid.* 31b), and they concur with the majority that the purpose of the *hatta't* is for ritual purification.

The discussion on the parturient is decisive: "But according to R. Simeon son of Yahai who holds that a woman in confinement is a sinner, what can be said (concerning the purpose of her *hatta't*)? The sacrifice she brings is, nevertheless, for the purpose of permitting her to partake of consecrated food and *is not expiatory*" (*Ker.* 26a). Finally, the categorical statement of the Talmudic commentators, the tosafists (on Lev 12:8), leaves no doubt concerning the rabbinic view: "According to the literal meaning of the text her (the parturient's) sacrifice is not brought for sin."

> The advantage of freeing the *hatta't* from the theologically foreign notion of sin and restoring to it its pristine meaning of purification is that now it is possible to see this sacrifice in its true ancient Near Eastern setting. Israel was part of a cultic continuum which abounded in purifications both of persons and of buildings, especially sanctuaries. The *hatta't*, I aver, is the key that opens the door to this world.[26]

This concept of a purification offering is the basic construct of sacrifice with which Jews operate. In the sacrificial process, wherever the blood is applied is then cleansed. "Atonement" (כִּפֶּר/*kpr*) vicariously "accomplishes cleansing" (Lev 12:8; 14:18–21, 31, 53; 15:15, 30; 16:30; Num 8:32; Heb 9:18–23).[27] Usually this atonement is returning the tabernacle or altar to a pure condition, but occasionally people are also sprinkled with blood and thus cleansed, and if they have committed sins, then they are forgiven. Such cleansing includes atonement forgiveness for sins committed in ignorance (Lev 4:2, 13, 22, 27; 5:2–4; Num 15:30–31; Heb 5:2; 9:7). God's forgiveness within the Mosaic covenant everlastingly forgives past sins (Exod 34:6–7; Ps 103:12; Mic 7:18–20). When the object of atonement (כִּפֶּר) is people, then its meaning includes forgiveness, rendering the people cleansed to their appropriate level of holiness and righteous.[28] Jacob Milgrom contested that persons are only spoken as indirect objects in sacrifice settings, but Roy Gane has successfully answered him, that the preposition מִן/*mn* consistently indicates a purification (of the people) "from" their sins (which are mentioned following the preposition מִן/*mn*) in forgiveness (Lev 4:26; 14:19; 15:15, 30).[29] An individual whose sin is atoned

---

26. Milgrom, *Leviticus 1–16*, 253–54; in addition to the rabbinic texts cited in the quote of m. Yoma 3.9; 4.1.

27. At times, this cleansing is accomplished before כִּפֶּר so that כִּפֶּר is not actually the purification (Lev 12:7–8). At times, כִּפֶּר is either synonymous or synthetically parallel with cleansing and consecrations (Lev 16:18–19; Ezek 43:20, 26). Obviously, some sense of ceremonial purity is accomplished by כִּפֶּר, esp. since some of its uses render clean a house or person when no sin had made them unclean (Lev 14:53; 15:15, 30).

28. The parallel arrangement with forgiveness, which is evident in Lev 4:20, 26, 31, 35; 5:10, 13, 18; 6:7; 10:17; 16:30; and Ps 79:9, indicating that forgiveness is included within כִּפֶּר. Additionally, כִּפֶּר deals with people's sins such that forgiveness is included within its semantic field (Lev 16:32–34; Num 15:25, 28; Deut 21:8; Pss 65:3; 78:38; 79:9; Isa 6:7; 27:9; Ezek 16:63). See Gane, *Cult and Character*, xx, 47–49, 299; Gammie, *Holiness in Israel*, 39.

29. Milgrom, "Preposition מִן in the חַטָּאת Pericopes," 161–63; Gane, "Private Preposition מִן," 209–22; 11QT (11Q19–21; 4Q524; 4Q365ª) 25.14; 26.9–10; and 27.1 defend Gane's conclusion that the people are forgiven in atonement; m. Yoma 8.8–9 supports

(כִּפֶּר) has his iniquity pardoned (Isa 6:7; 27:9), whereas an individual who does not have atonement does not have forgiveness and is thus still under judgment (Num 16:46–47; 25:11–13; 1 Sam 3:14; Isa 22:14; 28:18; 47:11). So, vicarious "atonement" (כִּפֶּר) appeases divine wrath of covenant curse, returning them again to covenantal blessings (Deut 32:43; 2 Sam 21:3; Pss 78:38; 79:9).[30] Gane summarizes his view that purification through the year is primarily personal cleansing and forgiveness, while the corporate cleansing on the Day of Atonement is largely a cleansing of the tabernacle and corporate forgiveness of the nation.[31] Occasionally, in Ezekiel, the LXX refers to this purification offering as "propitiation," dealing with uncleanness, forgiveness of sin, and God's covenant curse (ἱλασμόν; Ezek 43:20; 44:27). That is, even in these eschatological purification offerings, there is still appeasement, which makes the unclean condition vicariously favorable or atoned (כִּפֶּר) with God (Ezek 45:15, 17, 20).

One passage explains that the critical feature to obtain atonement in all the offerings is the life (נֶפֶשׁ/npš) that is given, for which the blood stands as an emblem (Lev 17:11). The life (נֶפֶשׁ) vicariously offered benefits our life (נֶפֶשׁ). So, the blood in sacrifice is not magical, for it merely indicates that the offering is given. In the instance of murder, the dead can't be atoned (כִּפֶּר) for by sacrifice, but only by the murderer's death as a penal sacrifice for his own crime and the ensuing affects (Num 35:33). However, there are instances when the offering is completed without any blood, and yet vicarious atonement (כִּפֶּר) is accomplished (Exod 21:30; 30:15; Num 31:50; Heb 9:22[32]). Even in one instance, atonement (כִּפֶּר) is accomplished by lovingkindness and truth without an offering at all (Prov 16:6).[33] This indicates that no deed accomplishes atonement (כִּפֶּר). Instead, one's life focus to follow the narrow way and the divine enablement within this narrow way are

---

Gane's conclusion that people forgiven in atonement are provided the sin or guilt offering, which is accompanied with repentance.

30. 11QT (11Q19–21; 4Q524; 4Q365a) 25.14; 26.9–10 and 27.1; m. Yoma 8.8–9; Kennard, *Biblical Covenantalism*, 1:151–313.

31. Gane, "Private Preposition מִן," 217.

32. Notice that Hebrews 9:22 acknowledges that blood is "almost" (σχεδὸν) always used in cleansing, but this admits that there are instances when other means cleanse, such as an exchange of money, or if the worshipper is poor, a grain offering will suffice as a purification offering (Lev 5:11).

33. This כִּפֶּר is parallel to the fear of the Lord, which keeps one from evil and its ensuing punishment.

important for atonement to be realized through the available means. That is, atonement is accomplished by whatever means that God designates.

Milgrom underscores that, "As shown (Lev 4:13–14), the *hatta't* laws are based on the assumption that the inadvertent offender becomes aware of his act and feels remorse for it, expressed by the verb *'asam*. Repentance is thus a precondition for the *hatta't*."[34] That is, external deeds are not effective without one's personal commitment to follow God's law. God established this as a feature in relationship; God is not a vending machine.

The guilt offering (אָשָׁם/*'asam*, or ἐπλημμέλησεν in LXX) is a special case of purification offering which deals with an individual who feels his guilt (Lev 5:6–7; 6:17; 7:1–7, 37; 19:21–22; Num 18:9). Such an offering atones and propitiates (Num 5:8, כֹּפֶר, or in LXX it is ἱλασμόν). That is, this offering is very much like the purification offering, in that the clean Nazarite completes his time of purity with a guilt offering when no sin or uncleanness has rendered him impure (Num 6:12). In such guilt offerings, the blood is placed on the altar, and if necessary on the one who is to be cleansed, indicating that both sancta and person are to be cleansed in this atonement (Lev 7:5; 14:12–28). Rabbi Rabad claims that such a guilt offering requires a confession (Num 5:7–8).[35] At times, such a guilt offering mentions an object taken and requires that it be returned, along with twenty percent added, before this guilt offering is effective in atoning for the person's sin (Lev 5:15–19; 6:6). However, if no object is mentioned, then the offering is the appropriate response for one who feels his guilt and confesses it before God. Jacob Milgrom summarizes the guilt offering (אָשָׁם/*'asam*) as follows:

> In sum, the cultic texts reveal four usages of the root *'sm*, as follows: the noun "reparation" and "reparation offering," and the verbs "incur liability [to someone]" and "feel guilt" (without a personal object). These meanings derive from the consequential *'asam*, the punishment or penalty incurred through wrongdoing. The fourth meaning, "feel guilt" refers to psychological guilt. These findings are best summarized by citing two passages in which all four meanings appear (indicated by italics): "He shall pay it to its owner as soon as he *feels guilt* (*beyom 'asmato*). Then he shall bring to the

---

34. Milgrom, *Leviticus 1–16*, 264; 1QS 3.3–6, 8–9; 4.5; 5.13; b. Šeb 1.16.2/13AD; m. Yoma 8.8A; t. Kippurim 4.8A; m. Sanh. 6.2D; Chilton and Neusner, *Classical Christianity*, 199–203.

35. Sipra Hobah 7.3; Sipre Zuṭa on Num 5:5; t. Menaḥ. 10.12; Milgrom, *Leviticus 1–16*, 344–45.

priest, as his reparation (*ʾasmato*) to the Lord, an unblemished ram from the flock, or its assessment, as a reparation offering (*leʾasam*)" (Lev 5:24b–25); and "When that person feels guilt (*weʾasemâ*), he [lit., 'they'] shall confess the wrong he [lit., 'they'] has done, make reparation (*ʾasamo*) in its entirety, add one-fifth to it, and give it to the one to whom he has incurred liability (*leʾaser ʾasam lo*)" (Num 5:6b–7).[36]

Both of these offerings (purification and guilt offerings) vicariously bear the uncleanness or guilt away from the sancta and the one (or group) for whom they are offered. Each of the purification and guilt offerings accomplishes vicarious "atonement" (כִּפֶּר; Lev 14:18–19; Num 5:8)[37] or "propitiation" (LXX: ἱλασμόν; Num 5:8; Ezek 44:27). For example, these offerings, along with the scapegoat[38] in the Day of Atonement, bear the guilt away from the nation (Lev 10:17; 16:22; Heb 9:7). Through such atonement, Israel continues with Yahweh in a relationship of peace, as evidenced by the continuing Mosaic covenant benefits. If Israelites violate the stipulations of the covenant and don't resolve their uncleanness by these available means, then the Israelite and the nation continue to bear the guilt of their sin (Lev 5:1, 17; 17:16; 20:19; Num 9:13; 14:34).

Corporate national atonement to deal with this continuing uncleanness occurs at the establishment of the Mosaic covenant and its renewal at the Day of Atonement. Moses established Israel as clean in the ritual of cleansing, initiating the Mosaic covenant (Exod 24; Heb 9:7). Within the Mosaic covenant, Yahweh demands that Israel be kept clean and holy (Lev 11:44–45). If Israel does not deal with their uncleanness, then it becomes a sin. Ultimately, sins defile Yahweh's holy name and bring covenant curse, as was previously developed (Deut 28:15–29:29; Ezek 43:7–8). For Israel to ignore this mandate and to become unclean defiles the tabernacle and puts Israel at risk to be cut off in covenant curse (Lev 15:31; Num 19:13). This defilement of tabernacle includes the holy place and altar as well (Lev

---

36. Milgrom, *Leviticus 1–16*, 345.

37. m. Yoma 8.8–9.

38. The scapegoat ritual is similar to the Hittite substitution ritual, where the uncleanness and sin is sent away from the cult and people. However, in the Hittite situation, it is sent to a designated region of the offended god, and there is no clear Biblical teaching that the demon Azazel is being placated; rather, the focus is on the removal of the iniquities to an undesignated wilderness location (Lev 16:8, 20–22), and there is a greater variety of animals used in this pattern (van Brock, "Substitution Rituelle," 117–46; Kümmel, "Ersatzkönig und Sündenbock," 289–318; Gurney, *Some Aspects of Hittite Religion*; Wright, *Disposal of Impurity*; Hoffner, "Hittite-Israel Cultural Parallels," xxxii.

16:16, 18; Num 19:20). For example, high-handed unrepentant sin (such as refusing to purify oneself after touching a dead body) defiles both the tabernacle and the holy place (Num 19:13, 20).

Jacob Milgrom develops the idea that the defiled tabernacle is cleansed in three stages.[39] First, the individual's inadvertent misdemeanor or severe physical impurity defiling the courtyard altar requires that the courtyard altar be cleansed by covering its horns with the blood of the purification offering (Lev 4:25, 30; 9:9).[40] The LXX occasionally refers to this altar as the place of "propitiation" (ἱλαστήριον; Ezek 43:14, 17, 20; Amos 9:1).

Secondly, any inadvertent misdemeanor by the high priest or the entire community polluting the shrine is cleansed by the high priest placing the blood of the purification offering on the inner incense altar before the veil that divides the holy place from the Holy of holies (Lev 4:5–7, 16–18; Heb 9:7).[41]

Finally, any high-handed unrepentant sin, polluting both the outer altar and penetrating the veil to the holy place and the Holy Ark, must be cleansed through the Day of Atonement (Lev 16:16; Num 19:20; Isa 37:16; Heb 9:7).[42] Usually, the LXX primarily refers to the mercy seat on the Ark as "the place of propitiation," alluded to on the Day of Atonement (LXX: ἱλαστήριον; Exod 25:17–22; 31:7; 35:12; 38:6–9; Lev 16:2, 13–15; Num 7:89; Heb 9:5). Since the high-handed, rebellious sinner is barred from bringing a purification offering (Num 15:27–31), the uncleanness wrought by his offense must await the cleansing of the sanctuary on the Day of Atonement. This cleansing consists of two steps: the purification offering and the scapegoat. The purification offering cleanses the holy place, the high priest, and the nation of Israel by placing blood of a goat on and in front of the mercy seat and on the horns of the altar (Lev 16:15–19). Next, the scapegoat bore the iniquities of the high priest and Israel away from Israel and the land (Lev 16:20–24).[43] This vicarious "bearing" (נָשָׂא/nš') iniquity identifies the scapegoat as a vicarious substitute to avert covenant curse (Lev 16:22 with 5:1, 17; 7:18).[44] Both scapegoat and purification offering

---

39. Milgrom, *Numbers*, 445–46; Milgrom, *Leviticus 1–16*, 256–61.

40. m. Yoma 5.3, 5–6.

41. m. Yoma 5.5–6.

42. m. Yoma 5.4; though Judah's version has the sprinkling on the curtain inside the holy of holies (m. Yoma 5.4b).

43. m. Yoma 6.1–8.

44. m. Yoma 6.4; Bar 7.7, 9. The scapegoat averts the covenant curse, but is not

are identified as atoning, and the blood clearly cleanses (Lev 16:16–20, 24). However, rabbinic sources resist blending these sacrifices by clarifying that the blood cleanses and the scapegoat forgives all other transgressions.[45] Additionally, some early Jewish sources went beyond Leviticus to see this scapegoat offering as attempting to placate the rebellious demon Azazel, or perhaps the Canaanite god of death.[46] However, rabbis instead consider that this likely refers to the place, namely a precipice, to which the goat is led.[47] However, semantically, the word "probably" is just a compound of the words "goat" (*'ez*) and "lead away" (*'azal*).[48] Biblically, this scapegoat is a means by which God provides vicarious atonement; there is no syncretism with paganism. There is no development of curse or destruction of the scapegoat, so this propitiation is not developed as penal. The process of cleansing first begins with the purification offering cleansing the tent, the outer altar, and the people with atonement (Lev 16:16–19, 30).[49] This is motivated by an abiding fear of temple pollution and divine curse, as evident by the frequency of the purification offering in the public cult. Rabbi Simeon notices this concern, and recognizes that tabernacle cleansing even developed into a monthly recovery to further protect Israel from the build-up over the year:

> More grievous is imparting pollution to the sanctuary and its sancta than all other transgressions in the Torah. All other transgressions that are listed in the Torah are atoned for with a single goat, but imparting pollution to the sanctuary and its sancta is

---

described in a legal penal substitution as is claimed from Hellenistic sources (*Oedipus Rex* 1290–93) but these are foreign to the Jewish Day-of-Atonement pattern.

45. m. Šeb. 1.6; m. Yoma 4.2; 6.1–8; Milgrom, *Studies in Cultic Theology*, 81. There is also a third goat eaten during the Yom Kippur ritual (Philo, *Spec. Laws* 1.190; m. Menaḥ. 11.7; Stökl Ben Ezra, "Fasting with Jews," 174.

46. Azazel as a divine being (3 En. 4.6; Pirqe R. El. 46), which 11QT 26.12 read as *'zz'l*, identifying it as the Canaanite god of death Mot (Barthélemy and Milik, *Discoveries in the Judaean Desert*, 180, ln. 7; parallel to Neh 7:28; 12:29) or rebel angel Raphael (1 En. 10.4–5), and the wilderness as the habitation of demons (Isa 13:21; 34:14; Bar. 4.35; Tob. 8.3; Matt 12:34; Luke 11:24; Rev 18:2); or the devil (LXX; Josephus; Kaiser, "Leviticus," 1112); Helm, "Azazel in Early Jewish Tradition," 217–26; Levine, *In the Presence*; Milgrom, *Leviticus 1–16*, 1020–21; Neusner, *Idea of Purity*, 9–11.

47. Tg. Neb. 5.10.

48. Kaiser, "Leviticus," 1112.

49. Averbeck (in VanGemeren, *New International Dictionary of Old Testament*, 2:344) and m. Yoma 8.8–9 support my claim that the people as well as the tabernacle are cleansed at the Day of Atonement, contrary to Milgrom, who only sees the tabernacle as cleansed.

atoned for through thirty-two goats (Lev 23:19; Num 28–29). All other transgressions in the Torah are atoned for one time in the year (Yom Kippur), but imparting pollution to the sanctuary and its sancta is atoned for every month (Num 28:15), as it is written: 'Surely because you have polluted my sanctuary with all your detestable things and abominations that you did, more grievous than all of them was imparting impurity to the sanctuary.[50]

Thus all the sin and uncleanness of the most holy place and that of the people are cleansed on the Day of Atonement with the purification offering blood. Likewise, the scapegoat has all the national iniquities confessed on its head so that, when it is led out into a solitary land, it bears Israel's iniquities away (Lev 16:21–22).[51] Averbeck develops the idea that the ritual of the scapegoat here is of great significance in that it symbolizes the vicarious removal of all iniquity and transgressions from Israel, cleansing the tabernacle (Lev 16:19) and the people (Lev 16:30).[52] Both the purification offering and the scapegoat contribute to the Day of Atonement, accomplishing atonement or propitiation (כִּפֶּר, Lev 16:6–34; LXX, ἱλασμοῦ, Lev 25:9) from Israel's uncleanness and sin.[53] In this way, the nation of Israel was able to continue on for another year in the Mosaic covenantal relationship of peace with Yahweh because their corporate unclean condition had been atoned for at the yearly Day of Atonement. Wheeler Robinson summarizes how sacrifices maintain covenantal relationship for Israel with God.

> None of the sacrifices implies penal substitution, or makes any provision, at least in theory, for those who have sinned intentionally against God. Intentional sin is itself an act of self-exclusion from the covenant of God with Israel, and ideally, deserves death. The sacrifices operate within the covenant; they were "offered to a God already in relations of grace with His people. They were not offered in order to attain His grace, but to retain it."[54]

---

50. t. Šebu. 1.3.

51. In Second Temple Judaism, this scapegoat was pushed off a precipice to its death in a ravine (1 En. 10.4–8; Philo, *Planting* 61; m. Yoma 6.6). There is no clear statement that penal wrath has come upon *azazel*, for it awaits eschatological judgment (1 En. 10.6).

52. Averbeck (in VanGemeren, *New International Dictionary of Old Testament*, 2:344) and Gane (*Cult and Character*) follow Milgrom on Tabernacle atonement but also add individual atonement and forgiveness that Milgrom ignores (Lev 4:26; 14:19; 15:15; 16:30, 34a; Num 6:11; m. Yoma 8.8–9).

53. Further confirmed as atoning by rabbinics (m. Šebu. 1.6; m. Yoma 5.3–6; 6.1–8; 8.8–9; Sipra Aḥare 5.8).

54. Robinson, *Religious Ideas of the Old Testament*, 166; end of quote quotes Davidson,

Early Judaism expected a Jewish temple to be functioning in Jerusalem to provide this cleansing and atonement, grounded in the Abrahamic and Mosaic covenants.[55] After the Babylonian captivity, during the Day of Atonement ceremony, the high priest would cleanse himself and, dressed in special garments, enter the holy of holies to pray and sprinkle blood on the stone where the Ark of the Covenant had stood.[56] Rabbis saw that all sins between the worshipper and God were forgiven through these Day-of-Atonement sacrifices.[57] To supplement these Day-of-Atonement offerings, the Testament of Levi expected archangels to also offer propitiatory sacrifices in the heavenly temple.[58]

The Qumran community joined the prophets in considering that the temple cult in Jerusalem was corrupt, but they did not reject it altogether because they considered that, in the future, the temple cult would be re-established and provide atonement in the eschatological context (Jer 33:18; Ezek 44:15—46:24).[59]

ISAIAH 53 AND SERVANT AS SACRIFICE

Eschatological atonement was expected through the Messiah in his priestly ministry.[60] One possibility of this eschatological atonement was through the concept of Isaiah's "servant of the Lord."

Theology of the Old Testament, 316–17. These convey sentiments later embraced in the new perspective of Paul, but are affirmed decades earlier.

55. 4Q414 col. 7, frag. 29–32; 11Q19 col. 11–35; 29.7–10, esp. 9–10; Jub. 1.27–29; 1 En. 90.28–29.

56. Philo, *Dreams* 1.216–17; Philo, *Embassy* 306; m. Yoma 5.

57. m. Yoma 8.9; y. Yoma 8.9, 45c; b. Yoma 65 ab; Sipra Ahere Mot 8.5.

58. t. Levi 3.4–6.

59. Early Judaism continues the hope of the construction of the temple as identified with the new creation at the end time (1 Chr 17:12–14; Ezek 40:1–43:5; Jub. 1.27–28; 1QS 8.6–7; 4Q174), the temple being indwelt by the presence of God (Pss 11:4; 79:1; Isa 6:1; 66:6; Ezek 43:2–5; 11QTa 29.7; 45.12–14; 46.3–4) and populated by functioning priests in a covenant relationship with God where sacrifices atone and forgive (Ezek 44:11–31; Sir. 45.25; 47.11; 1QM 2.5; 11QT 25.10—27.10; *Shemoneh 'Esreh* benediction 14; Pirqe R. El. 46). This central focus of temple in eschatological Israel becomes a metaphor for the community of Israel (1QS 8.5–6; 9.6).

60. 1QS 7 1.19; 11Q13 12.7–8; 4Q541; 1 En. 39.4–6; 41.2 (much like Rom 8:28–30; Col 3:1–4); 48.1–4; 51.4–5; 61.4; 62.14; t. Levi 18; Kennard, *Messiah Jesus*, 302–5; Pate and Kennard discuss other possible allusions Paul may have made to Isaiah 52–53 (*Deliverance Now and Not Yet*, 173–76). Some of these claimed allusions, such as Rom 4:25,

Differing interpretations of the suffering servant in Isaiah 53 are reflected in the translations; however, David A. Sapp and Otto Betz present convincing cases for the following development: (1) the servant's afflictions

---

"justification," as reflecting Isaiah 53:11, "justify," only work on the level of Vulgate or English text—neither the MT nor the LXX have any similarity in phrase or theology to that of Paul. For an explanation of and an apologetic for this "Isaac Typology," see Wood, "Isaac Typology in the New Testament," 583–89; Daly, "Soteriological Significant," 45–75; Gubler, *Die Frühesten Deutungen*, 336–75; Rosenberg, "Jesus, Isaac and the Suffering Servant," 381–88; Riesenfeld, *Jesus Transfiguré*, 86–96; Strack and Billerbeck, *Kommentar zum Neuen Testament*, 3:746; Vermes, *Scripture and Tradition in Judaism*, 193–97; 217–27; Schoeps, *Paul: The Theology of the Apostle*, 141–49. An important issue that emerges from the concerns of chapters two and three of this study is whether or not pre-Christian Judaism expected a suffering Messiah. Those who say "yes" include Cullmann, *Christology of the New Testament*, 55–56, 60; Lohse, *Märtyrer und Gottesknecht*, 104–6; Jeremias, "παῖς θεοῦ." The last-mentioned author summarizes the evidence for the Messianic interpretation of the Isaianic servant in Palestinian Judaism: (1) this interpretation was confined to Isaiah 42:1–9; 43:10; 49:1–2 and 6–7; and 52:13—53:12; (2) in relation to Isaiah 42:1–9 and 52:13—53:12, the Messianic understanding is "constant from pre-Christian times"; (3) the Messianic interpretation of the passion sayings of Isaiah 53 can be traced back at least with a high degree of probability to the pre-Christian period, though not with the same certainty. Those who do not think pre-Christian Judaism gives evidence of a suffering Messiah expectation include Hooker, *Jesus and the Servant*, 56–67; Strack and Billerbeck, *Kommentar zum Neuen Testament*, 2:273–74; Menard, "Pais Theou as a Messianic Title," 83–92, esp. 84–85; Longenecker, *Christology of Early Jewish Christianity*, 105; Fitzmyer, *Luke X–XXIV*, 156–66. The latter summarizes the evidence for this view, whereas the notion of a suffering messiah is not found in the OT, or in any texts of pre-Christian Judaism. Strack and Billerbeck (*Kommentar zum Neuen Testament*, 2:273–99) say that the "Old Synagogue" knew of "a suffering Messiah, for of whom no death was determined; i.e., the Messiah ben David" and a "dying Messiah, of whom no suffering was mentioned," the Messiah ben Joseph (273–74). Yet when they cite the passages from Rabbinic literature (282–91) that speak of the suffering Messiah ben David, they are all drawn from late texts, which scarcely show that the expectations of such a figure existed among Palestinian Jews in or prior to the time of Jesus. The same has to be said of the texts about the dying Messiah ben Joseph (292–99). Strack and Billerbeck rightly reject the implication found at times in Christian commentators that Mark 8:31 and Matt 16:21 refer to a "suffering Messiah," and the latter is not a "messianic" title without further ado. Where in pre-Christian Judaism does one find a "Son of Man" as an agent of Yahweh anointed for the salvation, deliverance of his people? True, in Tg. Jonathan the "servant" of Isaiah 52:13 is identified as "the Messiah": "See, my servant, the Messiah, shall prosper; he will be exalted, great, very mighty," and 53:10c is made to read, "They will look upon the kingdom of their Messiah, many sons and daughters will be theirs." Yet no use of "Messiah" is made in the crucial verse, 53:12. It is not surprising that the "Servant" of Isaiah 52–53 was eventually identified with a messiah in the Jewish tradition; but it still remains to be shown that this identification existed in pre-Christian Judaism or in Judaism contemporary with the NT (Fitzmyer, *Luke X–XXIV*, 156–66); Wright, *Jesus and the Victory of God*, 591.

and death are portrayed as vicariously atoning in the MT, (2) and the LXX tones down the servant's suffering (he does not die, but is divinely rescued), almost to the point of being representative atoning, (3) while Targum Jonathan to the prophets transposes suffering from the servant/messiah to Israel's enemies.[61] This reinterpretation makes Israel's enemies become the sacrifice of atonement. There is perhaps an "Isaac Typology" (based on Genesis 22:1–14) that lies behind Isaiah 53, and its influence is to be seen in the Intertestamental period, as well as throughout the New Testament, where the motif of suffering and death in an atoning and vicarious sense emerges.[62] Sometimes adherents of a pre-Christian origin of the suffering

---

61. For numbers 1 and 2, see Sapp, "LXX, 1QIsa, and MT Versions ," 170–92; while Betz treats the *Targum* in "Jesus and Isaiah 53," 70–87, esp. 73.

62. For an explanation of and an apologetic for this "Isaac Typology," see Wood, "Isaac Typology in the New Testament," 583–89; Daly, "Soteriological Significant," 45–75; Gubler, *Die Frühesten Deutungen*, 336–75; Rosenberg, "Jesus, Isaac and the Suffering Servant," 381–88; Riesenfeld, *Jesus Transfiguré*, 86–96; Strack and Billerbeck, *Kommentar zum Neuen Testament*, 3:746; Vermes, *Scripture and Tradition in Judaism*, 193–97; 217–27; Schoeps, *Paul: The Theology of the Apostle*, 141–49. An important issue that emerges from the concerns of chapters two and three of this study is whether or not pre-Christian Judaism expected a suffering Messiah. Those who say "yes" include Cullmann, *Christology of the New Testament*, 55–56, 60; Lohse, *Märtyrer und Gottesknecht*, 104–6; Jeremias, "παῖς θεοῦ." The last-mentioned author summarizes the evidence for the Messianic interpretation of the Isaianic servant in Palestinian Judaism: (1) this interpretation was confined to Isaiah 42:1–9; 43:10; 49:1–2 and 6–7; and 52:13—53:12; (2) in relation to Isaiah 42:1–9 and 52:13—53:12, the Messianic understanding is "constant from pre-Christian times"; (3) the Messianic interpretation of the passion sayings of Isaiah 53 can be traced back at least with a high degree of probability to the pre-Christian period, though not with the same certainty. Those who do not think pre-Christian Judaism gives evidence of a suffering Messiah expectation include Hooker, *Jesus and the Servant*, 56–67; Strack and Billerbeck, *Kommentar zum Neuen Testament*, 2:273–74; Menard, "*Pais Theou* as a Messianic Title," 83–92, esp. 84–85; Longenecker, *Christology of Early Jewish Christianity*, 105; Fitzmyer, *Luke X–XXIV*, 156–66. The latter summarizes the evidence for this view, whereas the notion of a suffering messiah is not found in the OT, or in any texts of pre-Christian Judaism. Strack and Billerbeck (*Kommentar zum Neuen Testament*, 2:273–99) say that the "Old Synagogue" knew of "a suffering Messiah, for of whom no death was determined; i.e., the Messiah ben David" and a "dying Messiah, of whom no suffering was mentioned," the Messiah ben Joseph (273–74). Yet when they cite the passages from Rabbinic literature (282–91) that speak of the suffering Messiah ben David, they are all drawn from late texts, which scarcely show that the expectations of such a figure existed among Palestinian Jews in or prior to the time of Jesus. The same has to be said of the texts about the dying Messiah ben Joseph (292–99). Strack and Billerbeck rightly reject the implication found at times in Christian commentators that Mark 8:31 and Matt 16:21 refer to a "suffering Messiah," and the latter is not a "messianic" title without further ado. Where in pre-Christian Judaism does one find a "Son of Man" as an agent of Yahweh anointed for the salvation, deliverance of his people? True, in Tg.

messiah appeal to three texts thought to be important exceptions to the rule: 4 Ezra 7:28–30; Targum of Isaiah 53; and the "Pierced Messiah" text (4Q285). The first mentions the death of the messiah as the climax of the temporal messianic kingdom. However, it is important to note that there the messiah does not suffer; rather, after having lived long and well for four hundred years, he simply dies with the rest of humanity. His death, therefore, has no apparent theological significance. Likewise, the Aramaic translation (*Targum*) of Isaiah 53 is not evidence for the concept of a suffering messiah when it transposed (probably in reaction to Christianity) the afflictions of the suffering servant of Isaiah 53 *from* the messiah *to* Israel (or to the surrounding gentile nations). Moreover, both texts are dated after the birth of Christ and cannot be used as testimony for pre-Christian Jewish messianic understanding. With regard to the Pierced Messiah Text, it cannot for grammatical reasons be invoked to support the idea of a suffering messiah.[63] Thus that text should read, "The leader of the community [the Prince of the Congregation] will kill him [the leader of the *Kittim*]." N. T. Wright's comments represent a fair-minded solution to the issue:

> There was not such a thing as a straightforward pre-Christian Jewish belief in an Isaianic 'servant of YHWH' who, perhaps as Messiah, would suffer and die to make atonement for Israel or for the world. But there was something else, which literally dozens of texts attest: a large-scale and widespread belief, to which Isaiah 40–55 made a substantial contribution, that Israel's present state of suffering was somehow held within the ongoing divine purpose; that in due time this period of woe would come to an end, with divine wrath falling instead on the pagan nations that had oppressed Israel (and perhaps on renegades within Israel herself); that the explanation for the present state of affairs had to do with Israel's own sin, for which either she, or in some cases her righteous representatives, was or were being punished; and that this suffering and punishment would therefore, somehow, hasten the moment when Israel's tribulation would be complete, when she would

---

Jonathan the "servant" of Isaiah 52:13 is identified as "the Messiah": "See, my servant, the Messiah, shall prosper; he will be exalted, great, very mighty," and 53:10c is made to read, "They will look upon the kingdom of their Messiah, many sons and daughters will be theirs." Yet no use of "Messiah" is made in the crucial verse, 53:12. It is not surprising that the "Servant" of Isaiah 52–53 was eventually identified with a messiah in the Jewish tradition; but it still remains to be shown that this identification existed in pre-Christian Judaism or in Judaism contemporary with the NT (Fitzmyer, *Luke X–XXIV*, 156–66); Wright, *Jesus and the Victory of God*, 591.

63. Schiffman, *Reclaiming the Dead Sea Scrolls*, 346.

finally have been purified from her sin so that her exile could be undone at last. There was, in other words, a belief, hammered out not in abstract debate but in and through poverty, exile, torture and martyrdom, that Israel's sufferings might be, not merely a state *from* which she would, in YHWH's good time, be redeemed, but paradoxically, under certain circumstances and in certain senses, part of the means *by* which that redemption would be affected.[64]

Let us then return to the MT and unpack what is meant by the "servant of Yahweh" from the servant songs. The term "servant" is used several ways throughout Isaiah, but in the four servant songs it refers to a spiritually instructed individual in the midst of a sinful and blind nation (Isa 40:2; 42:1, 19; 53:9). This servant as an individual trusts Yahweh throughout discouragement and suffering for others sins, of which he is innocent (Isa 42:1; 49:4; 53:4–6, 9–11), whereas Israel corporately is spiritually deaf and dumb, doubting Yahweh in discouragement and suffering for their own sins (Isa 40:2, 27; 42:19). This concept of a "servant" is one who is chosen for a special ministry by God. Regal description "prohibits an understanding of 'servant' as slave or lackey, but determines its meaning as 'trusted envoy' or 'confidential representative.'"[65] Qumran noticed these features and even changed aspects in 1QIsa and 4Q541 from the MT to be more Messianic with regard to offering himself as atonement for humanity.[66]

In summary form, the servant songs convey a good overview of the servant's role. As a humble prophet, Yahweh's servant will bring salvation and the proper order to the earth (Isa 42:1–4). Yahweh, through the new covenant, guarantees his servant's mission for accomplishing salvation (Isa 42:5–9). The servant, called by Yahweh, rejected by his own people, will bring salvation to the gentiles, and at the proper time will restore Israel to the land and to Yahweh (Isa 49:1–13). The righteous servant declares that, by his being rejected while trusting Yahweh, he learned to comfort the weary (Isa 50:4–9). Yahweh applies the lessons from his servant's experience to others by reminding believers to live by faith, while unbelievers are warned about judgment (Isa 50:10–11). Yahweh promises to exalt his

---

64. Wright, *Jesus and the Victory of God*, 591.

65. Williams, "Poems About Incomparable Yahweh's Servant," 75.

66. 1QIsa 52:14 replaces the MT "marring" (מִשְׁחַת) with a Qal singular, "I have anointed," indicating that God established the sacrifice role for his Messiah, and 1QIsa 51:5 replaces the MT first-person "My righteousness" with a third person "His arm," also indicating Messianism; also 4Q541 9.1.1.2, "he will atone" (Hengel and Bailey, "Effective History of Isaiah 53," 101, 103, 108, 146).

servant because he voluntarily provided a "substitutionary atonement," having died as a vicarious sacrifice on behalf of guilty people to cleanse and save them (Isa 52:13–15). Israel responds in a confession of their sin and belief in the servant's atoning death (Isa 53:1–9; Zech 12:10–11). Israel's confession probably takes place as the servant is honored in kingdom. This confession fits the pattern of the servant offering himself as purification and guilt offering *on their behalf*, thus "vicarious atonement." Because of the effectiveness of the guilt (MT) or sin (LXX) offering by the servant, the servant will be blessed with a continuing inheritance (Isa 53:10–12).

Israel understands that the human abuse and death of the servant was ultimately because Yahweh placed their iniquity and covenant curse upon the servant as a vicarious substitutionary atonement, an expression of guilt or purification offering (Isa 53:3–6, 10). Especially in Isaiah 53:4, the people declare that God smites the servant. The basic root נכה usually means "striking" or "violent killing" in OT and early Jewish contexts (Exod 21:12; Num 35:11, 15; Isa 14:6; 66:3),[67] unless the object of the beating does not kill, like Balaam's staff (Num 22:23–32). Thus the emphasis is "violent killing," but the term does not essentially mean killing. The hophal passive participle מֻכֵּה ("smitten") in Isaiah 53:4, when used as coming from God, is identified by emphasis as broadly smiting with covenant curse in the OT, early Judaism, and in Isaiah (Lev 26:21; Num 11:33; Deut 28:59; Isa 1:6;[68] 10:26; 27:7; 30:26; 53:4).[69] However, in Ezekiel, God claps (נכה) his hands together, and no covenant curse is conveyed (Ezek 21:19 [Eng v. 14], 22 [Eng v. 17]; 22:13), showing that the term from God does not essentially mean death by covenant curse. However, in this Isaiah 53:4 instance, based on emphasis, God doing the striking implies "penal atonement." Thus the servant receives the covenant curse from God which would have come upon humans, resulting in the servant's death. This is a softer but compelling case for penal death here because the evidence splits and it expresses the confessed understanding of Israelites, rather than either a claim of reality or God's assessment.

---

67. *TDOT*, 9:415–8; this term (נכה), if accomplished by humans, does not carry the semantic field of covenant curse, merely "killing," which term in Zechariah 13:7 conveys that the Shepherd will be struck (נכה) by humans and his followers will scatter.

68. Perhaps Isa 1:6 מֻכֵּה is self-inflicted wounds rather than the covenant curse due to Israel's sins.

69. "Covenant curse" when from God—see Van Dam in VanGemeren, *New International Dictionary*, 3:103–4; CD 19.8; 4Q166 2.12; 4Q169 frag. 3–4 1.5; 11QT^a 55.6–8.

The theological meaning of the servant's death is carried by the sacrificial terminology. The servant atones for many nations and Israel in their sin through the pattern of covenantal atonement (purification or guilt offering). In his marred appearance, he is identified as "He will sprinkle many nations" (Isa 52:14–15; יַזֶּה/*yzh*). Such a concept of corporate sprinkling indicates the establishment of a covenant and the atonement forgiveness which accompanies this relationship (Exod 24:8; Heb 9:13; 1 Pet 1:2). To effect this atonement forgiveness, eschatological Israel confesses they understood that the servant was cursed by God (Isa 53:4–6). This concept of divine curse would become an instance in the life of the servant where he might take upon himself the cup of God's wrath (which penal imagery is in the context; Isa 51:17, 22) or become like the scapegoat at the Day of Atonement (Lev 16:20–22, vicarious but not developed as penal sacrifice; Isa 51:17, 22; 53:4). The sins of the people are confessed upon the scapegoat to bear them away into the wilderness. This vicarious "bearing" of the people's sin is what the Servant accomplishes (Isa 53:4, 10). The Servant's death is to deal with our corporate iniquities—that is, to bring atonement and peace with God. Such atonement and reconciliation are what one would expect as benefits from a "guilt offering" (Isa 53:10 MT identifies אָשָׁם/*'sm*, "guilt offering," though the LXX identifies it as a purification or "sin offering": δῶτε περὶ ἁμαρτίας). There is no object taken, so no reparations are required—only Israel's conscious confession of their sin, which is in fact the voice of Isaiah 53:1, saying, "Who has believed our message?" Isaiah presents this confession of corporate Israel as in the future kingdom era (Isa 52:7–10; 54:1–17). Presumably, individual Israelites could confess their sin earlier than that expression of kingdom and have the atonement benefits of the servant applied to them. John Oswalt describes this substitution sacrifice from Isaiah 53:4–6, 10–12.

> It is here and in vv. 10–12 that the issue of the substitutionary suffering of the servant, and thus his capacity to deliver his people, comes to the fore. He does not suffer merely as a result of the people, but in the people. He suffers *for* them, and because of that, they do not need to experience the results of their sins.[70]

---

70. Oswalt, *Book of Isaiah*, 385, and for contextual development see 386–87, 401; for a discussion on a range of interpretations of Isaiah 53, see Pate and Kennard, *Deliverance Now and Not Yet*, 92–96.

As has been shown, the servant's substitutionary sacrifice is informed especially by the language of the cult, not a courtroom situation (especially Lev 5:1, 17; 10:17; 16:22; 17:16; 20:19; and Num 9:13; 14:34).

In Isaiah 53:5, the "piercing," "crushing," "chastening," and "scourging" are each metaphors of the death of the servant, along with the "slaughter" and "cut off" of Isaiah 53:7–8. We should not focus on the "pierce" and "scourge" as though they were specifically descriptive of Roman scourging and spear piercing on a cross, for neither was Rome present, nor was this means of death being used in Isaiah's eighth century BC. For example, "scourging" (בַּחֲבֻרָתוֹ/*bḥbrtw*) of Isaiah 53:5 simply means "stripe," "blow," or "strike," as in Genesis 4:23. The word has no conscious allusion to Roman scourging. Likewise, we should not ignore the other metaphorical terms, especially "crushing," which is repeated again when this is identified as a guilt offering (Isa 53:5, מְדֻכָּא/*mrk'*; 10, דַּכְּאוֹ/*dk'*). I take these terms as metaphors of the servant's death.

The NT refers to Isaiah 53 directly in several places, but the amazing thing is that none of these references develop the atonement which Isaiah's servant of the Lord undertakes. For example, Matthew 8:17 describes the miracles accomplished by Christ as his carrying of our infirmities (quoting Isa 53:4). First Peter 2:22 indicates the silence that Jesus maintained before his accusers as a mimetic[71] atonement pattern for Christians to follow (quoting Isa 53:9). Luke 22:37 identifies (through Isaiah 53:12) that Jesus was to be classified with criminals. Acts 8:32–35 quotes some of the physical surroundings (such as, Jesus is silent in his death) to recognize the servant's death as Jesus' death (quoting Isa 53:7–8). Paul makes two direct citations following the LXX and being rather dissimilar to the MT.[72] Isaiah 52:15b is quoted in Romans 15:21, and Isaiah 53:1a is quoted in Romans 10:16. Neither quote has Christological or sacrificial value. Of these passages, only 1 Peter adds in the context that Jesus "bore our sins in his body

---

71. Mimetic atonement is where an example sets a pattern to emulate. Such a view was common in early Judaism and Greco-Roman literature (Pate and Kennard, *Deliverance Now and Not Yet*, 22–71; 2 Macc 6.18–7.42; 4 Macc 10.10; 11.12, 20, 27; 16.24–25; 17.2, 11–12, 18; Wis. 3.5–6; 7.14; 11.19; 12.22; deaths of Socrates, Cato, Diogenes, Demonax, and Seneca: Seneca, *Ep.* 24.6–7; Epictetus, *Diatr.* 4.1 168–72; Plutarch, *Tranq. an.* 475D–F 1.11; Tacitus, *Ann.* 15.62; Seeley, *Noble Death*).

72. Pate and Kennard discuss other possible allusions Paul may have made to Isaiah 52–53 (*Deliverance Now and Not Yet*, 173–176). Some of these claimed allusions (such as Romans 4:25 "justification" as reflecting Isa 53:11 "justify" only work on the level of Vulgate or English text, neither the MT nor the LXX have any similarity in phrase or theology to that of Paul).

on the cross" with imagery of the Christians having strayed like sheep (1 Pet 2:24–25, probably alluding to Isa 53:4–6, 10). So at least Peter probably recognized that Isaiah 53 describes Christ's death as vicarious substitutionary atonement, though his emphasis in the context is on instruction for servants suffering to follow Jesus in silent mimetic atonement (1 Pet 2:18–23). Additionally, with no clear statement using Isaiah 53 in the NT for vicarious atonement, the synoptic and Acts pattern identifies more with mimetic atonement. There is no mention of Isaianic servant atonement in Hebrews, but both Isaiah and Hebrews develop their views reflecting Mosaic covenant language.

In 1 Enoch and some Qumran texts, the teachings about the Isaianiac suffering servant combine[73] with Merkabah[74] mysticism. First Enoch joins mainstream Judaism in announcing the afflictions of the righteous are to be seen as mimetic atonement, especially at the culmination of the Messianic woes.[75] In this context, the Son of Man as Messiah[76] employs a representative role of suffering on behalf of the elect.[77] That is, the heavenly Son of Man appropriates to himself the afflictions of the elect so that the elect on earth may enjoy in heaven the glory of the Enochian Son of Man. This

---

73. Pate and Kennard (*Deliverance Now and Not Yet*, 75–77) follow Nickelsburg (*Resurrection, Immortality, and Eternal Life*, 71–72) in connecting these imageries in contrast to Sjöberg's (*Der Menschensohn im ältiopischen Henochbuch*, 116–39) contentions.

74. Or Jewish divine chariot presentations of a real divine temple in heaven, simultaneous to that of God inhabiting the temple on earth. That is, both the heavenly and earthly temples are real, and different things may be occurring in these different realities. For example, the heavenly temple is normally thought to be where God's presence dwells (Isa 6:4), but the amazing thing is that with the cleansed tabernacle God dwells on earth, with the ark of the covenant serving as his throne (Exod 40:34–38). However, the uncleanness of the earthly temple dislodges the divine presence from the earthly temple, while it remains in the heavenly temple (Ezek 1:4–28; 11:22–25). The different conditions of the pure heavenly temple and the occasionally unclean earthly temple show that they are both real in this multidimensional Hebraic framework rather than the idealism of the earthly shadows, which a Platonism would portray (1 En. 14; 37–71; 2 En. 15–17; 4 Ezra 9.26–10.59; 13.35–36; 2 Bar. 4.2–7; 6.9; 32.4; Gal 4:26; Heb 12:22; Rev 3:12; 21:2, 10; Ascen. Isa. 9; LAE 37; Apoc. Ab. 29; Exod. Rab. 43.8; m. Hag. 2.1; b. Hag. 14a; 15a; Hec. Ab. Rab. 20.1; b. Sanh. 38b; Pate and Kennard, *Deliverance Now and Not Yet*, 98–103; Sholem, *Jewish Gnosticism*; Lincoln, *Paradise Now and Not Yet*, 9–32, 169–95; Dean-Otting, *Heavenly Journeys*; Gruenwald, *Apocalyptic and Merkavah Mysticism*, 29–72; Schafer, *Kehhalot-Studien*; Chernus, "Visions of God," 123–46; Isaacs, *Sacred Space*, 59–61; Koester, *Hebrews*, 97–100).

75. 1 En. 43.4; 47.1–2; 48.6; 103.9—104.8.

76. 1 En. 46.1–7; 48.2–10; 52.4.

77. 1 En. 39.6; 48.1–4; 51.4–5; 61.4; 62.14.

glory already exists in heaven,[78] but the public resurrection of the elect will vindicate them before the wicked.[79]

However, meanwhile, the teacher of righteousness viewed himself as Isaiah's suffering servant, providing vicarious atonement for his community.[80] Thus to be associated with him is to experience divine forgiveness.[81] The Qumran covenanter identified the teacher of righteousness with Melchizedek, who was expected to atone for the Qumran covenanter's sins,[82] which meant deliverance of the righteous from the age of the Messianic woes into kingdom.[83] After the teacher of righteousness died, his followers recalculated that deliverance to occur at the end of forty years would entail their mimetic suffering, in order to fill up what was lacking from the teacher's sufferings.[84] However, after the forty years came and went with no rescue, the Qumran covenanters reinterpreted their deliverance mystically to mean that they were caught up to heaven in the worship setting with and because of the vicarious atonement of the teacher of righteousness.[85]

Additionally, because of Qumran's separation, they also considered that the community itself atoned for its members through a sacrifice of humility, prayer, and mystical community worship, provided that the member repents of sin and submits to the community discipline (Pss 51:17; 141:2);[86]

---

78. 1 En. 39.4–5; 41.2, much like Rom 8:28–30; Col 3:1–4.

79. 1 En. 62.14–16.

80. 1QH^a 15.8–27, esp. 15.18 and 16.4–17.36; 11Q13. 6–25. The teacher of righteousness probably understood himself to be on the verge of exaltation in Jerusalem (1QH^a 14.28–36; 15.24–28). However, the Damascus Document suggests that the teacher of righteousness died before he could deliver on his promises (CD 19.34–35; 20.13–16). Deliverance was recalculated to be forty years later (CD 20.13–16; 11Q13; 1QS 8.1–16).

81. Esp. 1QH^a 15.18.

82. 11Q13 6–8.

83. 11Q13 9–25.

84. The teacher of righteousness probably understood himself to be on the verge of exaltation in Jerusalem (1QH^a 14.28–36; 15.24–28). However, the Damascus Document suggests that the Teacher of Righteousness died before he could deliver on his promises (CD 19.34–35; 20.13–16). Deliverance was recalculated to be forty years later (CD 20.13–16; 11Q13; 1QS 8.1–16).

85. 1QH^a 11.19–38; 15.26–36.

86. Prayer: 1QS 3.8; 5.6–7; 8.5–6, 10; 9.4–5; 1Q34 1+2; 4Q400 frag. 1 lines 15–16; 4Q508 frag. 2 2–3; 22+23; 4Q509 frag. 16 3; 5–6 ii, 7; 11Q5 27.2–11; Jub. 5.17–18; 34.18–19; *Festival of Prayers*; Pss. Sol. 3.8; 9.6; Philo, *Moses* 2.23–24; Philo, *Spec. Laws* 2.196, esp. within 193–203; Philo, *Embassy* 306; LAB 13.6; b. Ber. 26b; mystical worship: 1 En. 14.8–25; T. Levi 3.4–5; *Songs of the Sabbath Sacrifice*; 1QH^a 11.19–38; 15.26–36.

nonmembers remained unclean as sinners. 1QS identifies that God's merciful justification occurs at the eschatological judgment for those who reflect the narrow way from their heart.[87] Actually, the Babylonian Talmud considered that confessional prayer and the study of the Torah was more effective in atoning than animal sacrifice, so those practices replace burnt offerings for atonement.[88]

Furthermore, mimetic atonement is celebrated among Jews. For example, ben Sir considers that a virtuously righteous life atones.[89] Additionally, Maccabean and other Jewish martyrs were seen to propitiate the sins of the people as mimetic deaths and suffering redeem Israel from the domination of foreign powers.[90]

With the destruction of the Jerusalem temple in 70 and 135 AD, some forms of early Judaism continued to offer purification sacrifices, including those of the Day of Atonement in synagogues[91] and in alternative Jewish temples, such as the Jewish Elephantine temple (near the Aswan high dam in Egypt).[92] Several other Jewish frameworks without a functioning Jewish temple practiced modified purification sacrifices and Day of Atonement sacrifices from their synagogues.[93] While these approaches were acknowledged, Yoḥanan ben Zakkai additionally proposed (similarly to Prov 16:6) that acts of mercy and loving kindness remained as an effective atonement to cleanse and forgive on the basis of Hosea 6:6.[94] Philo identified that con-

---

87. 1QS 11.2–3, 12,13–15; also 4Q394ᶜ 31.

88. b. Ber. 32b; b. Menaḥ. 110a.

89. Sir 3.3; 35.5–6, 9.

90. 1 En. 43.4; 47.1–2; 48.6; 103.9—104.8; 4 Macc 6.29; 17.21–22; 4Q171 frag. 1–10 ii 8–11.

91. Philo, *Moses* 2.23; *Seder 'Abodah*; b. Meg. 31a.

92. Porten, *Archives from Elephantine*, 128–33, 279–82, 311–14.

93. The Jewish practice would have sacrifice complete the reconciliation process (Lev 1–7; Ep. Aristeas 170–71; Sir. 34.18–19; 35.12; Philo, *Spec. Laws* 1.236–37). Continuing this practice, Matthew 5:23–24 and Acts 18:18; 21:23–27 support Jewish Christian participation in Jewish sacrifices. In contrast, Gos. Eb. 7, as recorded by Epiphanius in *Pan.* 30.16.4–5, has Jesus condemn such practice of Jewish sacrifices. Of course, the law prescribes the Levitical sacrifices for Israel (Lev 1–7, 16:1–17:9). Additionally, the OT describes the kingdom era under the Messiah as continuing to practice these sacrifices that atone (Jer 33:18; Ezek 43:18–46:24), though Hebrews 10:1–8 ceases the sacrifices for now for any people following the new covenant who would be disturbed by their reminder, and Lev. Rab. 9.7, written four centuries after the destruction of the temple (fifth century AD), ceases the ritual sacrifices in the Messianic kingdom.

94. *The Fathers according to Rabbi Nathan*, cited by Neusner, *Idea of Purity*, 68.

fession atones,[95] as does repentance,[96] affliction,[97] and prayer.[98] Pinḥas ben Yair drew all these categories together as a narrow way of salvation unto everlasting life for holiness, cleanness, righteousness.

> Heedfulness leads to [physical] cleanness, cleanness to purity, purity to separateness, separateness to holiness, holiness to humility, humility to the shunning of sin, the shunning of sin to saintliness, saintliness to the Holy Spirit, the Holy Spirit to the resurrection of the dead.[99]

Obviously, Christianity takes things into a Messianic sacrifice and kingdom, but that is beyond the bounds of connections made by Isaiah.[100]

MESSIANIC ATONEMENT IN HEBREWS

The atonement in Hebrews is definite[101] or "direct application" to the community of followers of Christ, but is applied indefinitely[102] or "available but not immediately applied" on an individual basis with regard to forgiveness and definitely with regard to a cleansed conscience. Two things should be immediately apparent: 1) Hebrews has crafted a view of atonement between the limited atonement of Calvinism and the unlimited atonement of

---

95. Philo, *Posterity* 70–72.
96. Philo, *Spec. Laws* 1.188.
97. Philo, *Alleg. Interp.* 3.174; Philo, *Prelim. Studies* 107.
98. Philo, *Moses* 2.24.
99. m. Soṭah 9.15; y. Šeqal. 3.3.
100. For further discussion, see Kennard, *Messiah Jesus*, 107–56 for Jesus' development of law and traditions concerning cleansing and sacrifice, 293–332 for Jesus' Messianic sacrifice, and 377–414 for Jesus' Messianic rule.
101. "Definite" is a technical term indicating "direct application to" the individual for whom Jesus died and is normally identified with limited atonement in the wake of the Dortian Calvinistic reaction to Arminianism.
102. "Indefinite" is a technical term indicating "available for but not immediately applied" to the individual for whom Jesus died and normally identified with a form of unlimited atonement which is advocated by Arminians, Wesleyans, and Amryaldians. That is, either the human choice or God's additional grace is needed to apply Jesus' death for the individual's sins.

Arminianism[103], Wesleyanism[104], and Amyraldianism[105], and 2) Hebrews' concept of salvation is primarily communal (as in the Jewish covenant), rather than the Western reformation concept of salvation as primarily individuals obtaining everlasting life. Unpacking this further, the atonement in Hebrews should be understood as definitely accomplished by Christ for the new covenant community. The book of Hebrews applies this new covenant in two ways. The first application of Hebrews' new covenant atonement identifies that it is the community that is everlastingly forgiven. However, individuals who identify with this community are obligated to continue to believe in the supremacy of Christ to enter into the rest (or everlasting salvation) and the forgiveness that this new covenant relationship provides, thus reflecting an indefinite aspect of the atonement for the individual. Hebrews' view frames an experiential assurance later identified with William Perkins's "temporary faith" from 2 Peter 1:10 or Richard Rogers's believing heart in contrast to an "unbelieving heart" from Hebrews 3:12.[106] This sets up a two-way soteriological strategy of faith in Christ, in contrast to their temptation to depart from new-covenant benefits.

The other feature that Hebrews focuses upon with regard to the new covenant is that of an individually definite application of Christ's atonement similar to Calvin's confirming of individual election through a good conscience of holy life[107] or a kind of Edwardsian religious affection identified as a cleansed conscience.[108] Christ's atonement internally cleanses the conscience that the Mosaic covenant sacrifices could never accomplish (Heb 10:2, contrasting with 9:14).

---

103. Jesus' death is a substitute for sinners in the sense that it is available for the sinners to believe and then have it applied by God to remedy their sin condition.

104. Jesus' death is a substitute for sinners in the sense that it is available for the sinners, who are elevated by God's prevenient grace so that they might believe and then have it applied by God to remedy their sin condition.

105. Jesus' death is a substitute for sinners in the sense that it is available for the sinners to have the divine efficacious grace applied to them, which evidences itself in believing, and then this sinner has Christ's atonement applied by God to remedy their sin condition.

106. Perkins, *Workes of that Famous and Worthy Minister*, 1:125, 358, 3:271; Rogers, *Seven Treatises*, 102, 109, 136, 243, 298, 308, 322, 401; John Rogers also advocates "temporary faith" in *Doctrine of Faith*, 10; Kendall, *Calvin and English Calvinism to 1649*, 69, 81–82.

107. Calvin, *Calvin's Commentary*, 376–78, on 2 Pet 1:10; *Institutes of the Christian Religion* 3.15.8, "judged by their fruits."

108. Edwards, *Treatise Concerning Religious Affections*.

In contrast to the traditional individual reformation soteriology of the Reformed, Lutheran, or Arminian traditions, Hebrews paints a communally covenantal background. We need to be careful in applying modern constructs of individualism on a text. A better strategy is to notice the constructs available in the historical-cultural context and allow them to evidence something of the range of the possible views. Then, more specifically, we should prefer those constructs that the text itself floats as models that set up the foundation for the teaching it develops. And, of course, in this, any clear statement in the text takes priority over these inclinations of the possible and the likely.

The context of Hebrews is clearly that of Jewish followers of Jesus who need to think through the covenantal frameworks that govern them. The book of Hebrews draws out discussions about the Mosaic covenant and builds its teaching on the new covenant in part against and in part as extending the Mosaic covenant. Entering Hebrews' thought forms is to enter into an analysis of the aspects of the Mosaic covenant that Hebrews builds upon. This analysis emphasizes a corporate covenantal perspective that sets up an exclusive two-way view of salvation.

As was developed in the preceding chapter, the new covenant emphasizes corporate and internal transformation for the nation Israel; "'Behold days are coming' declares Yahweh, 'when I will make a new covenant with the house of Israel and with the house of Judah'" (Jer 31:31; also quoted in Heb 8:8). The whole of the people of Israel were to be regathered by God into their land again (Isa 49:6; Jer 31:27–28).[109] The new covenant is predicted to be a work of God, with corporate Israel internalizing the law: "this is the covenant which I will make with the house of Israel after those days, 'I will put My Law within them, and on their heart I will write it; and I will be their God and they will be My people'" (Jer 31:33; also quoted in Heb 8:10; 10:16). In the wake of their regathering from the Babylonian captivity in Israel, some Jews saw passion for the law as a realization of the new covenant in which God was giving them a "new heart" and a "new spirit."[110] However, the LXX retranslates the MT singular "law" into a plural "My laws," which internally transform them into broadening obedience to whatever God commands. This new covenant was a transformation of the

---

109. Sir 35.11; 48:10; Bar 4:37; 5:5; 2 Macc 1:27; 2:18; Jub. 1:15; Pss. Sol. 11:2; 17:28–31, 50; 8:34; 1QM 2.2, 7; 3.13; 5.1; 11QT 8.14–16; 57.5; Philo, *Rewards* 164; Kennard, *Biblical Covenantalism*, 2:79–89, 129–30.

110. As in Jeremiah 31:31–34 and Ezekiel 36:24–37:28, so too in Jub. 1:22–25; 1Q3 4, 5; 1QH^a 4, 5, 18; and 4Q400.

whole community: "they shall not teach again, each man his neighbor and each man his brother, saying, 'know Yahweh,' for they shall all know Me, from the least of them to the greatest of them,' declares Yahweh" (Jer 31:34; also quoted in Heb 8:11). The forgiveness to be found in this new covenant is understood to be a corporate one as well; "I will forgive their iniquity, and their sin I will remember no more" (Jer 31:34; also quoted in Heb 8:12; 10:17). The individualism of Western approaches is often assumed in individually applied forgiveness, but the corporate pronouns and contextual emphasis better fit into a premodern and oriental corporate construct of the group as being regathered and forgiven as a corporate entity.

New covenant corporate forgiveness is developed by Hebrews as mirroring the corporate atonement of the Day of Atonement (Heb 9:7, 11). The pattern by which Hebrews extends Christ's new-covenant atonement is built upon that of corporate Israel at the Day of Atonement. Within the Mosaic covenant, Yahweh demands that Israel be kept clean and holy (Lev 11:44–45) or sins defile Yahweh's holy name and the tabernacle, and puts Israel at risk to be cut off in covenant curse (Lev 15:31; Num 19:13; Ezek 43:7–8). This defilement of tabernacle penetrates to defile the holy place and altar as well (Lev 16:16, 18; Num 19:20); thus the discussion of cleansing the tabernacle vessels and the heavenly originals with blood sacrifice to inaugurate both as cleansed (Heb 9:19–24). Jacob Milgrom developed that this uncleanness defiling the tabernacle is cleansed in stages.[111] First, with a sin offering, the heavenly courtyard alter would be cleansed by the blood of the sacrifice, which in this case is Christ's blood (Lev 4:25, 30; 9:9; Heb 9:15, 23–25). Secondly, in the pattern of the Day of Atonement, Christ as high priest would place his own sin-offering blood on the incense altar and the ark of the covenant, which cleanses the heavenly tabernacle and the people (Lev 16:16–19, 30; Num 19:20; Isa 37:16; Heb 9:15, 23–25). Hebrews 9:7 acknowledges this process and develops the idea the high priest enters the holy place once a year with the blood of the atonement "which he offers for himself and for the ignorance of the people." Such a phrase, τῶν τοῦ λαοῦ ἀγνοημάτων, retains this corporate emphasis (of the people's ignorance or sin) from the Mosaic description of the Day of Atonement so that the people and tabernacle are cleansed to continue in the relationship with Yahweh for another year; however, the new-covenant promise of a perfected conscience does not get accomplished by the Day of Atonement (Heb 9:9, 22–23).

---

111. Milgrom, *Numbers*, 445–46; Kennard, *Biblical Covenantalism*, 1:277–303.

Christ's new covenant corporate atonement is also developed by Hebrews as mirroring the corporate atonement practice that Moses applied to initiate the Mosaic covenant cleansing in the first place (Heb 9:19–21; Exod 24:5–8; also 1 Pet 1:2). All the different tabernacle implements and the people are sprinkled with blood[112] to initially cleanse them and to serve as in the beginning of the Mosaic covenant. The statement in which Hebrews 9:20 reports Moses as saying ("This is the blood of the covenant which God commanded you") is a shortened form combining Moses' Exodus 24:8 statement ("Behold the blood of the covenant, which Yahweh has made with you in accordance with all these words") with Israel's complete submission in obedience ("All Yahweh's spoken word we will do, and we will be obedient"). Both the shortened and longer forms are clearly describing the group as Israel and thus have a corporate role of binding Israel to this Mosaic covenant. In accomplishing this cleansing, this atonement initiates Israel as a group into the fearful experience with the glory of God (Exod 24:9–18). Hebrews conflates this initiation of the Mosaic covenant with the experience of Moses cleansing the earthly tabernacle parts constructed by the Spirit-empowered craftsmen after the heavenly pattern (Exod 40:9). So this later corporate event of tabernacle initiation and cleansing is seen by Hebrews as an extension of the divine covenant binding on the corporate community. Such a covenant blessing of the "blood of the covenant" remains with Israel as a marker that God is faithful to his governing Mosaic covenant, having Zechariah remind Israel that he will rescue them from captivity because of this "blood of the covenant" (Zech 9:11). In a similar manner, rabbis use the same phrase to reassure Israelites that they are included within the blessing of the combined Abrahamic and Mosaic covenants because of their circumcision (the source of this blood) as a baby or at conversion.[113] By extension, Hebrews indicated that Jesus Christ's

---

112. This is an opportunity for Hebrews to discuss that blood is the dominant means of cleansing in the Mosaic covenant (Heb 9:22); however, Christian tradition often reads this as the only way to cleanse, and thus emphasizes further the need for Christ's death. Hebrews is, however, very explicit with the use of σχεδὸν at the start of the clause that "one may *almost* say, that all things are cleansed with blood." There are other Mosaic means of cleansing including time, cleaning, removing the material, destruction of the object, and a baptism in the *mikvot*, or ritual baths, as developed by Leviticus 13–15. Additionally, the poor could bring a sacrifice of grain without blood and be cleansed by atonement (Lev 5:11). There is even an odd instance in which Israel is atoned for by bringing gold instead of animal sacrifice (Num 31:50). However, the usual way of cleansing is through animal sacrifice, and that is what this verse says.

113. m. Sipra 123.1.8a; m. Pesaḥ. 8.8; Instone-Brewer, *Traditions of the Rabbis*, 57–58.

atoning blood functions in a similar manner as an initiating "blood of the covenant" to mark the beginning and continuing of the blessing believers have because Jesus initiated the everlasting new covenant to include them (Heb 10:24; 13:20). Having the agency of the "blood of the [new] covenant" is to essentially have the agency of Jesus Christ and his atonement working on the believer's behalf to equip them in every good thing so that believers will do Christ's will to his glory (Heb 13:20–21).

Hebrews presents Christ as a new Melchizedek high priest who has also entered the heavenly tabernacle to atone after these two patterns of Day of Atonement and initial covenantal cleansing (Heb 9:11–28).[114] The initial cleansing by Moses served to support the initiation of a covenant by blood, of which Christ's new covenant is initiated with his sacrifice. Christ's death in the new covenant is toward redemption so that the called may receive everlasting salvation inheritance (Heb 9:15 with 1:14). However, Christ's death deals with transgressions under the first covenant (τῶν ἐπὶ τῇ πρώτῃ διαθήκῃ παραβάσεων); it does not satisfy something of the inadequate Mosaic covenant.[115] The initiation of the new covenant is also identified with a brief discussion of a will and testament in which Hebrews explains that Christ must die or this covenant cannot take effect (Heb 9:16–17). The Day-of-Atonement pattern served to develop the priestly role with tabernacle and thus set up the inadequacies of repeated Mosaic covenant Day of Atonement. Christ's once-for-all new-covenant atonement goes against both Mosaic covenant patterns (Mosaic covenant initiation and Day of

---

114. Kennard, *Messiah Jesus*, 353–75.

115. The placement of the article τῶν associated with transgressions, παραβάσεων, identifies that the transgressions were committed under the Mosaic covenant by wrapping around the phrase (ἐπὶ τῇ πρώτῃ διαθήκῃ), not that Christ's death was under or governed by the first covenant (Heb 9:15).

Atonement) because Christ brings a better sacrifice[116] in a better place,[117] a heavenly tabernacle. Such Day-of-Atonement imagery of carrying Jesus'

116. Christ's death is a better sacrifice, but Christian tradition often overstates this by reinterpreting Hebrews 10:4, "For it is impossible for the blood of bulls and goats to take away sins," to mean that no forgiveness is possible at all on account of such animal sacrifices, and thus the absolute need for Christ's death or all Jews before Christ remain unforgiven. This common view ignores the clear statement of the biblical text that, in the divine provision of the animal sacrifices, atonement and forgiveness is in fact declared to be realized (Lev 1:4; 4:20, 26, 31, 35; 5:6, 10, 13, 16, 18, etc.). So, if animal sacrifices can forgive sin in God's Mosaic covenant framework, "take away sins" in Hebrews 10:4 needs to be interpreted in light of its place in the argument of the Hebrews context. The point being made about the new-covenant sacrifice is that Christ's sacrifice occurs once and that settles the matter for all time; Heb 9:28; 10:12. In contrast to this complete atonement, even for the future sins, the Mosaic covenant sacrifices must continue to be done on a yearly basis (alluding to the Day of Atonement again), and thus never finally "take away sins." That is, forgiveness for past sins wonderfully accomplished by God through the Mosaic covenant sacrifices don't settle the future issue regarding sins, like Christ's sacrifice does. Therefore, Christ provides a greater sacrifice than the Mosaic covenant, meaning that Christ's sacrifice forgives all the community's sins for all time, while the Mosaic sacrifice only provides forgiveness for past sins (Kennard, *Biblical Covenantalism*, 3:162).

117. Often the idea of heaven is developed through a Platonic framework (Philo, *Alleg. Interp.* 3.102, 94–96; Philo, *Moses* 2.74; Origen, *Princ.* 4.2.4, 6, 9; *Biblia Patristica*, 3:453–55; Clement of Alexandria, *Strom.* 1.5, 9; 6.7–11; 7.16; Cody, *Heavenly Sanctuary and Liturgy*, 78–84), but this is foreign to the text. In Platonism, the heavenly forms are the only reality, with the earthly objects being merely a shadow of this reality imposed upon our senses through our souls' recollection of pre-incarnate life among those heavenly forms. Thus, if the truth is present in the heavenly, then it is present in the earthly as well, because the earthly is a mere shadow of the heavenly. Here in Hebrews 9:23–25, both the heavenly tabernacle and the earthly copies of the heavenly tabernacle are real, as evidenced by the Hebraic pattern of *Merkabah* mysticism—that is, both the heavenly and earthly temples are real, and different things may be occurring in these different realities. For example, the heavenly temple is normally thought to be where God's presence dwells (Isa 6:4), but the amazing thing is that, with the cleansed tabernacle, God dwells on earth, the ark of the covenant serving as his throne (Exod 40:34–38). However, the uncleanness of the earthly temple dislodges the divine presence from the earthly temple, while the presence remains in the heavenly temple (Ezek 1:4–28; 11:22–25). The different conditions of the pure heavenly temple and the occasionally unclean earthly temple show that they are both real in this multidimensional Hebraic framework rather than being the idealism of the earthly shadows which Platonism portrays (Josephus, *Ant.* 3.123, 181; Josephus, *J.W.* 5.213; 1 En. 14; 37–71; 2 En. 15–17; 4 Ezra 9.26—10.59; 13.35–36; 2 Bar. 4.2–7; 6.9; 32.4; Gal 4:26; Heb 12:22; Rev 3:12; 21:2, 10; Ascen. Isa. 9; LAE 37; Apoc. Ab. 29; Exod. Rab. 43.8; m. Ḥag. 2.1; b. Ḥag. 14a; 15a; Hec. Ab. Rab. 20.1; b. Sanh. 38b; Pate and Kennard, *Deliverance Now and Not Yet*, 98–103; Sholem, *Jewish Gnosticism*; Lincoln, *Paradise Now and Not Yet*, 9–32, 169–95; Dean-Otting, *Heavenly Journeys*; Gruenwald, *Apocalyptic and Merkavah Mysticism*, 29–72; Schafer, *Kehhalot-Studien*; Chernus, "Visions of God," 123–46; , Isaacs, *Sacred Space*, 59–61; Koester, *Hebrews*, 97–100).

blood into the heavenly tabernacle further identifies that the cleansing is not complete in Jesus' substitutionary death, as would be the case in a forensic model. Rather, Jesus as Melchizedek priest carries his blood into the heavenly tabernacle to cleanse it[118] so that it can facilitate cleansing for the Christian community and for the cleansed heavenly tabernacle to support Jesus' continuing ministry as priest (Heb 9:23–24).

Hebrews' atonement applies the new covenant to the Christian with two accomplishments: perfected conscience and everlasting forgiveness. These two issues are where the text requotes aspects of the Jeremiah 31 quote again (Heb 8:10, 12; and 10:16–17) and thus shows the selection and emphasis of the new covenant atonement in Hebrews.

The Day of Atonement (Heb 9:7–9) and the initiation of the Mosaic covenant (Heb 9:18–22) are developed as the framework through which Christ's new covenant atonement is to be viewed (Heb 9:11–14, 23–28). Both these frameworks of the Mosaic covenant bring corporate atonement and belonging. Thus, the individual is a beneficiary of this corporate Mosaic-covenant atonement by continuing in the covenant way with faithfulness and loyalty. This Mosaic covenant pattern would mean that Christ's atonement after this pattern would be an indefinite atonement for individuals and yet definite atonement for the community of the new covenant. This definiteness for the new covenant community is apparent in such statements as Christ "obtained everlasting redemption" and Christ died "once to bear the sins of the many" (Heb 9:12, 26, 28; 10:10, 12). That is, Christ's death has accomplished the atonement for the group. From this corporate pattern, and perhaps the indefiniteness of "the many," there is indefiniteness with regard to individuals in this new covenant forgiveness. In such a covenantal structure, one would expect a two-way strategy to launch, and that is what occurs in especially the warning sections of the book.[119] Therefore, the readers should heed Jesus' miraculously attested great salvation and obediently press on into the rest by continuing to trust God (Heb 2:3–4; 3:8, 11–13, 15, 19; 4:2–4, 11; 11:1—12:13). This is also said in the negative "do not harden your heart," as when Israel provoked God in the wilderness, for such rebellion and disbelief brings judgment, as when Israelites died on the wilderness journey (Heb 3:8, 13, 15–19; 4:5–7; 6:6; 10:26–31). Faithfulness in the narrow new-exodus way is a disposi-

---

118. Schweitzer, *Lordship and Discipleship*, 72; deSilva, *Despising Shame*, 237.

119. Kennard, "Warnings in the Book of Hebrews"; see chapter 11 of this book on warnings in Hebrews.

tion of continuing faith for those who God has called to inherit everlasting salvation, which he will generously give (Heb 1:14; 6:12; 9:15). Jesus and Abraham are provided as positive examples of continuing faithfully to inherit (Heb 1:4; 11:8), and Esau provides a warning pattern of an unrepentant rebel to avoid, for he could not inherit even though he wished inheritance (Heb 12:17). The issue is not obtaining the gospel message in the first place, but rather maintaining a loyal relationship to Jesus as the Christ and his new covenant instead of merely returning to Judaism with its Mosaic covenant (Heb 7:1—10:31). So the Jewish framework of atonement brings a Jewish perspective on life that requires continuing belief in Christ, which is an exclusive soteriological strategy. For those who continue in this faith, forgiveness is their benefit, along with kingdom rest. For those who do not continue, they identify themselves to be unbelievers and rebels, much like Israel did, consequently dying in the wilderness (Heb 3:16–19). This means that the issue is not a conversion point or a moment of faith, but it is continuing faith. Remember that Hebrews' construction frames faith in the future for benefits that have not been realized yet for those who are believers (Heb 11:1–39). This emphasis of future-looking faith further supports a two-way strategy unto salvation. Thus, the Jewish followers of Jesus are called to continue in future-looking faith, for that is the way that they as individuals each experience the corporate new covenant benefit of everlasting forgiveness.

The new covenant is superior over the Mosaic covenant as the heavenly pattern, but the Mosaic is a close earthly copy of the heavenly tabernacle shown to Moses on the mountain (Heb 8:5; 9:23). The priestly and sacrificial functioning of the Mosaic tabernacle train the Jews in basic concepts that the new covenant completes in the one sacrifice of Jesus Christ. Jesus' once-for-all sacrifice is emphasized in Hebrews (Heb 7:27; 9:12, 14, 25, 28; 10:10, 12, 14, 18); so why, when the heavenly things are cleansed for new covenant effectiveness, does Hebrews say that they are cleansed with "sacrifices" (plural: θυσίαις) instead of Jesus' one sacrifice (Heb 9:23)?

Might these plural sacrifices hint at the burnt offerings and sin offerings which the Levitical priests use to cleanse Ezekiel's eschatological altar (Ezek 43:18–27)? With Hebrews' emphasis, the plural cleansing sacrifice should be argued to be the singular sacrifice of Jesus—here rendered plural "sacrifices" (θυσίαις) out of attraction to the plural "with these" (τούτοις)[120]—or Gutherie's theological appeal that Christ's single sacrifice sufficiently replaces all of the Levitical sacrifices (Heb 9:23).

> The plural is used in the sense that the one sacrifice stands as the complete fulfillment of all the different sacrifices in the old order. It may be said that the sacrifice of Christ is so many sided that it required a whole range of sacrifices to serve as adequate copies.[121]

Hebrews develops Christ's one sacrifice as the one in the context that was accomplished in the heavenly temple.

Amid the final exhortations of Hebrews, a devotional homily reminds the reader to follow her Christian leader's faith in grace, thereby worshipping God and doing good in the new covenant (Heb 13:7–16). The rationale reminds the reader that we live in grace, so the faith of Christian leadership should be emulated (Heb 13:7–9). Such a gracious life contrasts with that of those diminishing grace with strange teaching that see real benefit in food. Perhaps this food issue refers to a Jewish liturgical meal with a peace offering because of the Jewish context in which the worshippers eat major portions of the sacrifice and the priest officiating obtains the right thigh of the sacrifice for his food (Heb 13:9–10; Lev 7:15–17, 32–33).[122] Such eating was festive as an expression of thanks to God, often with the blessing that the food strengthens the heart (Ps 104:14–15).[123] The use of the plural "foods" (βρώμασιν) in Hebrews 13:9 may also indicate the issue of kosher, which was a significant Jewish issue at that time,[124] and because the LXX only uses the plural βρῶμα to refer to kosher food in contrast to that which is impure (Lev 11:34)[125] and the other instance of the plural word in Hebrews is broader than a sacrificial sense (Heb 9:10). However, in either option,

---

120. Lane, *Hebrews 9–13*, 247.
121. Guthrie, *Letter to the Hebrews*, 196.
122. m. Pesaḥ. 10.6; Jub. 22.3–9; 32.7; 49.6.
123. m. Ber. 6.1, 3.
124. Dan 1:1–21; Esth 3:28; 4:16; Tob 1.9–12; 4.12–13; Jdt 10.5; 12:1–2, 9–19; 13:8; 2 Macc 7, esp. 7.9 and 8.2; 3 Macc 3.4–7; 7.11; 4 Macc 1.8, 10; Jos. Asen.; Let. Arist. 139–42; Josephus, *Ant.* 14.185–267; Josephus, *Vita* 14 includes Jewish priests imprisoned in Rome in 61 AD abstaining from meat on kosher grounds; T. Isaac 4.5; Macrobius, *Sat.* 2.4.11; Riggenbach, "Die Starken und Schwachen," 655–68; Strathmann, *Geschichte der frühchristlichen Askese*, 1–13; Rauer, *Die "Schwachen" in Korinth*, 138–69; Behm, "ἐσθίω," 694; Dunn, *Romans 9–16*, 799–802; Elliott, "Asceticism among the 'Weak,'" 231–51, but esp. 239–45; Winter, "Roman Law and Society," 90–91; Pucci Ben Zeev, *Jewish Rights in the Roman World*, 381–408; Hellerman, "Purity and Nationalism," 401–21.
125. Lane, *Hebrews 9–13*, 534.

the food was merely physical food passing through one's body, polemicing such food without lasting benefit to the one who partakes of it (Heb 13:9), a theme for which Philo expressed value in the transformation of one's heart as far more important than food.[126] The polemic continues in that new-covenant Christians have an altar, presumably Christ's original heavenly altar, which is aligned with the new covenant, so those Levitical priests of the Mosaic covenant do not have a right to eat from it (Heb 9:23–24; 13:10, in contrast to Lev 7:32–33).

The Day-of-Atonement sacrifice from which the high priest took blood into the holy place had its remains burned outside the camp (Heb 13:11; 9:7–8; Lev 16:27).[127] By connecting Jesus' sacrifice with the blood sacrifice at the Day of Atonement, Hebrews identifies Jesus' sacrifice as a vicarious substitution. Since Jesus was excluded and killed outside the Jewish camp, the Jewish Christians could relate to his exclusion. By similarity, Jesus suffered outside the gate in his death so as to sanctify the people (Heb 13:12). Upon this basis, the author exhorts, "let us go outside the camp, bearing his reproach," presumably calling his readership to remove themselves from mainstream Judaism by identifying with Jesus as their Messiah and atonement, with its hope of an everlasting kingdom to come (Heb 13:13–14).

Ignatius extends these phrases in his *Letter to Magnesians* to argue for abstinence from kosher and Jewish sacrifices.

> Gather together—all of you—to the one temple of God, as it were, to one altar, to one Jesus Christ ... Do not be led away through strange teachings and outmoded fables, which are not useful. If we still go on observing Judaism, we acknowledge that we never received grace.[128]

However, the metaphor of "going outside the camp" (ἔξω τῆς παρεμβολῆς) may function on a level of positively identifying with Christ in "bearing His reproach," rather than necessarily leaving Jewish practices, since this metaphor also is used positively in LXX Exodus 33:7–8 three times for where the tabernacle is set up and where Moses met Yahweh in this tabernacle.[129]

---

126. Philo, *Spec. Laws* 2.193–94, 198–99.

127. Rabbinics saw that the Day of Atonement forgave all sin between the worshipper and God (m. Yoma 8.9; y. Yoma 8.9, 45c; b. Yoma 65 ab; Sipra Ahere Mot 8.5).

128. Ignatius, *Magn.* 7.2–8.2.

129. Lane, *Hebrews 9–13*, 542–44.

With our Messianic kingdom hope, the Christian's life should be characterized by worship, doing good and sharing with others "for with such sacrifices God is pleased" (Heb 13:15–16). In aligning with Christ, we should continually offer up a sacrifice of praise to God, especially giving thanks to Christ's name. Joining these sacrifices are those that meet practical needs like doing good and sharing with others. All these forms of worship and doing good are sacrifices that please God.

Hebrews' perspective realizes many factors of the Davidic and new covenants so that its readers see that the Mosaic covenant has been superseded, prompting them to not place their trust in it. For example, Jesus is already the Davidic King over his house of believers in Christ (Heb 1:5—2:8; 3:6). Additionally, the new covenant makes believers already partakers of rest if we continue in faith (Heb 4:3). This new covenant establishes a lasting relationship with Yahweh in forgiveness (Heb 8:12; 10:17) and matures the conscience by internalizing God's laws (Heb 10:14–16).

Jeremiah 31:33 (in the Hebrew text) left the whole Mosaic law as a binding internalized code within the new covenant for the Jew heading into the kingdom. However, in the LXX (which is Jeremiah 38:33), the dispersion Jewish community saw God's generic commands as internally binding without identifying them as the Mosaic covenant. Hebrews indicates that the Mosaic covenant is obsolete for the Jewish Christian, but is less clear as to what are the continuing internalized laws of God. However, Jeremiah and Ezekiel (in Hebrew and LXX) left behind the hope of Levitical priests offering Mosaic sacrifices within a temple. These sacrifices include burnt offerings and sin offerings so that forgiveness and atonement (כִּפֶּר/*kpr*) for sins will be obtained from God by these means (Jer 33:18; Ezek 43:18–27; 44:11, 15, 29; 45:15, 17–20, 21–25; 46:2, 4, 12–15). Hebrews identifies that, with Jesus' sufficient sacrifice to obtain forgiveness, "there is no longer any offering for sin" (Heb 10:18).

How are these tensions between the Levitical sacrifices in Ezekiel (and Jeremiah) and Christ's sacrifice in Hebrews to be worked out? Most attempts to resolve these issues ignore or leave out various features, showing that they are inadequate solutions. One way to resolve this is to merge all the factors together with clear indicators as to when and whom they refer. When this is done, we find that Hebrews has clear teaching on Jesus' sacrifice as sufficient to obtain forgiveness so that the Jewish Christian does not need to offer another sacrifice for sin. The new covenant is in place, perfecting the conscience of the Jewish Christian so that he does not have the external Mosaic covenant as binding upon him. Laws of the Mosaic covenant may float freely from the Mosaic covenant into the new covenant and into the conscience and life of the Jewish Christian. Any transfer of laws, like faithfulness and obedience to enter into rest, excel beyond a suzerainty treaty framework as they penetrate into the conscience and life of the Jewish Christian under the covenant grant of the new covenant. Within this new covenant, there is the necessary identification with Jesus as the Messiah for kingdom. Ultimately, when national Israel is benefited by the new covenant, they will find themselves as a national group forgiven and transformed in their hearts to do the Mosaic law within the new covenant grant framework. In this kingdom state, the Levitical priests may offer sin and guilt offerings for forgiveness and atonement purposes (because God did not make a mistake when he established the Mosaic covenant framework). When such obedience and sacrifice is done regarding the Mosaic covenant, there is a redundant affirmation from both Mosaic and new covenants that Israel is blessed and forgiven. The individual responsiveness under this new covenant transformation supersedes any need for multi-generational judgment, so individual responsibility and judgment is what is affirmed in the new covenant. In this new covenant, the relationships of a Jewish Christian and kingdom Israelite with Yahweh are forever in forgiveness.

The other new-covenant application is the perfected conscience. The warning charge to the readers rings out: "don't harden your hearts" (Heb 3:8, 11, 15; 5:5). In light of this call and Israel's failure to obey it, the law is seen to be impotent. The inability of the law to perfect a person's conscience is the basis for the Mosaic covenant being set aside or annulled (Heb 7:18–19). Since this perfection is not through the Mosaic covenant and the Levitical priesthood, then the law is changed from the Mosaic covenant to the new covenant. Likewise, the Mosaic covenant's cleansing of the flesh left it impotent to cleanse the conscience (Heb 9:13–14). Part of the problem is that the Mosaic covenant repeatedly reminds the sinner with the need to sacrifice, so the consciousness of sins remains before the individual. However, Christ perfects those who are sanctified or set apart in the new covenant (Heb 10:14). This sanctification alludes to those sanctified by Christ's atonement (Heb 10:10). Again, this sanctification should be seen through the contextual lens of the Mosaic covenant, which is the condition for sanctification to set apart Israel (in the flesh) as holy (Heb 9:13; Exod 19:14). Thus, for the Mosaic covenant, the cleansing of the people identifies them as appropriately in the covenantal community (Exod 19:14; Lev

12–16). However, in the new covenant, an internal cleansing is realized of the heart, which Hebrews identifies as the cleansing of the conscience (Heb 8:10; 9:14; 10:2, 16). Additionally, Hebrews 8:10 (Jeremiah 31:33, or LXX 38:33), "teaching my laws to their mind and upon their heart," is requoted in Hebrews 10:16 with phrases left out and the order flipped to more blatantly emphasize that Christ's new-covenant transformation is "in their heart and mind." This rearrangement emphasizes the heart-conscience transformation over one of teaching legal information. This transformation is also stated as perfecting conscience (Heb 10:1–2) in contrast to the lack of perfecting of conscience from the Mosaic covenant (Heb 9:9). This cleansing or perfecting of conscience is done to the follower of Jesus as part of Jesus' new-covenant atonement cleansing. So the perfecting of conscience is a definite work of Christ for those within the new covenant. However, such divine perfecting continues to cultivate maturing an affirming conscience. It serves to balance the human-responsibility side of continuing to be faithful within this divine work, which is noticeable in the mind of the believer. It is then like an Edwardsian religious affection and thus provides reassurance to the cleansed in conscience, that they are among the community of everlastingly forgiven. Perhaps this cleansed conscience is part of the way that we believers already enter rest (responsively believing instead of hardened in heart), even though the dominant expression of rest is still in the future and would be identified with Christ's kingdom (Heb 1:8–13; 3:14; 4:1–11). Additionally, this cleansed conscience also provides the basis of a new-covenant command to draw near to God and his cleansed community with a future-looking faith (hope) because God is himself faithful (Heb 10:22–25). The fact that the cleansed conscience becomes a basis for appeal to continue in the faith may softly hint at this cleansed conscience as Hebrews' analog to the new birth (in John and Peter) or that of becoming a new human (in Paul). That is, it looks like the cleansed conscience is Hebrews regeneration-transformation metaphor. As such, it fits rather well as an Edwardsian religious affection, evidencing where authentic salvation is being realized and thus provides assurance for this salvation.

In summary, in Hebrews, Christ's new covenant atonement is definite for the community of Jesus followers in a two-way strategy which provides 1) everlasting forgiveness as an indefinite blessing to those in the community who continue in the faith, and 2) cleansed conscience as a definite blessing corroborating their faith.

10

The Narrow Exodus Way of Faith to Salvation

Jesus' narrow way toward the kingdom was earlier explained to frame Jesus' roles as apostle and king over the house of Israel. There the contrast was made for Jesus' superiority over Moses. However, in this chapter, the emphasis develops the trajectory for Jesus' narrow way using a continuation of the exodus theme that Moses initiated for Israel. Jesus' new-covenant exodus continuation is more empowered than Moses', but as on Moses' exodus there is still the need to be faithful believers persevering toward kingdom.

Emerging from Mosaic leadership within the house of Israel, the exodus begins leading to the promised land (Heb 3:2, 16–17; Exod 3–4). Moses refused to be identified with Pharaoh's household, but instead identified with Israel in leading the exodus (Heb 11:23–27; Exod 2:11–12; 9–12). The journey was begun by faithfully keeping the Passover, as Egyptian firstborn died in the last plague (Heb 11:28; Exod 12). Continuing by faith, Israel passed through the Red Sea on dry ground, as the Egyptian soldiers were drowned (Heb 11:29; Exod 14:2—15:21). The repeated use of words of "faith" (Heb 3:12, 19, 4:2–3; 11) and obedience (Heb 3:18, 4:6, 11) emphasize fusion of faith with faithfulness in obedience. The exodus frames salvation in a two-way strategy for Israel, where the narrow way of faithfulness leads to the promised land and kingdom (Heb 3:6).[1] In contrast, rebellion leads to destruction (Heb 3:16).

1. Jub. 1.15–16, 20, 22–25; 5.11, 15; Sir 11.26; 16.12, 14; 17.23; 1 En. 95.5; 100.7; Pss.

The Narrow Exodus Way of Faith to Salvation

Several commentators develop parallels, especially with the LXX text of Numbers 14 and Hebrews, especially Israel's rebellion against the report of spying out the promised land and the warning passages of Hebrews to show how extensive the exodus theme is present in this section of the book of Hebrews.[2] The closest parallels take up verbal similarity of Israel on exodus travels and the narrow exodus way for Jewish Christians, to whom the author of Hebrews writes. Both groups are at risk of being evil unbelievers (πονηρὰ ἀπιστίας, LXX Num 14:11, 27; Heb 3:12) who apostatize (ἀποστῆναι, LXX Num 14:9; Heb 3:12) and thus turn back, failing to enter (ἀπειθείας, LXX Num 14:43; Heb 3:18; 4:6, 11) in the context of rebellion and die on the way to the promised land (Num 15–16; Heb 3:17–19). While these are impressive verbal similarities from this chapter in Numbers, the fact that the OT citations in Hebrews do not come from this Numbers text but from Psalms 95 likely broadens the exodus imagery to the whole of the exodus way rather than a particular rebellion at Kadesh. Thus, Hebrews' warning concerning the exodus way is generalized to the whole exodus journey and Christian life unto kingdom.

Moses' Exodus account brought Israel to a fire-covered Mount Sinai, providing ample warning to not let anything touch the mountain (Heb 12:18–21; Exod 19:12, 16; Deut 9:19). Such a fearful threat reminds those embracing the law of God that God judges from Cain's murder of Abel to the shaking of the earth in eschatological judgment, for God is a consuming fire (Heb 12:24–27, 29). By contrast, Apostle-King Jesus brings new-covenant Christians (especially mature spirits) to Mount Zion, where God the Judge sprinkles the people with new-covenant blessing of atonement blood (Heb 12:22–24). This new-covenant kingdom cannot be shaken and thus prompts gratitude, service, reverence, and awe (Heb 12:28).

At the conclusion of the exodus, Jericho was destroyed, while Rahab, who lived within the city, was rescued because she identified by faith with the Israelite spies and protected them (Heb 11:30–31; Josh 2:1–7; 6:22–25). However, the pattern of Israel's journey during the exodus travel was full

---

Sol. 2.7, 16, 25, 34–35; 17.8–9; Jos. Asen. 28.3; Philo, *Spec. Laws* 4.164; LAB 3.10; 44.10; 64.7; 2 Bar. 54.21; 1QS 2.7–8, 11–14; 10.11, 17–18; 1QH^a 4.18–19, 31–32; 5.5–6; 14.24; 1QM 6.6; 11.3–4, 13–14; 18.14; CD 3.4–5; 5.15–16; 7.9; 19.6; 20.24; 1QpHab 12.2–3; 4QpPs37 4.9; 4Q266 18.6 (= 4Q270 11 I.19–20) exclude "disobedient" from "people of God"; Josephus, *Ant.* 10.138; Josephus, *J.W.* 1.378; Gathercole, "Torah, Life, and Salvation," 126–39.

2. Hofius, *KATAPAUSIS*, 117–37; Ellingworth, "Old Testament in Hebrews" 110; Gheorghita, *Role of the Septuagint*, 79–84.

of Israel's rebellion. This journey becomes the pattern for new-covenant Christians in pursuing the heavenly agenda to follow Christ unto the kingdom (Heb 1:14; 6:12; 9:15).³

3. Nairne, *Epistle of Priesthood*, 205, 226–28; Käsemann, *Wandering People of God*, 86; Spicq, *L'Epître aux Hébreux*, 1:243–46, 269–80; Johnston, "Pilgrimage Motif," 239–51; This judgment according to deeds is continued in the two-way teaching of the church: Did. 1.1.1–4; 4.14b; 1 Clem. 34–35; 2 Clem. 6.8; 8.4; Polycarp, *Phil.* 10; Ign. *Phil.* 5.1; Ign. *Eph.* 3.1; Barn. 16.7–8; 18.1–2; 19; Justin, *Dial.* 3.4; Justin, *1 Apol.* 16.8–9; Justin, *2 Apol.* 9; Irenaeus (*Haer.* 3.1.10) maintained this as the universal teaching all Christians held at the time; Herm. Mand. 2.7; Herm. Sim. 3.8.6–11; Clement of Alexandria, *Strom.* 4.6; Clement of Alexandria, *Quis div.*, esp. 1.6–7; 16.5; Commodianus, *Instr.* 28; Origen, *Comm. Matt.* 14.10–13; Origen, *Fr. Prin.* 2.9.7–8; 3.1.12; Cyprian, *Fort.* 12–13; Dionysius of Alexandria, *Exegetical Fragments* 7, "Reception of Lapsed"; Methodius of Olympus, *Banquet of the Ten Virgins* 9.3; Methodius of Olympus, *Oration Concerning Simeon and Anna* 8; Lactantius, *Inst.* 3.12; 6.3–7; 7.10; Lactantius, *Epit.* 73; Lactantius, *Constitutions of the Holy Apostles* 7.1.1–2; Lactantius, *Clementine Homilies* 18.17; Eusebius, *Hist. eccl.* 2.19; 3.20.6–7; 5.1.10, 48; 5.8.5; 5.13.5; Eusebius, *Council of Sardica Lengthy Creed*: Socrates Scholasticus, *Hist. eccl.* 2.19 = Athanasius, *Syn.* 26; 351 = Hilary of Pointers, *On the Councils* 34 and 359 AD *Sirmium Creed*: Socrates Scholasticus, *Hist. eccl.* 2.30 = Athanasius, *Syn.* 27 = Hilary of Pointers, *On the Councils* 38; *Synod at Ariminum Creed*: Socrates Scholasticus, *Hist. eccl.* 2.37; 359 AD *Seleucia Creed*: Socrates Scholasticus, *Hist. eccl.* 2.40 = Athanasius, *Syn.* 8; 359 AD *Confession at Niké* and 360 AD *Constantinople Creed*: Athanasius, *Syn.* 30; 359 AD *Ariminum Creed* and modified for the 381 AD Council at Constantinople: Socrates Scholasticus, *Hist. eccl.* 2.41; Athanasius, *Inc.* 57; Cyril, *Catechetical Lectures* 15.1, 24–25, 33; Gregory of Nyssa, *On Pilgrimages*, paragraph 1; Gregory of Nyssa, *Great Catechism* 40; Gregory of Nazianzus, *Or. Bas.* 4; Ambrose, *Off.* 1.16.59; Augustine, *Conf.* 1.11.17; Augustine, *Civ.* 13.8; 14.25; 19.11; 20.1–8, 12, 14, 22; 21.1; Augustine, *Trin.* 8.7–8; Augustine, *Enchir.* 15; 31–32; 55; 107; 113; Augustine, *Doctr. chr.* 1.12.10; Augustine, *Perf.* 42–44; Augustine, *Ennarat. Ps.* 31.25; 112.5; Augustine, *Tract. Ev. Jo.* 124.5; Hilary of Poitiers, *On the Trinity* 12.45; Leo the Great, *Sermons* 46.3; 49.2, 5; 63.2, 7; 67.5–6; 72.1; 95.1–9; Vincent of Lérins, *Commonitory* 23.57–59, which he claims is the teaching everyone held at that time: 23.4–6; John Cassian, *Cassian's Conferences* 1.1.5; 1.6.3, 8; 1.40.9; 2.13.13, 18; 2.14.3, 9; John Cassian, *Seven Books of John Cassian* 3.13–14; Leo the Great, *Sermons* 23.5; 24.1–5; 26.2; 66.7; 90.2; 95.1–9; Saint John Climacus, *Ladder of Divine Ascent*, 9.1; summary on step 30; Thomas à Kempis, *Of the Imitation of Christ*, esp. 1.23; 2.7; 3.44, 56; Bunyan, *Pilgrim's Progress*, esp. 18, 187; Reiche, "New Testament Concept of Reward," 195–206; Jeremias, *Neotestamentliche Theologie*, 209; Willard, *Divine Conspiracy*; Yinger, *Paul, Judaism, and Judgment*, 285—summary, but argued through the book; Grindheim, "Ignorance is Bliss," 313–31; Kim, *God Will Judge Each One*; Dunn, *New Perspective on Paul*, 72–73; Dunn, "If Paul Could Believe," 135, and Dunn, "Response to Thomas Schreiner," 106–8. However, this view can be granted from outside the two-way tradition, such as from the Reformed tradition: Calvin, *Institutes of the Christian Religion*, 3.15.8; 3.16.1; "we are justified not without works, and not by works, since in the participation in Christ, by which we are justified, is contained not less sanctification than justification" (16.3); 18.1; Schreiner, "Justification," 78–79.

The Narrow Exodus Way of Faith to Salvation

Intertextually, Psalms 95:7–10 combines with a *midrash* or retelling of the exodus journey toward the promised land to provide a call to join a persistent faith toward kingdom rest (Heb 3:7—4:13).[4] Faithfulness in the narrow new-exodus way is a disposition of continuing faith for those who God has called to inherit everlasting salvation, which he will generously give (Heb 1:14; 6:12; 9:15).[5] Jesus and Abraham are provided as positive examples of continuing faithfully to inherit (Heb 1:4; 11:8). In contrast, Esau provides a warning pattern of an unrepentant rebel to avoid for he could not inherit even though he wished inheritance (Heb 12:17). Likewise, the wilderness warning, "do not harden your heart" as when Israel provoked God in the wilderness, for such rebellion and disbelief brings judgment, as when Israelites died on the wilderness journey (Heb 3:8, 13, 15–19; 4:5–7; 6:6; 10:26–31). Hebrews' view frames an experiential assurance later identified with William Perkins's continuing faith (so one's life is not described by merely "temporary faith" from 2 Pet 1:10) or Richard Rogers's believing heart (in contrast to an "unbelieving heart" from Heb 3:12).[6] The issue is not obtaining the gospel message in the first place, but rather maintaining a loyal relationship to Jesus as the Christ and his new covenant instead of returning to Judaism with merely the Mosaic covenant (Heb 7:1–10:31). This sets up a narrow new-Exodus way where continuing faith in Christ is essential to obtaining kingdom rest.

The concept of "salvation" (σωτηρία) in Hebrews is a future everlasting rescue akin to and greater than entering the promised land (Heb 2:3). Hebrews utilizes the concept as a physical rescue, as in Noah's ark rescuing his household (Heb 11:7).[7] However, the rescue Jesus provides from death

---

4. Buchanan (*Hebrews*, xxiii–xxiv) explains Hebrews' discussion of the exodus within Hillel's first rule as a strong *a fortiori* argument: what applies in a minor case also applies in a major case; Josephus, *Ag. Ap.* 2.175–81; Jerusalem synagogue Theodotus inscription; Philo, *Embassy* 311–13; Meg. Ta'an.; y. Hor. 3.5 (48c); b. Tem. 14b; b. B. Meṣ. 59a–b; Sipre Deut. 351; Sipra 193.1.1–11; *Iggeret Rav Sherira Gaon* 1–2; Zeitlin, "Midrash: A Historical Study," 21–36; Wright, *Midrash*, 52–59, 64–67; Ellis, "Midrash, Targum and New Testament," 61–69; le Déaut, "Apropos a Definition of Midrash," 259–82; Miller, "Targum, Midrash," 29–82; Bloch, "Midrash," 29–50; Porton, "Defining Midrash," 55–95; McNamara, "Some Issues and Recent Writings," 136–49.

5. Käsemann, *Wandering People of God*, 86.

6. Perkins, *Workes*, 1:125, 358, 3:271; Rogers, *Seven Treatises*, 102, 109, 136, 243, 298, 308, 322, 401; John Rogers also advocates "temporary faith" in *Doctrine of Faith*, 10; Kendall, *Calvin and English Calvinism to 1649*, 69, 81–82.

7. *TDNT*, 7:966–67, 970–71.

probably entails resurrection,[8] so the concept of "salvation" also includes spiritual and physical vindication and recovery (Heb 5:7). Christ's salvation for Christians rescues them to a solution and life that is better than the warned damnation (Heb 6:9). Christian salvation is grounded in Christ's obedience, maturing, and sacrificial sufferings (Heb 5:9; 2:10), but not fully realized for the Christian until Christ returns at his second coming (Heb 9:28). That is, "salvation" in the book of Hebrews is realized in a future time than Christ's past sacrifice. With Hebrews future orientation, salvation is something to be inherited in the future when Christ brings many sons to glory (Heb 1:14; 2:10).[9] Thus the protecting ministry of angels is significant in enabling the Christian to arrive at this inheritance. Therefore, everlasting salvation is designated as the goal of life for those who draw near to God in obedience (Heb 5:9; 7:25). So the Christian is heading toward salvation (Heb 1:14; 5:9; 7:25) and activity can be said to be presently salvific if it leads toward that end (Heb 7:25, present infinitive).

The concept of "rest" (κατάπαυσίν) is a stopping and a calm rest.[10] Otfried Hofius argued that in Hebrews the meaning of the concept is dependent upon the OT Exodus citations in Hebrews 3–4 rather than Käsemann's view reflecting later Alexandrian Gnosticism.[11] As such, rest in Hebrews is an extension of the promised land and blessings of the Mosaic covenant (Ps 95:8–11; Heb 3:8–11). The exodus imagery is explicit in the citation from Psalms 95, where Israel's forty years of testing God resulted in a whole generation killed in the wilderness under God's wrath (Ps 95:8–11; Heb 3:8–11).

Such a kingdom-oriented view of rest is itself an extrapolation of a sacred time concept of Sabbath rest, grounded in the divine creation account (Gen 2:2–3; English and LXX with MT 2:4; Exod 20:8–11; Heb 4:4, 10).[12] God "ceased" (*yklw*/וַיְכֻלּ֣וּ) creating the heavens and the earth, and all their hosts that he had created (Gen 2:1–2; Heb 4:4, 10). *Yklw*/וַיְכֻלּ֣וּ is best seen as the ending of a phase of creation, which then permits further develop-

---

8. See discussion of the effectiveness of Jesus' prayer under the discussion of Melchizedek priest.

9. *TDNT*, 7:996.

10. Liddel and Scott, *Greek-English Lexicon*, 904; *TDNT*, 3:627–28.

11. Hofius, KATAPAUSIS; Wray, *Rest as a Theological Metaphor*, 11–49; contrary to Käsemann, *Wandering People of God*.

12. Philo, *Cherubim* 87; Philo, *Unchangeable* 12; Philo, *Alleg. Interp.* 1.16; Philo, *Spec. Laws* 2.64; Philo, *Flight* 5.173–74; Odes Sol. 16.12–13 view is echoed in early Christian literature (Origen, *Cels.* 6.61).

ment within nature. While *yklw*/יְכֻלּוּ can mean a complete finish, within the Pentateuch in the piel imperfect as here (Gen 2:1–2; 49:33; Exod 40:33), it usually means a finishing of the preceding narrative or finishing a phase, of which there is more to come.[13] William Domeris and Cornelis Van Dam define the word "in a positive sense to denote the end of a period of time."[14] For example, the word is used of God *finishing* talking at that time with a person, but God returned to talk with that individual again (Gen 17:22 with 22:1–2; similarly in Gen 24:45 with 34–49; Exod 34:33 with 34; Deut 32:45 with 33:1–29). Similar to this is when camels have *finished* drinking at that occasion, but will drink again (Gen 24:19), or when the Israelite is finished gathering his tithe, so that he can give it and then do so again the next year or when appropriate (Deut 26:12). Likewise, Moses *finished* setting up the tabernacle several times in series at different locations (Exod 40:33; Num 7:1). In fact, Moses' statement of this *completion* of the tabernacle (Exod 40:33) may be parallel and occurring at about the same time as Moses' description that God *completes* his creation as sacred space, thus establishing sacred time (Gen 2:1).

So the choice of *yklw*/יְכֻלּוּ in the creation account (Gen 2:1–2) indicates that this phase of divine creation is complete, not that all divine creation is complete. For example, in the kingdom, God creates (*br'*/בָּרָא) a new heaven and new earth, and within them he creates (*br'*/בָּרָא) a new Jerusalem (Isa 65:17–18; also Jer 31:22). In forgiveness, God creates (*br'*/בָּרָא) a new heart (Ps 51:10[12]). Furthermore, in miracles, God creates manna, wine, fish, and bread that had not been there before (Exod 16:4, 15; Matt 14:14–21; 15:32–39; Mark 6:34–44; 8:1–9; Luke 9:12–17; John 2:7–10; 6:5–13; Heb 2:4; 6:4). That is, God miraculously provided "manna" (meaning "what's it?") in the wilderness for Israel's journey, where it hadn't been before or since. These are actual creation miracles because God can continue to create today, and God and Jesus have continued to create whenever miracles occur. However, this initial phase of the creation was finished in six days. The choice of *yklw*/יְכֻלּוּ permits continued development produced by the Creator God, though this six-day phase of creation is complete.

With the close of the creation account in Genesis 1 there is the development of sacred time, which serves as the temporal climax for this first

---

13. Kautzsch, *Gesenius' Hebrew Grammar*, 328 calls this instance an imperfect and describes it as finishing the preceding narrative. Some creationists insist that the word means "finality" so as to not develop anymore, but this is an assumption on their part (Kennard, *Critical Realist's Theological Method*, 339–40).

14. Domeris and Van Dam, "3983 כלה," 2:641.

creation account, structured as it is by the repeated temporal framework (Gen 2:1–3).[15] God set this Sabbath day apart as a day in the calendar, which reflects God's stopping (*ykl*/יְכַל, *yšbt*/יִשְׁבֹּת) the creation process, not that he needed to rest (Exod 20:11). Later as the sign of the Mosaic covenant for Israel, this sacred seventh day of creation is incorporated as the rationale for the Sabbath day (*šbt*/שָׁבַת; Exod 20:8–11; 31:12–17; Heb 4:4). This Sabbath day becomes the pattern for the Sabbatical year, freeing people from servitude, need, and giving the land rest (Exod 21:2–4; Lev 25:2–7; Deut 15:1–18). After seven sevens of years, there was then to be a super-sabbatical year, the Year of Jubilee, which again freed people from servitude, debt, and prior sale, and gave the land rest (Lev 25:8–55). All land and houses were to be redeemed to the rightful tenant, since God said, "the land is mine; for you are but aliens and sojourners with me" (Lev 25:23), which of course means that even after Israel is living in the land, they are still sojourning on to a grander Sabbatical rest of kingdom (Isa 61:1–3; Luke 4:18–19). Other words might indicate more of a resting place (מְנֻחָה), but these words for rest (שְׁבִיעִי, יָנַח, κατέπαυσεν, ἑβδόμῃ, σαββατισμός) indicate sacred time, such as the Sabbath or an era of sacred time, such as the kingdom. Early Judaism developed the concept of "rest" eschatologically as the kingdom era: Paradise for the blessed in contrast to Hell for the damned.[16] The kingdom is the era when "God's people will join God in his 'rest' penultimately at death and finally at the judgment."[17] However, the rest is both temporally present and eschatologically future.[18] Judith Wray summarized Hebrews concept of rest as "a to-be-maintained participation

---

15. To preserve the Sabbath as completely work free in Genesis 2:2 LXX, the Samaritan Pentateuch, Peshitta, Jubilees 2.1.16a, and Genesis Midrash Bereshith Rabbah reads "On the sixth day God ended his work."

16. Wis 4.7; t. Dan 5.12; Philo, *Cherubim* 90 building an argument in 87 from God's present character and Sabbath rest available to those in relationship with him (similarly: Philo, *Unchangeable* 12; Philo, *Embassy* 1.16; Philo, *Spec. Laws* 2.64; Philo, *Flight* 5.173–74; also Odes Sol. 25.9–12); LAB 19.12; 4 Ezra 7.36, 38, 120, 123; 8.52; Jos. Asen. 8.9; 15.7; 22.13; T. Isaac 2.6, 12; T. Jac. 2.26; 5.5–6; 2 Bar. 73.1; 85.9; Odes Sol. 25.9–12); b. Ketub. 104a; b. Šabb. 152; this view is extended in fringe Christianity (2 Clem. 5.5; 6.7; Ep. Barn. 4.12–13; 15; Irenaeus, *Haer.* 1.2.6; 2.29; 34.1–2; Clement of Alexandria, *Strom.* 5.14.122.3; 5.6.36.3; 7.10.57; Origen, *Cels.* 3.63; Gos. Eg. 65.21–22; 76.19–24; Tri. Trac. 121.23–29; Treat. Res. 43.32–44.3; Dial. Sav. 120.1–8; Gos. Thom. 50–51; Thom. Cont. 145.8–16; Gos. Truth 36.30–39); Laansma, *"I Will Give You Rest,"* 102–251.

17. Cockerill, *Epistle to the Hebrews*, 199; Hofius, *KATAPAUSIS*, 59–90; contrary to a present state developed by Attridge, "Let Us Strive to Enter," 279–88.

18. Laansma, *"I Will Give You Rest,"* 278–79; Hofius, *KATAPAUSIS*, 33–41.

The Narrow Exodus Way of Faith to Salvation

in the completed cosmic work of God . . . a reward for faithfulness and not yet defined as an integral result of participation in Christ."[19]

William Manson and L. D. Hurst develop that Hebrews' two-way exodus reflects similarities from the Christian tradition with Stephen's defense in Acts 7.[20] They especially make comparisons between these respective accounts concerning the exodus as follows:

1. The living God comes with the living word (Acts 7:32, 38; Heb 3:12; 4:12).
2. God calls to go out (Acts 7:3, 7; Heb 11:8, 13; 13:13).
3. The law is given by angels (Acts 7:30, 38, 53; Heb 2:2).
4. The tabernacle pattern is in heaven (Acts 7:44, 48; Heb 9:23–24).
5. Israel's life shifts direction (Acts 7:3–50; Heb 11; 13:14).
6. The faithful are homeless (Acts 7:5, 36, 44; Heb 11:8–10, 13–16).
7. The faithful head toward the promised land (Acts 7:5,7; Heb 11:14–16).
8. Joshua promised rest (Acts 7:49; Heb 4:2–5, 7–9).
9. Israel always resists the Holy Spirit (Acts 7:42, 51–52; Heb 4:7–11).
10. Jesus is after Moses' pattern (Acts 7:37; Heb 3:3–6).
11. The situation must change after Jesus (Acts 7:37, 51–52; Heb 8:6–13).
12. The law must change (Acts 6:13–14; Heb 8:6–13).
13. Believers focus on Jesus (Acts 7:55; Heb 12:2; 1; 5; 7).
14. Believers head toward heaven (Acts 7:55–56; Heb 11:10; 13:14).

From these points, the book of Hebrews works within a two-way framework that reflects the consistent Christian model as articulated by Stephen in Acts 7. In this, the believers in Christ undergo a new exodus of a narrow way toward kingdom.

---

19. Wray, *Rest as a Theological Metaphor*, 91.

20. Manson, *Epistle to the Hebrews*, 25–46, esp. 36; Hurst, *Epistle to the Hebrews*, 89–106, esp. 94; the list is Kennard's rearrangement to reflect their point, with verses added. Hurst (*Epistle to the Hebrews*, 114–30) also analyzed parallel arrangement with Hebrews and the Christological hymn of Phil 2, and Hurst and Kennard were unconvinced of this parallel contra Hofius, *Der Christushymnus Philipper 2.6–11*, 75 and Bornkamm, "Das Bekenntnis im Hebräerbrief," 56–66.

Several commentators also develop parallels concerning the exodus in 1 Peter and Hebrews.[21] Parallels between 1 Peter and Hebrews regarding these exodus plans include the following:

1. Believers are ransomed by blood of a spotless lamb (1 Pet 1:18–24; Heb 9:12, 14; 10:10).
2. Believers are sprinkled by Christ's blood (1 Pet 1:2; Heb 12:24).
3. Believers are strangers and aliens (1 Pet 1:1; Heb 2:11).
4. Believers are heading toward heavenly inheritance (1 Pet 1:4; Heb 9:15; 12:17).
5. Believers have an undefiled inheritance (1 Pet 1:4; Heb 7:26; 13:4).
6. Believers are in suffering to test them (1 Pet 1:6–8; Heb 2:9–18).
7. Prophets predict Christ's suffering (1 Pet 1:10–12; Heb 12:1–2).
8. Angels look into salvific things (1 Pet 1:12; Heb 1:4, 14).
9. Believers must discipline themselves toward goal (1 Pet 1:13; Heb 12:1).
10. Believers are to hope in grace (1 Pet 1:13; Heb 11:1–30).
11. God's people are ignorant and erring (1 Pet 1:14; 2:25; Heb 5:2; 9:7).
12. Believers pray with fear through exodus (1 Pet 1:17; Heb 4:1; 10:30; 12:7–9).
13. Believers should love and be kind to strangers (1 Pet 1:22; 4:9; Heb 13:1).
14. Believers have living word (1 Pet 1:23; Heb 4:12).
15. The community of believers is a "house" (1 Pet 2:5; Heb 3:6).
16. Believers are a "holy and royal priesthood" (1 Pet 2:5, 9; Heb 7:1, 26).
17. Believers are to offer spiritual sacrifices to God (1 Pet 2:5, 9; Heb 7:1; 13:10).

From this summary of their points, the thrust of Hebrews' pilgrimage works within a two-way framework that reflects the consistent Christian model as articulated by 1 Peter. Once again, the exodus is a Christian

---

21. Gräßer, "Der Hebräerbrief, 1938-63," 138–236; Moffat, *Introduction to the Literature*, 440; Masterman, *First Epistle of St. Peter*, 36–38; Hurst, *Epistle to the Hebrews*, 126–30.

The Narrow Exodus Way of Faith to Salvation

framework evidencing the two ways believers can live, emphasizing the narrow way of virtues in following Christ to the kingdom.

The promised-land imagery also includes a homeland that will be their own (Heb 11:13–16) and a celestial city to which they are traveling by faith (Heb 11:9–10; 12:22; Gen 12:1; 15:18–21).[22] So, when Abraham was called, he went out to a place where he was to receive an inheritance, not knowing where he was going (Heb 11:8). By faith he lived in the land of promise in tents, for he was looking for a city designed and built by God (Heb 11:9–10, 16; 13:14). Abraham, Isaac, and Jacob were fellow heirs of the promise of a homeland that they lived within, but they died having not receive the inherited land (Heb 11:13–16). They were temporary residents desiring a homeland provided by God from heaven (Heb 11:16).

Another image of believing pursuit of the goal is in a race (Heb 12:1–2). The athlete lays aside all encumbrances and sins which entangle so that in the games he might run as fast as he can, which in that Greco-Roman context was in the nude, with only males observing.[23] But the runner also develops endurance over time as they practice. The athlete runs with a clear goal of Jesus in view to focus his faith and endurance. In fact, Jesus becomes a prime example for how to run, as he ran the race before us and has already been elevated to the right hand of God.

The way of faith in Hebrews is one of a continuous, confident faith in God and his promises (Heb 1:1). Our author gathers a series of respected elders as testifying witnesses who gained approval with God by pursuing it by faith because God provided the better promise (Heb 11:2, 6, 39–40; 12:1). Judaism commonly established a community of faith through a list of historical witnesses from the people (Heb 11:2—12:1).[24] The first witness is the author and his Jewish Christian lineage, who understand that God created the world, bringing all things into being (Heb 11:3; Gen 1). By faith Abel offered the first and the best (fat portions) sacrifice, thus identifying himself as a righteous witness (Heb 11:4; Gen 4:4).[25] Likewise, Enoch walked with God within a pleasing relationship permeated with faith, so God took him directly into the afterlife continuing this relationship (Gen

---

22. 2 Bar. 4.2–5; 4 Ezra 3.13–14; T. Ab. [recension A]; Wray, *Rest as a Theological Metaphor*, 91.

23. Acts 7:58; Mart. Pol. 13.2.

24. Sir 44–50; Wis 10; Cov. of Damascus; Eisenbaum, "Heros and History in Hebrews," 380–96; Cockerill, *Epistle to the Hebrews*, 516.

25. Josephus, *Ant.* 1.53; T. Zeb. 5.4; T. Iss. 5.4; 4 Macc 18:11; Tg. Gen. 4.8, 10; Mart. Ascen. Isa. 9.8.

5:22, 24; MT "walked with God," LXX "pleased God," which is repeated in Heb 11:5).[26] In faith, Noah prepared an ark in obedience to God's salvation plan, thus showcasing his righteousness, when the world around was destroyed (Heb 11:7; Gen 6:8–22; 7:1; 8:20–9:17; 2 Pet 2:5).[27]

Abraham became a prime example of a witness to faith. Abraham left his homeland for God's promised land[28] and involved multiple generations in the role as fellow-heirs of this promise (Heb 11:7–10). Sarah joined Abraham in faith, trusting God's promise to remove infertility and provide a son by giving her the power to receive Abraham's disposition of generating seed (Heb 11:11–12).[29] Furthermore, when tested by God, Abraham was set to offer his uniquely born and beloved[30] son of the promise, perhaps expecting resurrection because God had promised Abraham's seed through Isaac (Heb 11:17–19).[31]

Other patriarchs join as faith witnesses. Isaac blessed Jacob and Esau regarding things to come (Heb 11:20). As death approached, Jacob blessed the sons of Joseph and worshiped God (Gen 47:31 MT; "bed" is replaced in the LXX with "worshipped on his staff," which Heb 11:21 follows). As Joseph was dying, he showed his faith by mentioning the exodus and ordering his bones to be taken with them when they left Egypt (Heb 11:22; Gen 50:24–25; Exod 13:19).[32]

---

26. Enoch believed (3 En. 6.3), was called righteous (T. Levi 10.5; T. Dan 5.6; T. Benj. 9.1; Wis 4:4, 7, 16; 1 En. 1.2; 12.1; Jub. 10.17), and was taken by God (Philo, *Names* 38; Philo, *QG* 1.86; Josephus, *Ant.* 1.85; Jub. 4.23; Wis 4:10).

27. Noah believed (1 Clem. 9.4; Sib. Or. 1.125–26) was called righteous (Wis 10:4; Sir 44:17; Jub. 5.19; 7.20; Philo, *Worse* 105; Philo, *Posterity* 48, 173–74; Josephus, *Ant.* 1.74; LAB 3.4; Sib Or. 1.125–36, 280; 1 Clem. 7.6; 9.4).

28. Sir 44.19–20; Jub. 19.8–9; 23.9–10; 1 Macc 2.52; Philo, *Migration* 127–30; Philo, *Abraham* 275–76; Philo, *Heir* 6–9; Josephus, *Ant.* 1.233–34; 4Q225 1.4; 2.1.9–11, 14; 2.7–8; 4Q226 7.1–2; m. Qidd. 4.14; m. Ned. 3.11; CD 3.2–4; de Roo, "God's Covenant with the Forefathers," 195–96. In contrast, Albrektson expresses a minority view that both the faith and the affirmation of righteousness can be handled as trust in Yahweh considering his promise as reliable ("Disputed Sense," 1–9).

29. Cockerill, *Epistle to the Hebrews*, 544–45.

30. Gen 22:2 MT and LXX have "beloved son" but Aquila substitutes μονογενῆ in Symmachus quoting Genesis 22:2 and Hebrews follows this substitution to describe Isaac; also Josephus, *Ant.* 1.222; Gen. Rab. 22.4; Lev. Rab. 23.4; Pesiq. Rab Kah. 23.

31. Philo (*Abraham* 177) anticipates resurrection, but Isaac was not actually sacrificed to death (Gen 22:12–13; 2 Macc 7:29; Josephus, *J.W.* 2.153).

32. Wis 10:13–14; 1 Macc 2:53; 4 Macc 18:11; T. Jos. 20.2; 1 Clem. 4.9.

The Narrow Exodus Way of Faith to Salvation

Moses himself became a prime example of a witness to faith. He was born in a believing family who hid him from Pharaoh's edict (Heb 11:23; Exod 2:2–3), and he embraced the same faith in aligning with Israel amidst their ill treatment rather than identifying with Pharaoh's household (Heb 11:24–26; Exod 5–15). Such a disposition is reapplied by the author through *pesher* to Christians who identify with Christ's suffering in seeking a reward of a new promised land (Heb 11:25–27). Within this *pesher*, Moses is presented as realizing that his sufferings include putting in motion the suffering of Christ, so that his reward was much more than Egyptian wealth or the promised land. Moses also believed in divine protection through miracles, such as occurred at Passover, the Red Sea, and even after he died at the defeat of Jericho (Heb 11:28–30).

Many more witnesses could verbalize benefits of a believing life. Some, including Gideon, Barak, Samson, Jephthah, and David, conquered kingdoms by faith (Heb 11:32–33). Others performed acts of righteousness, such as Rahab welcoming the spies in peace, and Samuel and the prophets joined as well (Heb 11:33). Many unnamed others are witnesses to faith by deed.[33] Some of them are recognizable, such as Daniel shutting the mouths of lions (Dan 6:23–24, with Theodotion's additions to LXX),[34] Daniel's friends (Hananiah, Mishael, and Azariah) quenching the fire of Nebuchadnezzar's furnace (Dan 3:19–28, 49–50 LXX with Theodotion), and Isaiah being sawn in two (Heb 11:33–34, 37).[35]

However, many of these witnesses are ambiguous with common deliverances or sufferings. Shifting to an ambiguous gathering of witnesses presents the voice of witnesses as overwhelming from many sides in Israel. These all gained approval by God through faith, even though they did not receive what was promised (Heb 11:39). The witnesses claim that God demonstrates that he has provided something better for the Christians (Heb 11:40). Therefore, maturity can only be obtained together in applying their witness into our lives.

Hebrew 13:7–17 reminds the readers to continue in this believing way of life. First, remember those leaders who led you so that you might consider the outcome of their way of life as a motive for imitating their faith

---

33. Lane, *Hebrews 9–13*, 2:382–92 conjectures helpfully who many of these figures might be with textual documentation.

34. 1 Macc 2:60; 3 Macc 16:3, 21; 18:13; Josephus, *Ant.* 10.262; 1 Clem. 45.6; Apos. Const. 7.37.2.

35. Ascen. Isa. 5.1–4, 11–14; Justin, *Dial.* 120.5; Tertullian, *Pat.* 14; Origen, *Ep. Afr.* 9; Hippolytus, *Antichr.* 30.

(Heb 13:7). Secondly, recognize that Jesus is immutable over time so that he can be trusted as the person you count upon in faith (Heb 13:8). With these two secure examples for life, do not be carried away by varied or strange teaching, such as specific foods, which do not benefit (Heb 13:9). Instead, strengthen one's heart by God's generosity, especially Christ's new covenant atonement (Heb 13:9). Jesus' heavenly sacrificial altar provides benefits beyond those provided by Jewish priests (Heb 13:10–11). For example, Jewish priests can eat selected portions of sacrifices offered in the tabernacle (Lev 6:19, 22, LXX 26, 29; 7:6; 10:17–18; Num 18:9–10),[36] but Jesus' body is not available for these priests to cannibalize (Heb 13:10–11; 9:7–28). This ban preventing Jewish priests from eating of this sacrifice does not intrude the Lord's Supper into this Jewish *pesher*, for the author continues to develop metaphors within the Jewish sacrificial setting. For example, the high priest, offering sacrifice for sin, sets up a pattern of removing the hides and burning them outside the camp (Heb 13:11; Exod 29:14; Lev 4:12, 21; 9:11; 16:27; Num 19:3–7). The author of Hebrews develops the theme of "outside the camp" as a *pesher* for why Jesus died outside the gate (Heb 13:12; Matt 27:31; Mark 15:20; Luke 23:26; John 19:20).[37] Hebrews extends this "outside the camp" rationale to a discussion of why Jewish-Christian readers must intentionally identify with Jesus Christ and his reproach outside the Jewish camp (Heb 13:12–13). However, Jesus' atonement death accomplished sanctification for his people, rendering Christians to be new-covenant holy people (Heb 13:12). Additionally, reproach is not an end in itself,[38] for identifying with Christ also identifies one with a life of serving others as he did (Heb 13:16).

In this life, Christians do not have a lasting geographic city, but because Christ's atonement sets Christians apart as sanctified, we have a city which is to come (Heb 13:14; 11: 9–10, 16). Such everlasting kingdom generosity should prompt Christians to join in worship via a "sacrifice of praise" to god verbally giving thanks to his name (Heb 13:15; 1 Pet 2:5, 9, 12, 17;

---

36. Philo, *Laws* 1.240; Josephus, *Ant.* 3.231; b. Zebaḥ 36a bar.; b. Mo'ed Qaṭ. 9a; b. Pesaḥ. 109a.

37. Josephus, *J.W.* 5.146; m. B. Bat. 2.9; Egeria Itin. 24.7; 25.9, 11; 27.3, 6; 30.1–2; 31.4; 35.2; 36.4.5; 37.1–8; 39.2; Jerome, *Epist.* 58.3; Eusebius, *Vit. Const.* 3.36, 39; Eusebius, *Onom.*

38. In contrast to Philo, who identified Moses as choosing virtue in pitching the tent "outside the camp" (Philo, *Alleg. Interp.* 2.54–55; 3.46; Philo, *Worse* 160; Philo, *Giants* 54; Philo, *Drunkenness* 99–101), Hebrews identifies Christ's death as a reproach and Christians joining him in service to others.

3:15). Such a sacrifice of praise is the verbal praise that would often accompany an animal sacrifice or grain offering (Heb 13:15; Lev 7:12–15). As such, Christian worship imitates priestly activity of corporate worship with a cleansed conscience (Heb 10:19–25). This praise should be accompanied in the Christian with sacrifices of doing good, submitting to authorities, and sharing, because these please God (Heb 13:16–17; 1 Pet 2:5, 12–3:2, 16). Specifically, this has the implication that Christians should submit to their Christian leadership because such submission enables leaders' joy while they watch over the spiritual condition of their believing family (Heb 13:17). Obviously, if one causes leaders grief through lack of submissiveness, then the Christian will not find these behaviors profitable for them. Joy with corporate growth is a much more encouraging outcome in this narrow exodus way.

11

Warnings in Hebrews

THE WARNING PASSAGES IN the book of Hebrews are often interpreted through the lens of developed Christian life traditions. In this way, regeneration and loss of salvation are often seen as alluded to in an Arminian traditional understanding of Hebrews 6.[1] In reform traditions, regeneration is recognized as a divine, definite, outworking, and extending election, which means that the warnings become either a hollow threat to the elect, and thus impossible to commit,[2] or merely warning the church participant who hasn't received such salvation benefits.[3] However, the warning is verbalized to all as motivation for believers. Additionally, from an Augustinian-Dispensational or Keswick Christian life tradition, some advocate that Hebrews describes a position of persistent, rebellious, carnal Christianity where those who will be saved need discipline.[4] If one of these traditional

---

1. Wiley, *Epistle to the Hebrews*, 210; Shank, *Life in the Son*, 229–34; Montefiore, *Hebrews*, 108–9; Marshall, *Kept by the Power of God*, 137–53; Osborne, "Soteriology in the Epistle to the Hebrews," 144–66; Osborne, "Classical Arminian View," 86–128, and Cockerill, "Wesleyan Arminian View," 257–306; Koester, *Hebrews*, 312–22; O'Brien, *Letter to the Hebrews*, 219–27; Cockerill, *Epistle to the Hebrews*, 270–74.

2. Westcott, *Epistle to the Hebrews*, 165; Hewett, *Epistle to the Hebrews*, 108, 111; Wuest, "Hebrews Six in the Greek," 52; Kent, *Epistle to the Hebrews*, 113; Guthrie, *Letter to the Hebrews*, 145–47.

3. Archer, *Epistle to the Hebrews*, 40; Hughes, *Hebrews*, 215; MacArthur, *Hebrews*, 136; Nicole, "Some Comments on Hebrews 6:4–6," 362, and Toussaint, "Eschatology of the Warning Passages," 68; Fanning, "Classical Reformed View," 172–219, and Gleason, "Moderate Reformed View," 336–77.

4. Dunham, "Exegetical Examination," 190; Kendall, *Once Saved, Always Saved*,

horizons is read onto the text, there is a real danger in missing the book's biblical thought forms. The proposal for this chapter is to read Hebrews' warning passages by restricting the meaning of the words to the sense in which they are utilized elsewhere within the book of Hebrews.[5] That is, this is a biblical theology study intentionally allowing Hebrews' distinctive voice to show itself in Hebrews' thought forms, without forcing traditional and contemporary Christian life concerns upon them.

When such a biblical theology approach is undertaken in Hebrews' warnings, these warnings of potential damnation best fit within a two-way salvation tradition.[6] Within such an approach, there is a narrow way of virtues (such as persistent faith, love, obedience, and good deeds of ministry) leading toward an eschatological glorification salvation at the second coming of Christ. The virtues provide significant assurance for the follower of Christ that she will arrive in the kingdom. However, the warnings remain authentic for all who travel this spiritual exodus, warning all not to lose the character of kingdom virtues, for to do so would mean expulsion from kingdom benefits. This is not a loss-of-salvation view, for kingdom or salvation benefits are only for those who remain on the narrow way. As such, assurance of salvation is for those who remain on the narrow way. Those who continue on the narrow way are already partakers (μετόχους) with Christ, but the only way to know if this eschatological salvation includes an individual is that they must continue. Thus, the warnings come for the whole community identified with Christ to urge them to do what it takes to miss damnation, the outcome of the broad way, by not departing from Christ.

HEBREWS 2:1–4

The first warning comes in Hebrews 2:1–4 in the wake of identifying salvation as something to be inherited in the future (Heb 1:14). This salvation (σωτηρίαν) is not yet inherited by the readers of Hebrews (Heb 1:14; 2:3),

---

175–82, 219–28; Gromacki, *Stand Bold in Grace*, 112; Pentecost, *Faith That Endures*, 10–13, 20–22; Dillow, *Reign of the Servant Kings*, 433–66; Eaton, *Theology of Encouragement*, 212–17; Gleason, "Old Testament Background," 62–91.

5. This approach was first introduced to Kennard by Edwin Blum at Dallas Theological Seminary in 1976.

6. John Chrysostom, *Hom. Heb.* 6–7, 10, 20–21; Käsemann, *Wandering People of God*, 86; Nairne, *Epistle of Priesthood*, 205, 226–28; Hofius, *KATAPAUSIS*; Buchanan, *To the Hebrews*, 106–8; Lane, *Hebrews 1–8*, 141–42; Wray, *Rest as a Theological Metaphor*, 11–49, 91; Laansma, "I Will Give You Rest," 278–79.

for it shall be realized by them with the second coming of Christ (Heb 9:28). Even though in his first coming Christ authored salvation in his sufferings (Heb 2:10; 5:9), this everlasting salvation is yet to be inherited in the future, which is why virtues (such as perseverance) should accompany salvation. Because salvation is to be inherited and Christ's enemies will be utterly defeated to become his footstool, the readers are warned not to depart the potential inheritance to join Christ's doomed foes (Heb 1:13–2:1).

The warning is to not "drift away" (παραρυῶμεν) as driftwood in a stream is passively carried away (Heb 2:1).[7] The word is also used for "paying attention" to a speaker and "holding fast" in accordance with what was said (Acts 8:6, 10; LXX Deut 32:46),[8] which makes it a synonym for "neglect" (Heb 2:3, ἀμελήσαντες). Such passivity is concerned about other things such as the law. Hebrews uses "legally binding" and "confirmed" terminology for both the law and Christ's message (Heb 2:2–3, "valid": βέβαιος, "validate": ἐβεβαιώθη).[9] This is a serious warning when put in contrast with the law, revealed by angels, but it can condemn (Heb 2:2; Acts 7:38, 53; Gal 3:19; in LXX, angels joined God in giving law; Deut 33:2).[10] That is, Christ is greater than these angels and speaks a greater salvation than comes through the law, so neglect of Christ's message renders one at greater risk than neglecting the law.

Not only was this salvation spoken by Christ, but it was actively witnessed by both God and the Holy Spirit through the use of various miracles (Heb 2:4). Hebrews uses an assortment of words (signs, wonders, works of power, and gifts of the Holy Spirit) to communicate repeatedly that divinely wrought attesting miracles corroborate Christ's message. These words should be seen in Hebrews' vocabulary as synonyms attesting to the authenticity, certainty, and greatness of Christ's salvation message.

So the first warning is for the readers to seriously attend to Christ's message of eschatological salvation attested by Father and Spirit. Since the readers have heard the message and seen the signs, they are obligated to heed its message.

---

7. Herodutus, *Hist.* 2.150; 6.20; Strabo, *Geogr.* 9.2.31.

8. Koester, *Hebrews*, 205.

9. Koester, *Hebrews*, 214.

10. Jub. 1.27, 29; 2.1, 17–19; CD 5.18; Josephus, *Ant.* 15.5.3 136; Sipre Num. 102; Mek. Exod. 20.18; Pesiq. Rab. 21; Kennard, *Biblical Covenantalism*, 1:104–243.

Warnings in Hebrews

HEBREWS 3:7—4:13

Christ the Son is shown to be superior over his house than Moses, the faithful servant builder within the house (Heb 3:1–6). Therefore, there is great need to persistently believe, as Israel should have during their wilderness wanderings toward the promised land under Moses' leadership in Exodus (Heb 3:9).

Psalms 95 is a hymn of prophetic exhortation calling Israel to worship Yahweh and to resist rebelling against him (LXX Ps 94:7–11). In Psalms 95:8, the Hebrew text identifies the time of provocation as *meribah* (rebellion) and *massah* (strife), which the narrative exodus texts describe as occurring in multiple locations (Exod 17:7; Num 20:13–14; 27:14; Deut 6:16; 9:22; 32:51; 33:8), especially as Psalms 95:9 declares that Israel tested God there over the forty-year exodus (Heb 3:8–9). Perhaps the supreme example of Israel's rebellion during the exodus was their refusal at Kadesh to go into the promised land and enter God's rest (Num 13:1–14:45). However, the exodus narratives indicate that there are additional instances of rebellion showing which make this a habitual pattern (Exod 15:22–25; 32:1–10; Num 14:21; as well as all the instances of *meribah* [rebellion] and *massah* [strife]). The emphasis on rebellion is not lost, for the LXX (Ps 94:10), cited by Hebrews 3:10, is more forceful in declaring Israel's rebellion habitual—"They always go astray in their heart; and they did not know my ways"—than the MT text (Ps 95:10). In the wake of Israel habitually testing God, Yahweh swore that Israel would not enter his rest in the promised land, so that generation perished in the wilderness (Num 14:23; Ps 95:11; Heb 3:11).

Even in Israel's rebellion, God was faithful in showing Israel his works for forty years (Heb 3:9). The MT text develops this divine faithfulness, but connects the forty years with the extent of time in which God's wrath made Israel wander the desert, whereas the LXX and Hebrews text shift the forty years to modify God's generous works before admitting divine anger because Israel repeatedly rebelled (Ps 95 [LXX 94]:9–10; Heb 3:9–10). From the emphasis of Hebrews and LXX, God's generous works are abundantly evident to the readers (Heb 2:4), so there are reasons not to rebel. However, Israel's habitual tendency to rebel (Heb 3:10, "they always go astray in their heart") raises the reason for the warning (Heb 3:10, διό); rebellion begets God's wrath.

The author is concerned that this Jewish history of rebellion would not repeat itself, so he exhorts the reader to personally "be watchful"

(Βλέπετε) that no one should permit "an evil unbelieving heart in falling away from the living God" (Heb 3:12). Such an unbelieving condition prompts the warning "don't rebel by pursuing your own way," because that outcome ends in destruction (Jer 16:12; 18:12; parallel to evil conscience, Heb 10:22).[11] Furthermore, the warning is also communal, urging each to "encourage one another" (παρακαλεῖτε) so that none would be "hardened by the deceitfulness of sin" (Heb 3:13).

Therefore, the warning is a *pesher* arrangement extending beyond the historical situation by its declaration of "Today" (σήμερον, Heb 3:7, 13, 15; 4:7), said in David's time, which shows that Joshua did not realize the rest in his day of conquest. The concept of rest in the books of Joshua and Judges is analogous to the kingdom, within which Mosaic covenant benefits of peace and blessing dominate. Joshua brought Israel into the land, and God gave them rest (Josh 21:44; 22:4), but it did not last, so that rest was only recoverable when judges recovered Israel in covenant faithfulness and blessing (Judg 3:11, 30; 5:31; 8:28; Heb 4:8). Unfortunately, Israel repeatedly departed in their sins, begot curse from Yahweh, and was troubled by her enemies. So rest from her enemies was a very fleeting experience for Israel, so what Israel experienced can't be said to be the kingdom rest to which the Mosaic covenant pointed. It is this Mosaic covenant kingdom rest which is still available as the Sabbath rest (the sign of the Mosaic covenant: Exod 31:12–18; Heb 4:9). Such a rest is realized when a person rests from her works as God has rested from his (Heb 4:10). Perhaps this pattern is reminiscent of God being finished creating, which set apart the sacred time of Sabbath rest (Gen 2:1–3; Exod 20:8–11; Heb 4:10). However, in the present condition of journeying toward the kingdom, such a blessing means that we have not arrived at the rest, similarly to Israel, which in the wilderness had not arrived at the promised land. The psalmist's repeated use of the word "today" rivets his readers to the realization that the risk is still present today. So, the warning does not resound to join the cursed apostates who "fall away" (ἀποστῆναι) from the Living God in having an evil unbelieving heart (Heb 3:12). Here, faith is seen as long-standing virtue and unbelief as vice rather than a definite event (as the Kadesh rejection alone). Some of the readers have had an event of faith, but there is cause to fear that possibly any one of the readers fall short of the promise of this rest (Heb 4:1). However, those characterized by the virtue of persistent "faith" (aorist) "enter" (perfect tense) that rest (Heb 4:3). The perfect tense indicates that the rest

---

11. Bar 1.22; 2.8; 4 Ezra 4.20–27; 4.4, 30.

is entered with lasting benefit. It could be that entering the rest will occur eschatologically with everlasting benefit, or perhaps there is already some rest benefit for those who will eschatologically experience rest, as indicated by their persistence of faith. This author prefers the second option because the first person plurals. "We who have believed" indicated that he and some of his audience have a continuing faith that involves them with rest already, whereas some others don't see that the past choice of faith has implications for continuing.

"We have become partakers of Christ" (Heb 3:14). The concept of "partaker" (μέτοχοι) is a distinctive term in the book of Hebrews meaning "co-sharer," and is lifted from Psalms 45:7—Christ is anointed "with the oil of gladness above his companions" (μετόχους, Heb 1:9). In this instance, the co-sharing identifies Christians with Christ as fellow travelers. In Hebrews 3:1, the "co-sharing" (μέτοχοι) carries the same meaning as "companions" or "brethren" (ἀδελφοί), because in that context the "calling" (κλήσεως) which they share is identified as Jesus "calling them brethren" (ἀδελφοὺς αὐτοὺς καλεῖν, Heb 2:11). This co-sharing identifies the brethren as those who confess Jesus as the verbal source and high priest of the belief system that orients their life (Heb 3:1). This same Jesus has been identified as God's Son, who will reign over the house in the kingdom (Heb 1:1–3:6) so that, in Hebrews 3:14, the announcement that "we have become co-sharers (μέτοχοι) with Christ"[12] should be seen as an announcement that the role of companions already co-sharing in the benefits of his reign has begun for those who persistently believe these things without casting away the confession. The co-sharing should not be seen as a technical term, for the context identifies what is shared in the relationship. For example, in Hebrews 12:8, discipline is what is shared, and in Hebrews 6:4, something from the Holy Spirit is shared which will be developed later.

In the context of Hebrews 3:14, we are co-sharers with Christ in his message and kingdom if we continue the journey, believing this assurance which his message and kingdom provide. The verse is a third-class conditional sentence; therefore, the ultimate outcome of co-sharer is uncertain, but still likely if the believer continues with persistent faith. "We have become partakers of Christ, if we hold fast the beginning of our assurance firm until the end" (Heb 3:14).

---

12. This should not be seen as Pauline death and resurrection imagery, such as Galatians 2:20 or being "in Christ," for these concepts are not developed in Hebrews.

This persistent faith should be mingled with fear for we, like the Exodus Israelites, had good news preached to us, and we have not yet arrived (Heb 4:1–2). They fell in the wilderness because they did not unite the message with faith to continue the journey to completion. The original Jewish-Christian audience of Hebrews seems to be tempted to leave the message of Christ and return to the Mosaic covenant. This is where fear can motivate their continuing with Christ. However, this fear should not dominate the faith, because as Hebrews 3:14 and 4:3 develop, there is already a kingdom benefit for those who are characterized by continuing faith.

HEBREWS 5:11—6:20

The author of Hebrews begins to develop the priesthood of Christ, but finds further need to warn his audience concerning their dullness. That is, they have identified with Christ for a while and they should be able to digest the solid food of the Melchizedek priesthood of Christ, and from maturity teach others as well. Instead, their dullness makes it difficult to go further. So, to help them get over this blockage, the author paints some of the characteristics of different levels of growth.

The baby Christian who identifies with Christ is able to handle elementary things, akin to milk. They deal with issues like repentance from a lifestyle of dead works to one of faith toward God. That is, to move through babyhood is to depart from the entanglements of a lifestyle unto death and to develop consistency in trusting God. In this transition, certain basic issues are clarified, such as the difference of baptisms (βαπτισμῶν) between Jewish proselyte John the Baptist and Christian baptism.[13] Likewise, instruction is provided regarding the laying on of hands, which bestows the Holy Spirit, healing (or authority), and empowerment for ministry.[14] Such basic teaching also includes the conceptual framework of the resurrection of the dead and everlasting judgment, and the practical implications like the realization of where one is in relation to resurrection and judgment, and what one ought to do about that.

---

13. Acts 2:38–41; 10:28; 19:3–4; 1QS 3.3–9; 4QTLevi[a] ar; Josephus, *J.W.* 2.150; Josephus, *Ant.* 14.285; 18.93–94, 117; T. Levi 2.3.1–2; Sib. Or. 4.162–70; Epictetus, *Diatr.* 2.9.19–20; Apoc. Mos. 29.6–13; b. Yebam. 46a–48b; Sipre Num. 15.14; m. Ṭehar 7.6; t. Yoma 4.20; t. Pesaḥ. 7.13.

14. Acts 6:6; 8:17–19; 9:12, 17; 13:3; 19:6; 28:8; 1 Tim 4:14; 5:22; 2 Tim 1:6.

The book's audience had enough time to have developed beyond these baby concerns, but they had not matured (Heb 5:12–13). So, likely, this is not an instance of the audience receiving baptism or the laying on of hands, for they experienced these a while ago without maturing beyond these issues. Such maturity entails training oneself in discerning and choosing good as opposed to evil. Such a condition enables one to teach others this discernment as well. However, the audience had not yet developed, so they were not accustomed to handling the word of righteousness which Hebrews was trying to convey. This word of righteousness follows Christ's pattern of loving righteousness and hating lawlessness (Heb 1:9). Such righteous living is identified with maturity (Heb 12:23). This righteousness is obtained by persistent faith (Heb 10:38; 11:4, 7, 33). Discipline from God helps to motivate such persistent faith and produce righteousness (Heb 12:11). Informed by this mindset of righteousness, he warns his audience to move on to maturity because they are in territory with dangerous alternatives.

To warn his readers, the author paints a scenario using traits which they have experienced. At this point, it is imperative to define these words by Hebrews' usage, not other biblical authors. The traits, when taken together will claim that the readers had heard a message and experienced its confirming signs, which we have seen is the starting point of the two previous warnings passages already developed.

The first trait, "having been enlightened" (φωτισθέντας), has occurred for them, resulting in some sort of *transforming life* that enabled them to undergo persecution (Heb 6:4; 10:32). Such enlightenment at least means that a message has opened their mind to some new things. However, the extent of the enlightenment needs to be determined by other phrases which accompany it.[15] One should not automatically assume that this is regeneration.

The phrase "tasted the heavenly gift" is best taken as having a full experience of signs which corroborate the message. The word "taste" (γευσαμένους) in Hebrews means to have a "full experience," as in Christ's full experience of death (Heb 2:9). So here it would claim a full experience of the object. That this object is described as "heavenly" identifies it as from God. The word for "gift" (δωρεᾶς) is not used elsewhere in Hebrews, but a related word, δῶρά, is used of animal sacrifice offered by the Levitical priests

---

15. Hebrews makes no claim that this is conversion, regeneration, or salvation, though the early church proposed that this might allude to baptism (Justin, *1 Apol.* 61.12; Justin, *Dial.* 39.2; 122.1–2, 6), but there is no clear evidence in Hebrews for this view.

and by Abel (Heb 5:1; 8:3–4; 9:9; 11:4). If this is how to define δωρεᾶς, here it would be a claim of his readers being fully religiously Jewish, having participated fully in animal sacrifice. A more promising option opens up when synonyms for "gift" (δωρεᾶς) are considered. The warning in Hebrews 2:1–4 includes "gift" (μερισμοῖς, Heb 2:4) as a confirming miracle to reassure in their existing condition in relationship to God. So both "gift" texts serve as the basis for the warning (Heb 2:4; 6:4). These synonyms functioning in the same purpose, for a parallel warning, make a similar meaning rather likely for δωρεᾶς in Heb 6:4. All the synonyms in Hebrews 2:4 refer to miracles which corroborate a message. So the phrase "tasted of the heavenly gift" is best taken as "having fully experienced the confirming signs which confirm a message."

The phrase "have been made partakers of the Holy Spirit" combines the unique word μετόχους with Hebrews' limited development of the Holy Spirit. The word μετόχους means "companion" or "co-sharer." It is usually identifying Christ's companions or co-sharers in kingdom, but the near context explains what is shared. For example, in Hebrews 12:8, divine discipline is what is shared by all Christians. So here the co-sharing of the Holy Spirit should be understood within the parameters of Hebrews' description of the Holy Spirit.[16] In Hebrews, the Holy Spirit is seen as the source of revelatory message (Heb 3:7; 9:8; 10:15) and as confirming miraculous powers (Heb 2:4). Both are likely alluded to in this phrase, since the revelatory role has the emphasis of use (66 percent), whereas in the warning of Hebrews 2:4 the Holy Spirit empowered the confirming signs. In a later warning, to reject the message about Christ is to spurn the Holy Spirit, probably the Spirit's message and confirming signs (Heb 10:29). Fifty percent of Hebrews' mention of the Holy Spirit occurs within warning passages. The clear parameters of Hebrews' description of the Holy Spirit is that the readers have experienced the Holy Spirit's revelatory message and confirming signs (Heb 6:4). To spurn the Holy Spirit is a rejection of his message and confirming signs (Heb 10:29). With this emphasis, there is no evidence in Hebrews to conjecture that "partaking of the Holy Spirit" alludes to regeneration, nor baptism with the Spirit.

The phrase "have tasted the good word of God and the powers of the age to come" is best taken as describing the readers having fully experienced

---

16. Hebrews does not develop Johainnine new birth by the Holy Spirit or Lukan reception of the Holy Spirit, or Pauline and Petrine spiritual concepts, so it is best not to read these other NT concepts into this context.

God's revelatory message and confirming signs (Heb 6:5). The word "taste" (γευσαμένους) should be taken as a full experience, as in the previous verse. The use of "word" (ῥῆμα) elsewhere in the book of Hebrews highlight the sovereign, creative, revelatory, and fearful message from God (Heb 1:3; 11:3; 12:19). Each instance of ῥῆμα expresses a message appropriate to the context. The breadth of the word relates the concept of God speaking a confirming message, such as the previous warning (Heb 2:3). The word "powers" (δυνάμεις) also has breadth of sovereign power, endless life, procreative strength, and destructive violence (Heb 1:3; 7:16; 11:11, 34). However, in the previous warning, δυνάμεις stands for confirming signs that accompany the word (Heb 2:4). In this context, "word" and "powers" are drawn together as well, so it is best to see this phrase as "full experience of god's revelatory message and confirming signs." In fact, the repeated point of Hebrews 6:4–5 has been the experience that the immature had with a message and confirming signs, for each was alluded to in this context three times. This fits with the pattern of the previous warning, where messages and confirming signs were each alluded to four times (Heb 2:1–4). The condition of the readers from Hebrews 6:4–5 is that they have had a full experience of hearing a message and its confirming signs. It is this message that has brought them into the foundational condition of immaturity, but they should have gone further.

If a reader apostatizes from this message and confirming signs, then it would be impossible (Ἀδύνατον) to renew him again to repentance (Heb 6:4, 6). In Hebrews, "impossible" (Ἀδύνατον) stands for a real impossibility, so God cannot be proven false, Jewish sacrifices do not bring about everlasting forgiveness, and people will not please God without faith (Heb 6:4, 18; 10:4; 11:6).[17] The term "fall away" (παραπεσόντας) is a unique word in the NT, but its meaning is quite clear in the context as a departure from the confirming signs and message, which have to do with the Son of God crucified. From this context, the "renewal" (ἀνακαινίζειν)[18] would be a return to the conditional already described, that of having a full experience of this message and its confirming signs. As has been previously mentioned, experience of the message included repentance or a turning from dead works (μετάνοιαν, Heb 6:1, 6). A later warning in Hebrews 12:16–17 uses the same

---

17. Koester, *Hebrews*, 312.

18. Hebrews does not develop a Pauline sanctification or regeneration idea (ἀνακαινοω or ἀνακαινωσις), so they must be kept out of this text in deference to the contextual emphasis here.

word, "repentance" (μετάνοιαν), in the same manner as here; Esau sold his birthright, but when he later wished to inherit a blessing, he found no place for repentance (μετάνοιαν), though he sought it with tears. So both these warnings corroborate each other. Once a person has turned from dead works and entered back into them by rejecting the message and its confirming signs, there is no coming back; apostasy damns (Heb 6:7–8).[19] The individual moves from an informed commitment following Christ's way to an informed rejection of Christ. After having been a follower in immaturity, impressed by the message and its confirming signs, they go over to the opposition, and it is as though they call for the Son of God to be crucified.[20] To leave such an informed embracing of the message and its confirming signs to apostatize to the opposition publically shames[21] the Son of God, who is the center of the message from which they are in danger of departing. Such an apostasy spurns the generosity of God and the Spirit, who gave the message and the confirming signs. It is akin to ground that drinks the rain and is cultivated but does not yield vegetation; rather, it yields thorns and thistles (Heb 6:7–8). Such a worthless crop is close to being cursed and ends up being burned. In these warnings, the judgment day is still future. So the apostate is close to being cursed and ends up damned.

After warning the whole group of the danger of apostasy, he reassures the whole group that he has reasons to believe that they will not apostatize. Hebrews discussed his readers' immature condition in the second person (Heb 5:11–12) before shifting to the third person (Heb 5:13–14; 6:4–8) for the extremity of infantile behavior and apostasy. Perhaps the third person is used to soften the accusation to the level of warning: this type of person apostasies and is damned. Will you join them? The first-person exhortation in the context encourages growing on to maturity (Heb 6:1–3). These first-person statements return with encouragement of the second-person address as well: "beloved, we are convinced of better things concerning you."

After warning his readers, the author of Hebrews reassures them that he is convinced that they show traits evidencing salvation. Salvation

---

19. Philo, *Alleg. Interp.* 3.213; Philo, *Worse* 149; Sir 34:30–31; 2 En. 62.3; m. 'Abot 5.18.

20. Such a sin of apostasy is at least as bad as that committed by the Pharisees who, after hearing Christ teach and seeing the Spirit's confirming signs, claim Christ's empowerment is from Satan and seek to kill Christ; such a sin, insulting the Spirit, is unforgiveable (Matt 12:14–37; Heb 10:29). However, those in danger of apostatizing in Hebrews went further into immaturity with the message before they were warned (Heb 6).

21. This public shame is akin to the exposure and death for immorality under the law (παραδειγματίζοντας, Matt 1:19; Heb 6:6).

(σωτηρίας) has been previously described as not yet inherited by the Hebrews readers (Heb 1:14; 2:3), for it shall be realized by them with the second coming of Christ (Heb 9:28). The readers continuing work and love in ministering to the saints in a manner that glorifies Christ evidences that they are heading toward this eschatological salvation (Heb 6:10). However, some do this better than others. The desire of the author of Hebrews is that each of his readers show the same diligence in love and service so that they may realize the full assurance of hope until the end (Heb 6:11). The virtues of diligence, continuing ministry work, and love provide the assurance that eschatological salvation will be obtained, so these virtues are precious indicators of being included in eschatological salvation for the one identified with Christ. Thus, the responsibility to be about these virtues is underscored for the reader. It is in living these virtues that the sluggishness of the readers will be broken (Heb 6:12). The readers need to realize that many others have trodden this path toward salvation before them, so that the readers might imitate the faith and patience of those ahead who inherit the promises. Outstanding examples to imitate are Abraham, who believed God's promise (Heb 6:13–19), and Jesus, our forerunner and everlasting priest (Heb 6:20—7:17). God is unchangeable so that we who have fled for refuge in laying hold of the hope set before us may be strongly encouraged that our hope anchors us[22] surely and steadfastly (Heb 6:18–19).

HEBREWS 10:19–39

The author develops a contrast within concepts of holy place (ἁγίων), priesthood, sacrifice, and sanctification (ἁγιάζει) outcome. The Levitical priest repeatedly enters the earthly sanctuary (ἁγίων, Heb 9:1–3, 8, 25; 13:11) with an animal sacrifice to sanctify (ἁγιάζει, Heb 9:13) or cleanse the flesh in relation to the Mosaic covenant. Such purification offerings cleansed the entryway into the sanctuary.[23] However, in this Mosaic setting, the sanctuary (ἁγίων) must mean something like the place of worship, rather than a banned area, such as the holy of holies, whereas Jesus Christ, as Melchizedek priest, with his new covenant sacrifice, enters the true sanctuary (ἁγίων, Heb 8:2; 9:12, 24) to sanctify (ἁγιάζει, Heb 2:11; 9:13–14; 10:10, 14, 29; 13:12) or cleanse once and for all in a new covenant

---

22. This is a wholistic use of ψυχῆς, analogous to the "whole person;" Kennard, *Critical Realist's Theological Method*, 379–88; Kennard, *Biblical Covenantalism*, 1:245–59.

23. Philo, *Spec. Laws* 1.261; Josephus, *Ant.* 19.332.

manner. Once cleansed, the believer is encouraged to enter the sanctuary (ἁγίων, Heb 10:19). In the context, this new covenant sanctification accomplishes this identification through the cleansing or perfecting of the conscience for those who are Christ's so that they can, in a new-covenant manner, live a life with their own conscience affirming their choices (Heb 9:13–14; 10:10, 14). For those who are Christ's, everlasting forgiveness is obtained in Christ's death (Heb 10:17). This everlasting forgiveness is a community benefit, which after the pattern of the Day of Atonement (Heb 9:7–14) atones for the sin of the people but leaves individual rebellious ones still guilty for their sins if they reject Christ's way. As a community with forgiveness-obtained everlasting and a new covenant-cleansed conscience, they are no longer to offer Mosaic sacrifices (Heb 9:14; 10:2, 16–17, 22), since it would put the Mosaic covenant against the new-covenant cleansing of conscience by reminding them of their sins. The new-covenant cleansed conscience motivates doing what is right internally without distracting externals such as Mosaic sacrifices.

At this point, the author provides a warning of positive exhortations, the negative consequences of apostasy and encouragement about how far they have come. These three are significant because they serve to show the need for continuing when one has such a new-covenant cleansed conscience. The positive exhortations show the way in which such a cleansed conscience should continue. The warning of negative consequences of apostasy develop what will happen for someone who gives up their cleansed conscience and new-covenant benefit to try to return to the Mosaic law. The encouragement reminds them about how far they have come so that they might identify with the new covenant benefits in positive persistent living by faith.

The positive exhortations metaphorically extend Christ's role as priest into his followers by having them (perhaps as priests) enter the holy place (ἁγίων, Heb 10:19) with a cleansed conscience to focus on intrinsic new-covenant motivations worked out through deeds (Heb 10:22–25). The purified conscience, which may have occurred at baptism,[24] provides a non-condemning perspective that needs to be channeled to a positive assurance of faith. This faith often deals with the future, so faith shows itself by holding fast the confession of our hope without wavering. This faith can

---

24. The imagery of Hebrews 10:22 include an allusion to covenant sprinkling in Exodus 24:8, but now it is through the new-covenant heart and conscience. The washing with pure water picks up the Mosaic practice for becoming clean, and may transform it into a once-for-all baptism in new-covenant cleansing (as accomplished in 1 Pet 3:21).

be encouraged because God is faithful, and it needs to work itself out in trying to incite one another to love and good deeds; this means that we need to assemble together in order for such stimulation to occur. However, mere assembling is not the goal, but merely the circumstances for the encouraging of one another to take place. Such encouragement grows in intensity as the day of reckoning is seen to be drawing near.

With the presence of a severe warning of apostasy, there must have been some who began this journey, only to break off assembling together. When believers enter the kingdom, the enemies of God will be consumed by fire (Isa 26:11; Heb 10:27). However, the future day of reckoning has implications back to the present through a terrifying expectation of judgment, like the new-covenant, transformed, conscience-motivating encouragement to love and good deeds. This new-covenant terror works through the conscience, severely warning of judgment consequence to the one who departs this knowledge of the truth by going over the brink of apostasy. Such is guaranteed, for there no longer remains a sacrifice for sins for those who go on sinning willfully (Heb 10:26). The Mosaic covenant gave sacrificial provision for remedying sins of inadvertence (Num 15:30–31); defiant sins against God have no sacrificial provision for forgiveness. Such willful sinning under the Mosaic covenant sets one outside the covenant blessings to receive covenant curse with all its fury. The readership of Hebrews, in following Christ, have stepped outside the Mosaic covenant, in practice by not keeping up with the sacrifices, and more fundamentally because Christ's new covenant arrangement annuls the Mosaic covenant (ἀθέτησις, Heb 7:18). Any Jewish person who annuls or sets aside (ἀθέτησις, Heb 10:28) the law of Moses dies of capital punishment through the testimony of two or three witnesses (LXX Ezek 22:26; Mark 7:9; Heb 10:28).[25] So there is a devastating outcome for these readers if they continue to pursue a return to the Mosaic covenant. They would be condemned to die. They would only have the recourse of throwing themselves upon the mercy of God. However, such willful sinning (Heb 10:26) would violate the avenue through which God's mercy now comes: Christ and the new covenant. Apostates of this sort give up their identification with Christ, for they trample underfoot the

---

25. Also, corporate Israel will suffer under punitive judgment in rebellion (Deut 28:15–68; Isa 1:5–9; Jer 2:1–37; 7:28; Amos 4:8–12; Zeph 3:1–7; Bar 13.1–10; 79.1–4; 2 Macc 5.17; 6.12–16; 7.18, 31–33; 3 Macc 2.13–20; 6.10; Tob 13.2, 5, 10; Pss. Sol. 2.3–7; 10.1–3; T. Mos. 12.10–13; Josephus, *Ant.* 2.293–314; Josephus, *J.W.* 1.656; 5.378, 401–3; 6.110; 7.328–33, 359–60; Philo, *Moses* 1.90–95; 2.53–57; Philo, *Good Person* 34; Philo, *Rewards* 126–62; 1QH; m. ʾAbot 5.8–9; m. Šabb. 2.6; y. Yoma 38a; b. Šabb. 32b; 33a; 55a).

Son of God, their king-priest. In rejecting Christ as their king-priest, they reject the Davidic and new covenants. In rejecting these, they show that they reject the new covenant cleansing of their conscience, their sanctification (Heb 9:13–14; 10:10, 14, 29). However, it was this cleansed conscience that identified them within the community of the forgiven, whereas apostates have given up that community and the mark that identified them with that community. This places the apostates into a place of insulting the Spirit of grace. As we have previously seen, the Holy Spirit is only developed in Hebrews as the source of revelatory message and confirming miraculous powers (Heb 2:4; 3:7; 6:4, with contextual emphasis; 9:8; 10:15). That is, such insult to the Holy Spirit is to reject the Spirit himself and his gift of revelatory message and confirming signs about Christ. The song of Moses as witness warns Israel to keep the Mosaic covenant under threat of curse, with phrases such as "vengeance is Mine, I will repay" and "the Lord will judge His people" (Deut 32:35–36; Heb 10:30). However, as apostates, they exclude themselves from both the Mosaic covenant and the greater new covenant, so they stand without forgiveness, ready for impending wrath. "It is a terrifying thing to fall into the hands of the living God" (Heb 10:31). In the fire of God's wrath, all the earth will be consumed (Jer 4:4; Zeph 1:18; 3:8; Ezek 22:21; 38:19; Pss 11:6; 21:9; 79:5; Matt 3:12; 1 Cor 3:13; Rev 20:9).[26]

In the same manner as in chapter 6, chapter 10 transitions from first and second person to develop the positive exhortation (Heb 10:22–25) to the third person as object of the warnings (Heb 10:26–31). Perhaps the third person is used to soften the accusation to the level of warning: that type of person apostatizes and is damned; will you join them? The use of an occasional first and second person in Hebrews 10:29 and 30 reminds that they know these things. When the encouragement is enjoined, the author returns to the warmth of second- and first-person address (Heb 10:32–39).

Hebrews encourages the readers with virtues from their life that evidences the enduring faith of salvation. The virtuous life begins with enlightenment (φωτισθέντες), an opening of one's mind to the message of Christ and confirming miracles and signs (Heb 10:32; 2:4; 6:4). Such a virtuous awareness is what it takes to endure great sufferings that come. These sufferings included personal tribulations as a public spectacle, such as the seizure of their property, and sympathy and sharing with others who were similarly persecuted (Heb 10:32–35). In such a condition, the readers need to evidence endurance to do the will of God so that they might receive

---

26. 1QS 2.15; 1QH^a 6.18–19; 1QpHab 10.6.15.

what was promised (Heb 10:36). LXX Habakkuk 2:3–4 reminds the reader that God is coming to judge and is pleased only with those righteous ones who live by God's faith(fulness) (quoted in Heb 10:37–38). In the Hebrew of Habakkuk, such "faith" (בֶּאֱמוּנָתוֹ) should be understood as a virtue of "faithfulness," either of God's faithfulness, which we operate within (such as God's covenant faithfulness), or the faithfulness of the human who follows God's narrow covenant way, in contrast to the vices of pride, haughtiness, and selfishness developed in the surrounding context.[27] Francis Anderson develops the idea that, throughout the OT, the use of "faith" (*'mwntw*/ אֱמוּנָתוֹ) as Divine faithfulness is about the same emphasis as instances of human faithfulness, so that he considers both to be live options for the Hebrew MT. However, the LXX identifies the faithfulness in Habakkuk 2:4 as "My faithfulness" (πίστεώς μου); that is, "God's faithfulness," since he is the One speaking.[28] However, Hebrews reframes "faith" as a believer's trust in God (Heb 10:38, in context with Heb 11). The author concludes that "we are not of those who shrink back to destruction, but those who have faithfulness to persevering of the soul" (Heb 10:39). Persevering faithfulness is a virtue that identifies one with salvation in both its trust and consistent practice (both are developed in Heb 11).

HEBREWS 12:3–29

Hebrews 12:3–29 continues the theme of the last warning. Christ sets the pattern for his followers to endure hostility, so that they might not grow weary and lose heart (Heb 12:3). Yet Christ died in this endurance, while his followers should continue, since they have not shed blood in striving against sin (Heb 12:4). Perhaps this "not shedding blood" is an allusion to boxing and wrestling matches,[29] or the fact that the Christians reading the letter are not martyred, as Christ was (Heb 9:14; Phil 2:8; Rev 12:11).[30] Proverbs 3:11–12 exhorts the readers to remember the discipline of the Lord as an expression of the Lord's love (Heb 12:5–6), so that their present

---

27. MT, supported by Mur 88, 4Q12g, 1QpHab, and Greek texts by Rom 1:17, Gal 3:11, Aquila, Theodotion, and Symmachus; Anderson, *Habakkuk*, 212–16; 1 Macc 2.52; Wright, "Paul's Gospel and Caesar's Empire," 170; Gheorghita, *Role of the Septuagint*, 148–224.

28. LXX is supported by *Naḥal Ḥever*; Gheorghita, *Role of the Septuagint*, 148–224.

29. Apollonius of Rhodes, *Argon.* 2.59; Homer, *Il.* 23.683–99; Virgil, *Aen.* 5.470.

30. Herodian, *Hist.* 2.6.14; 2 Macc 13:14; 4 Macc 17:10.

partaking (μέτοχοι, Heb 12:8) of discipline evidences them to be sons of God rather than illegitimate children (Heb 12:7–11). God provided such discipline for Israel to cultivate their maturity during the exodus (Deut 8:2–5), and he continues to provide for the Christian on the narrow way.[31] Though this discipline is painful, we can respect our Father, who brings it about for the purpose of producing peaceful fruit of righteousness, within which we are to live. This peaceful way includes strengthening the weak and making one's path straight (Heb 12:12–13). Peaceful living balances the pursuit of peace with all men and ensuring sanctification, without which no one will see the Lord (Heb 12:14). This implies a personal responsibility for oneself and for others (Heb 12:15). Make sure that no one misses God's gift by perhaps rejecting Christ from "a root of bitterness springing up to cause trouble," like Esau selling off his birthright (Heb 12:15–16; LXX Deut 29:17). Such a rejection places one in Esau's precarious outcome: "he found no place for repentance, though he sought for it with tears" (Heb 12:17). God's judgement through shaking extends from the threatening fire of Mount Sinai to that of an eschatological shaking-and-destroying motif (Heb 12:18–27; Hag 2:6).[32] That which can be shaken is destroyed and removed. Only those things which cannot be shaken may remain. "Therefore, since we receive a kingdom which cannot be shaken, let us show gratitude, by which we may offer to God an acceptable service with reverence and awe; for our God is a consuming fire" (Heb 12:28–29).

CONCLUSION

The warning passages in the book of Hebrews are best seen as addressing a community of Jews identified with Christ through at least the salvific message and corroborative signs. This community has the new-covenant benefits of everlasting forgiveness and cleansed conscience, so that they are to live the life that their cleansed conscience affirms. This walk follows the narrow way of virtues (especially persistent faith, love, and obedience) which show themselves in good deeds of ministry. Those continuing in this

---

31. God provides discipline for Israel to continue to mature them (4 Macc 10.10; 11.20; Wis 3.1–12; 11.1–14; 12.19–22; Sir 2.1–6; 4.17; Josephus, *Ant.* 3.13–16; Philo, *Moses* 1.191–99; Philo, *Providence* 55; Philo, *Prelim. Studies* 157–80; Philo, *Cherubim* 77–82; 4Q504 3; b. Ber. 5a; b. Ḥag. 4b–5a; b. Šabb. 55b). Such discipline continues to mature Christians (Croy surveys the patristics and history of commentaries on this point and passage in *Endurance in Suffering*).

32. 2 Bar. 32.1; 4 Ezra 6.16; 10.26; Sib. Or. 3.675.

way of virtues gain eschatological salvation. In the midst of persecution, individuals who try to return to the Mosaic covenant, departing from the new covenant, put themselves outside of the everlasting forgiveness wrought for Christ's community and are damned by God's wrath. Hebrews' hope and expectation is that readers will pursue the virtues unto eschatological salvation, and its warnings attempt to motivate them to that end.

12

Final Letter Features

LETTER FORMS HAVE STANDARD features in their closing that are found in the closing to the book of Hebrews,[1] namely, final exhortations (Heb 13:1–19, 22–23), final benedictions or blessings (Heb 13:20–21, 25), plan to visit recipients (Heb 13:23), and greetings (Heb 13:24). Such letters often have introductory features (author, recipients, and blessings) but these were absent from the book of Hebrews. However, the final letter-form features identify that, at least in the final written form, it was read by churches as a letter. As such, the book of Hebrews is personal communication, expressing concern and encouragement for the reader's wellbeing.

FINAL EXHORTATION

The final exhortation emphasizes brotherly love of the brethren (Heb 13:1–7). Their brotherly love was already present, so the exhortation is that such love might remain (Heb 13:1). Such a brotherly love (φιλαδελφία) shows a family bond and care within the community.[2]

Such a brotherly love also extends to the care (φιλοξενίας) of strangers (Heb 13:2).[3] In showing this hospitality to strangers, Abraham and Sarah

---

1. O'Brien, "Letters, Letter Forms," 551; Deismann, *Light from the Ancient East*; Francis, "Form and Function," 110–26; Klauck, *Ancient Letters*.

2. Rom 12:10; 1 Thess 4:9; 1 Pet 1:22; 2 Pet 1:7; 4 Macc 13:23, 26; 14:1; Philo, *Embassy* 87.

3. A Christian virtue (Acts 10:23; 28:7; Rom 12:13; 1 Tim 3:2; Titus 1:8; 1 Pet 4:9;

entertained angels without knowing it (Gen 18:1–8; 19:1–14).[4] Others followed with similar generosity (Judg 6:11–18; 13:3–22).[5]

Such brotherly love also extends to care for prisoners and the ill-treated as part of the body of believers (Heb 13:3). The body (σώματι) is a relational concept that includes physical presence with others. Care for prisoners would, at times, mean that others stayed in prison with the prisoner.[6] Ill-treatment includes these prisoners, as well as many from the list of witnesses, including those in Egypt (Heb 11:25), as well as Maccabean martyrs (Heb 11:37).

Honor marriage excluded all fornication and adultery because God will judge (Heb 13:4). Intercourse outside of marriage was considered to be defiling, among both Jews and Christians (Heb 13:4; Gen 49:4; Mark 7:21–22; 1 Cor 5:1, 9–11; 6:9; 7:14; Eph 5:5; 1 Tim 1:10; Rev 21:8; 22:15),[7] but broadly common in society.[8] The concept of "defilement" shows that Jews and Christians understand marriage within a covenantal strategy, including Jesus as our priest. As a consequence, God eschatologically judges such sins of immorality (Heb 13:4; 12:16; 1 Cor 6:9–11; Eph 5:5).

Be content with God's presence in life rather than pursuing love of money (Heb 13:5–6). God's promise in Deuteronomy 31:6, Joshua 1:5, and Psalms 118:6, and the divine presence undergirding this promise, shows the absurdity of pursuing the counterfeit love for money.

These final exhortations framed within two-way salvation emphasized a final warning concerning apostasy expounded in a previous chapter (Heb 13:7–16). Instead, the goal is to cultivate gratitude and godly fear.

A final exhortation is to obey your leaders, submitting to them because they keep watch over your souls (Heb 13:17). These community leaders left an example of faith to emulate and obey (Heb 11:2–12:3). Such obedience frames the relationship within joy and personal profitability, rather than grief (Heb 13:17).

Occasionally, prayer joins the final exhortations of Christian letters (Heb 13:18–19; Eph 6:18–20; 1 Thess 5:17; James 5:13–18; 1 Pet 5:7). Pray

---

Did. 12:1–2) which continues a Jewish virtue (Gen 18:1–8; 19:1–3; Judg 19:19–21; Job 31:32; T. Zeb. 6.4–5).

4. Philo, *Abraham* 107, 113; Josephus, *Ant.* 1.196.

5. Tob 3.17; 5.4–16; 12:1–20.

6. Lucian, *Peregr.* 12; Lucian, *Tox.* 32.

7. Wis 14:24; T. Reu. 1.6; Josephus, *Ant.* 2.55; 1 Clem. 2.1.

8. *Odes*, 3.6.17–32; Juvenal, *Sat.* 2.29.

for us as leaders who have a new-covenant conscience,[9] that we might continue with honorable conduct and be restored[10] to them sooner (Heb 13:18–19). In Hebrews 13:19 and 22, the author shifts to a more personal singular[11] reference of himself in need of restoration and desirous of coming with Timothy. By this grammatical shift, the author strengthens the connection he has with his readers.

The author calls the whole book "brief"[12] to encourage the readers to heed and not be annoyed with these "exhortations" (Heb 13:22). "Exhortation" is used in Jewish and Christian settings to promote faithfulness, comfort, and admonition (Heb 13:22; Rom 15:4; 2 Cor 1:3–7; Acts 15:3).[13]

FINAL BENEDICTIONS OR BLESSINGS

The final benediction comes as normal, not at the complete end of the book (Heb 13:20–21). The concept of peace is most evident in peace offerings requesting a restored relationship from God (Lev 3:1–6; 7:11–34; Ezek 46:2–12) and the prophetic promise of God's recovery of his people, regathering them into the kingdom (Isa 9:6–7; 54:10, 13; 57:2; 60:17; 66:12). The benediction praises the God of peace for resurrecting our Lord Jesus to be the Great Shepherd of the sheep (Heb 13:20). Jesus initiated atonement and the new covenant in his "blood of the covenant" after the pattern of Moses, initiating the Mosaic covenant and efficacy of the tabernacle (Exod 24:8; Heb 9:19–21; 10:24; 13:20). Both are tabernacle initiation (for earthly or heavenly tabernacles) and inclusion within the community (Israel or believers in Christ) by cleansing to bind the divine covenant (Mosaic or new covenants) upon the corporate community. Such a covenant blessing of the "blood of the covenant" remains with Israel as a marker that God is faithful to his governing Mosaic covenant, having Zechariah remind Israel that he will rescue them from captivity because of this "blood of the covenant"

---

9. New-covenant grounded conscience (Heb 9:9; 10:2; 1 Pet 3:16; Acts 23:1; 24:16; 1 Tim 1:19).

10. Maybe released from prison for restoration to occur (P. Oxy. 38.12; Phlm 22).

11. Apart from these two references and an authorship statement in Hebrews 11:32, the author includes themselves within plural "we" statements elsewhere in the book.

12. Some other authors call their works "brief," even though their books are longer than Hebrews (2 Macc 2:31–32; Barn. 1.5), so this comment does not merely apply to chapter 13.

13. 1 Macc 10:24; 2 Macc 7:24; 15:11.

(Zech 9:11). In a similar manner, rabbis use the same phrase, "blood of the covenant," to reassure Israelites that they are included within the combined Abrahamic and Mosaic covenants, and thus within its blessings, because of their circumcision as a baby or at conversion.[14] Hebrews indicated that Jesus Christ's atoning blood functions in a similar manner as an initiating "blood of the covenant" to mark the beginning and continued blessing believers are in because Jesus initiated the everlasting new covenant to include them (Heb 9:20; 10:24; 13:20). Praise of the God of peace continues as he equips Christians to do good and what is pleasing to Christ through the blood of the everlasting new-covenant atonement (Heb 13:20–21; Isa 53:5). This obedient consistency within a kingdom life of peace is accomplished through Jesus Christ, who should receive everlasting glory in this accomplishment (Heb 13:21).

A final blessing concludes with a prayerful blessing: "Grace be with you all" (Heb 13:25). This is a short prayer for God's generosity to be broadly dispersed to the whole community.

PLAN TO VISIT

The author plans to visit the readers with Timothy, who has been released from either jail or ministry (Heb 13:23). It is clear that the readers had some familiarity with Timothy, so he might have ministered there previously. The fact that there is no biblical record of Timothy having a prolonged imprisonment and the only prolonged ministry in the biblical text was in Ephesus (1 Tim 1:3; Acts 18:19), may indicate that the letter is written after Paul's letters to a region where Timothy had ministered, maybe even after Paul's death.

GREETINGS

The author greets the reader's leaders and all who have been sanctified to become saints by Christ's sacrifice (Heb 13:24). An additional group from Italy greet the readers, probably indicating that the author writes from somewhere other than Italy, since there are those with him who have come from (ἀπὸ) Italy.[15] There is too little evidence here to indicate the initial re-

---

14. m. Sipra 123.1.8a; m. Pes. 8.8; Instone-Brewer, *Traditions of the Rabbis*, 57–58.

15. ἀπὸ usually indicates "from," as in no longer in Italy (Matt 21:11; Mark 15:43; John

cipients. Perhaps not having the introductory features of a letter makes the book more universal for any Jewish Christians to consider their absolute need to continue faithfully following Christ.

1:44; 21:2; Acts 6:9; 21:27; 24:18).

Bibliography

Abraham, William J. "Epistemology of Jesus: An Initial Investigation." In *Jesus and Philosophy*, edited by Paul Moser, 149–68. New York: Cambridge University Press, 2008.
Albrektson, Bertil. "A Disputed Sense in a Covenant Context: On the Interpretation of Genesis 15:6." In *Covenant as Context: Essays in Honour of E. W. Nicholson*, edited by A. D. H. Mayes and R. B. Salters, 1–9. Oxford: Oxford University Press, 2003.
Allen, David. "The Lukan Authorship of Hebrews: A Proposal." *Journal of Translation and Textlinguistics* 8 (1996) 1–22.
Allen, Leslie. *Psalms 101–150*. Waco: Word Books, 1983.
Anderson, Francis. *Habakkuk*. New York: Doubleday, 2001.
Archer, Gleason. *The Epistle to the Hebrews*. Grand Rapids: Baker, 1957.
Attridge, Harold W. *The Epistle to the Hebrews: A Commentary on the Epistle to the Hebrews*. Philadelphia: Fortress, 1989.
———. "God in Hebrews." In *The Epistle to the Hebrews and Christian Theology*, edited by Richard Bauckham et al., 95–110. Grand Rapids: Eerdmans, 2009.
———. "'Let Us Strive to Enter That Rest': The Logic of Hebrews 4:1–11." *Harvard Theological Review* 73 (1980) 279–88.
Averbeck, Richard E. "כָּפַר." In *NIDOTTE* 2:689–710.
Balentine, Samuel. *Leviticus: Interpretation*. Louisville: Westminster John Knox, 2002.
Baltzer, K. *Das Bundesformular: Seine Ursprung und Seine Verwendung im AT*. WMANT 4. Neukirchen-Vluyn: Neukirchen, 1960.
Barber, Michael P. "A Catholic Perspective: Our Works are Meritorious at the Final Judgment Because of our Union with Christ by Grace." In *Four Views on the Role of Works at the Final Judgment*, edited by Alan Stanley and Robert Wilkin, 161–84. Grand Rapids: Zondervan, 2013.
Barr, James. *The Semantics of Biblical Language*. London: Oxford University Press, 1961.
Barth, Karl. Church Dogmatics. Translated by G. T. Thomson et al. Edinburgh: T. & T. Clark, 1936–1977.
Barthélemy, Dominique, and Joseph Milik, eds. *Discoveries in the Judaean Desert, Vol. 5*. Oxford: Clarendon Press, 1955.
Bateman, Herbert W., IV. *Early Jewish Hermeneutics and Hebrews 1:5–13: The Impact of Early Jewish Exegesis on the Interpretation of a Significant New Testament Passage*. New York: Lang, 1997.
———. *Four Views on the Warning Passages in Hebrews*. Grand Rapids: Kregel, 2007.
Bauckham, Richard. *Jesus and the Eyewitnesses: The Gospels as Eyewitness Testimony*. Grand Rapids: Eerdmans, 2006.

Bibliography

Bauckham, Richard, et al. *A Cloud of Witnesses: The Theology of Hebrews in its Ancient Contexts*. Edinburgh: T. & T. Clark, 2008.

———. *The Epistle to the Hebrews and Christian Theology*. Grand Rapids: Eerdmans, 2009.

Bauer, Walter, et al., eds. *Greek-English Lexicon of the New Testament and Other Early Christian Literature*. Chicago: University of Chicago Press, 1957.

Bauernfeind, Otto. "ἐντυγχανω." In *TDNT* 8:242–45.

Behm, Johannes. "ἐσθίω." In *TDNT* 2:689–95.

Bellinger, William, and William R. Farmer, eds. *Jesus and the Suffering Servant: Isaiah 53 and Christian Origins*. Atlanta: Trinity, 1998.

Berlin-Brandenburgische Akademie der Wissenschaften. *Die griechische Schriftsteller der ersten Jahrhunderte*. Berlin: Akademie Verlag, 1899.

Betz, Otto. "Jesus and Isaiah 53." In *Jesus and the Suffering Servant: Isaiah 53 and Christian Origins*, edited by William Bellinger and William R. Farmer, 170–92. Atlanta: Trinity, 1998.

Biblia Patristics: Index des citation et allusions bibliques dans la litterérature patristique. Paris: Éditions du Centre national de la recherché scientifique, 1975.

Bietenhard, Hans. "Lord, Master." In *DNTT* 2:508–20.

Blaising, Craig A. "Gethsemane a Prayer of Faith." *Journal of the Evangelical Theological Society* 22 (1979) 333–43.

Bleek, Friedrich. *Der Brief an die Hebräer*. 2 vols. Berlin: Dümmlern, 1838/1840.

Bloch, Renee. "Midrash." In *Approaches to Ancient Judaism: Theory and Practice, Vol. 1*, edited by William Scott Green, 29–50. Callaway: Scholars Press, 1978.

Bock, Darrell. *Proclamation from Prophecy and Pattern: Lucan Old Testament Christology*. Sheffield: JSOT Press, 1987.

Boda, Mark J. *A Severe Mercy: Sin and its Remedy in the Old Testament*. Winona Lake: Eisenbrauns, 2009.

Bornkamm, Günther. "Das Bekenntnis im Hebräerbrief." *Theologische Blätter* 21 (1942) 56–66.

Botterweck, G. Johannes, and Helmer Ringgren, eds. *Theological Dictionary of the Old Testament*. Translated by Geoffrey W. Bromiley et al. 14 vols. Grand Rapids: Eerdmans, 1974–2004.

Bray, Gerald. *Romans*. Downers Grove: InterVarsity, 1998.

Brichto, Herbert Chanan. "On Slaughter and Sacrifice, Blood and Atonement." *Hebrew Union College Annual* 47 (1976) 19–55.

Bruce, F. F. *The Epistle to the Hebrews*. Grand Rapids: Eerdmans, 1964.

Brueggeman, Walter. *A Pathway of Interpretation: The Old Testament for Pastors and Students*. Eugene: Cascade, 2008.

Buchanan, George. *To the Hebrews*. Garden City: Doubleday, 1972.

Bunyan, John. *The Pilgrim's Progress from this World to that World to that Which is to Come*. Edinburgh: Banner of Truth Trust, 1895.

Calvin, John. *Calvin's Commentary, Vol. 22: Hebrews, 1 John, 1 Peter, James, 2 Peter, Jude*. Grand Rapids: Baker, 1979.

———. *Institutes of the Christian Religion*. Philadelphia: Presbyterian Board of Christian Education, 1936.

Catechism of the Catholic Church. Vatican: Libreria Editrice Vaticana, 1997.

Charlesworth, James. *Old Testament Pseudepigrapha*. 2 vols. Garden City: Doubleday, 1985.

Bibliography

Chernus, Ira. "Visions of God in Merkabah Mysticism." *Journal for the Study of Judaism* 13 (1982) 123–46.

Chilton, Bruce, and Jacob Neusner. *Classical Christianity and Rabbinic Judaism: Comparing Theologies*. Grand Rapids: Baker, 2004.

Chrysostom, John. "Hom. Act." In *Patrologia Graeca, Vol. 48*. Edited by P. Migne. Seu Petit: Montrouge, 1859.

Cockerill, Gareth L. *The Epistle to the Hebrews*. Grand Rapids: Eerdmans, 2012.

———. "Hebrews 1:6: Source and Significance." *Bulletin for Biblical Research* 9 (1999) 51–64.

———. *Melchizedek Christology in Heb. 7:1–28*. Ann Arbor: University Microfilms International, 1979.

———. "A Wesleyan Arminian View." In *Four Views on the Warning Passages in Hebrews*, edited by Herbert W. Bateman IV, 257–92. Grand Rapids: Kregel, 2007.

Cody, Aelred. *Heavenly Sanctuary and Liturgy in the Epistle to the Hebrews: The Achievement of Salvation in the Epistle's Perspectives*. St. Meinrad, IN: Grail, 1960.

Collins, John. *Scepter and Star: The Messiahs of the Dead Sea Scrolls and Other Ancient Literature*. New York: Doubleday, 1995.

Combrink, H. J. B. "Some Thoughts on the Old Testament Citations in the Epistle to the Hebrews." *Neotestamentica* 5 (1971) 22–36.

Cosby, M. R. *The Rhetorical Composition and Function of Hebrews 11: In Light of Example Lists in Antiquity*. Macon: Mercer University Press, 1988.

———. "The Rhetorical Composition of Hebrews 11." *Journal of Biblical Literature* 107 (1988) 257–73.

Cragie, Peter. *Psalms 1–50*. Dallas: Word, 1983.

Cranfield, C. E. B. *A Critical and Exegetical Commentary on the Epistle to the Romans*. 2 vols. Edinburgh: T. & T. Clark, 1975 and 1979.

Crenshaw, James L., and Samuel Sandmel, eds. *The Divine Helmsman: Studies on God's Control of Human Events, Presented to Lou H. Silberman*. New York: KTAV, 1980.

Croy, N. Clayton. *Endurance in Suffering: Hebrews 12:1–13 in its Rhetorical, Religious, and Philosophical Context*. Cambridge: Cambridge University Press, 1998.

Cullmann, Oscar. *The Christology of the New Testament*. London: SCM, 1963.

Dabney, D. Lyle. "'Justified by the Spirit': Soteriological Reflections on the Resurrection." *International Journal of Systematic Theology* 3.1 (March 2001) 46–68.

Daly, Robert J. "The Soteriological Significant of the Sacrifice of Isaac." *Catholic Biblical Quarterly* 39 (January 1977) 45–75.

D'Angelo, Mary Rose. *Moses and the Letter to the Hebrews*. Missoula: Scholars, 1979.

Das, Andrew. *Paul, the Law and the Covenant*. Peabody: Hendrickson, 2001.

Davidson, Andrew B. *The Theology of the Old Testament*. Edinburgh: T. & T. Clark, 1904.

Dean-Otting, Mary. *Heavenly Journeys: A Study of the Motif in Hellenistic Jewish Literature*. New York: Lang, 1984.

Deismann, Adolf. *Light from the Ancient East: The New Testament Illustrated by Recently Discovered Texts of Graeco-Roman World*. Translated by Lionel Strachan. New York: Darron, 1927.

Delcor, M. "Melchizedek from Genesis to the Qumran Texts and the Epistle to the Hebrews." *Journal for the Study of Judaism* 2 (1971) 115–35.

Demarest, Bruce. "Hebrews 7:3, A Crux *Interpretum* Historically Considered." *Evangelical Q* 49 (1977) 141–62.

Bibliography

de Roo, Jacqueline C. R. "God's Covenant with the Forefathers." In *The Concept of the Covenant in the Second Temple Period*, edited by Stanley Porter and Jacqueline C. R. de Roo, 191–202. Leiden: Brill, 2003.

deSilva, David Arthur. *Despising Shame: Honor Discourse and Community Maintenance in the Epistle to the Hebrews*. Society of Biblical Literature Dissertation Series 152. Atlanta: Scholars, 1995.

———. *Perseverance in Gratitude: A Socio-Rhetorical Commentary on the Epistle "to the Hebrews."* Grand Rapids: Eerdmans, 2000.

Dey, Lala Kalyan Kumar. *The Intermediary World and Patterns of Perfection in Philo and Hebrews*. Society of Biblical Literature Dissertation Series 25. Missoula: Scholars, 1975.

Dillow, Joseph. *The Reign of the Servant Kings: A Study of Eternal Security and Final Significance of Man*. Miami Springs: Schoettle, 1992.

Domeris, William, and Cornelis Van Dam. "3983 כלה." In *NIDOTT & E* 2:641.

Dunham, Duane. "An Exegetical Examination of the Warnings in the Epistle to the Hebrews." ThD diss., Grace Theological Seminary, 1974.

Dunn, James D. G. *Christianity in the Making, Vol. 1: Jesus Remembered*. Grand Rapids: Eerdmans, 2003.

———. *Christology in the Making: A New Testament Inquiry into the Origins of the Doctrine of the Incarnation*. 2nd ed. Grand Rapids: Eerdmans, 1996.

———. "If Paul Could Believe both in Justification by Faith and Judgment According to Works, Why Should That be a Problem for Us?" In *Four Views on the Role of Works at the Final Judgment*, edited by Alan Stanley and Robert Wilkin, 119–41. Grand Rapids: Zondervan, 2013.

———. *The New Perspective on Paul*. Rev. ed. Grand Rapids: Eerdmans, 2007.

———. "Response to Thomas Schreiner." In *Four Views on the Role of Works at the Final Judgment*, edited by Alan Stanley and Robert Wilkin, 105–110. Grand Rapids: Zondervan, 2013.

———. *Romans 1–8*. Word Biblical Commentary 38A. Dallas: Word, 1988.

———. *Romans 9–16*. Word Biblical Commentary 38B. Dallas: Word, 1988.

———. *Unity and Diversity in the New Testament*. London: SCM, 1977.

Eaton, Michael. *The Theology of Encouragement*. Carlisle: Paternoster, 1995.

Edwards, Jonathan. *Freedom of the Will*. New Haven: Yale University Press, 1957.

———. *A Treatise Concerning Religious Affections*. New Haven: Yale University Press, 1959.

Eisenbaum, Pamela. "Heroes and History in Hebrews 11." In *Early Christian Interpretation of the Scriptures of Israel: Investigations and Proposals*, edited by C. Evans and J. A. Sanders, 380–96. Sheffield: Sheffield Academic, 1997.

———. *The Jewish Heroes of Christian History: Hebrews 11 in Literary Context*. Atlanta: Scholars, 1997.

Elliger, Karl. *Leviticus*. HAT 4. Tübingen: Mohr, 1966.

Ellingworth, Paul. "The Old Testament in Hebrews: Exegesis, Method and Hermeneutics." PhD diss., University of Aberdeen, 1978.

Elliott, Neil. "Asceticism among the 'Weak' and 'Strong' in Romans 14–15." In *Asceticism and the New Testament*, edited by L. E. Vaage and V. L. Wimbush, 231–51. London: Taylor and Francis, 2002.

Ellis, E. E. "Midrash, Targum and New Testament Quotations." In *Neotestamentica et Semitica*, edited by E. E. Ellis and M. Wilcox, 61–69. Edinburgh: Clark, 1969.

Bibliography

Evans, Craig A. "Covenant in the Qumran Literature." In *The Concept of the Covenant in the Second Temple Period*, edited by Stanley Porter and Jacqueline C. R. de Roo, 55–80. Leiden: Brill, 2003.

Fanning, Buist M. "A Classical Reformed View." In *Four Views on the Warning Passages in Hebrews*, edited by Herbert W. Bateman IV, 172–219. Grand Rapids: Kregel, 2007.

Feder, Yitzhaq. "On *kuppuru, kippēr* and Etymological Sins that Cannot be Wiped Away." *Vetus Testamentum* 60 (2010) 535–45.

Filium, C. Gerold, ed. *Corpus Scriptorum Ecclesiasticorum Latinorum, Vol. 3c*. New York: Johnson, 1972.

Finlan, Stephen. *The Background and Content of Paul's Cultic Atonement Metaphors*. Leiden: Brill, 2004.

Fisher, John. "Covenant, Fulfilment and Judaism in Hebrews." *Evangelical Review of Theology* 13:2 (1989) 175–87.

Fitzmyer, Joseph A. *The Genesis Apocryphon of Qumran Cave 1: A Commentary Biblica et Orientalia 1*. Rome: Pontifical Institute, 1966.

———. *The Gospel According to Luke X-XXIV: Introduction, Translation, and Notes*. Anchor Bible 28A. New York: Doubleday, 1985.

Ford, David F. "Paul Ricoeur: A Biblical Philosopher on Jesus." In *Jesus and Philosophy*, edited by Paul Moser, 169–93. New York: Cambridge University Press, 2009.

Francis, Fred. "The Form and Function of the Opening and Closing Paragraphs of James and 1 John." *Zeitschrift für die neutestamentliche Wissenschaft und die Kunde des Urchristentums* 61 (1970) 110–26.

Freedman, David Noel, and David Miano. "People of the New Covenant." In *The Concept of the Covenant in the Second Temple Period*, edited by Porter and Jacqueline C. R. de Roo, 7–26. Leiden: Brill, 2003.

Gammie, John. *Holiness in Israel*. Minneapolis: Fortress, 1989.

Gane, Roy. *Cult and Character: Purification Offerings, Day of Atonement, and Theodicy*. Winona Lake: Eisenbrauns, 2005.

———. "Privative Preposition מִן in Purification Offering Pericopes and the Changing Face of 'Dorian Gray.'" *Journal of Biblical Literature* 127 (2008) 209–22.

Gaon. *Iggeret Rav Sherira Gaon*. Berlin: Kehot, 1566.

Garland, David. "The Temple Tax in Matthew 17:24–25 and the Principle of not Causing Offense" In *Treasures New and Old: Recent Contributions to Matthean Studies*, edited by David Bauer and Mark Allan Powell, 69–98. Society of Biblical Literature Symposium Series 1. Atlanta: Scholars, 1996.

Gathercole, Simon. "Torah, Life, and Salvation: Leviticus 18:5 in Early Judaism and the New Testament." In *From Prophecy to Testament: The Function of the Old Testament in the New*, edited by Craig Evans, 126–39. Peabody: Hendricson, 2004.

Gese, Hartmut. "Die Sühne." In *Zur biblischen Theologie Alttestamentliche Vorträge*, 85–106. Munich: Verlag, 1977.

———. *Essays on Biblical Theology*. Minneapolis: Fortress, 1981.

Gheorghita, Radu. *The Role of the Septuagint in Hebrews: An Investigation of its Influence with Special Consideration to the Use of Hab 2:3–4 in Heb 10:37–38*. Tübingen: Mohr Siebeck, 2003.

Gieschen, J. Charles A. "The Different Functions of a Similar Melchizedek Tradition in 2 Enoch and the Epistle of Hebrews" In *Early Christian Interpretation of the Scriptures of Israel: Investigations and Proposals*, edited by Craig Evans and James Sanders, 364–79. Journal for the Study of the New Testament Supplement Series 148. Studies in Scripture in Early Judaism and Christianity 5. Sheffield: Sheffield Academic Press, 1997.

Gleason, Randall C. "A Moderate Reformed View." In *Four Views on the Warning Passages in Hebrews*, edited by Herbert W. Bateman IV, 336–77. Grand Rapids: Kregel, 2007.

———. "The Old Testament Background of the Warning in Hebrews 6:4–8." *BibSac* 155 (1998) 62–91.

Godet, Frederic. *Commentary on Romans*. Grand Rapids: Kregel, 1977.

Gordon, Robert P. "Better Promises: Two Passages in Hebrews against the Background of the Old Testament Cultus." In *Templum Amicitiae: Essays on the Second Temple Presented to Ernst Bammel*, edited by William Horbury, 434–49. Sheffield: Sheffield Academic Press, 1991.

Gräßer, Erich. "Der Hebräerbrief, 1938–63." *Theologische Rundschau* 30 (1964–1965) 138–236.

Greer, Rowan. *The Captain of Our Salvation: A Study in the Patristic Exegesis of Hebrews*. Tübingen: Mohr Siebeck, 1975.

Grindheim, Sigurd. "Ignorance is Bliss: Attitudinal Aspects of the Judgment according to Works in Matthew 25:31–46." *Novum Testamentum* 50 (2008) 313–31.

Gromacki, Robert. *Stand Bold in Grace*. Grand Rapids: Baker, 1984.

Gruenwald, Itamar. *Apocalyptic and Merkavah Mysticism*. Leiden: Brill, 1980.

Gubler, Marie-Louise. *Die Frühesten Deutungen des Todes Jesu: Eine motifgeschichtliche Darstellung aufrung der neuen exegetischen Forschung*. Orbis Biblicus et Orientalis 15. Freiburg: Universtatsverlag, 1977.

Gundry, Robert. *Mark: A Commentary on His Apology for the Cross*. Grand Rapids: Eerdmans, 1993.

Gurney, O. R. *Some Aspects of Hittite Religion*. London: Oxford University, 1977.

Guthrie, Donald. *The Letter to the Hebrews*. Downers Grove: InterVarsity, 1983.

Hagen, Kenneth. *A Theology of Testament in the Young Luther: The Lectures on Hebrews*. Leiden: Brill, 1974.

Hallo, William, ed. *The Context of Scripture, Vol. 3: Archival Documents from the Biblical World*. Leiden: Brill, 2003.

Harris, Murray. *Jesus as God: The New Testament Use of Theos in Reference to Jesus*. Grand Rapids: Baker, 1992.

Hawthorne, Gerald, et al. *Dictionary of Paul and His Letters*. Downers Grove: InterVarsity, 1993.

Hayman, A. P. "The Image of the Jew in the Syriac Anti-Jewish Polemical Literature." In *"To See Ourselves as Others See Us": Christian, Jews, "Others" in Late Antiquity*, edited by Jacob Neusner and Ernest S. Frerichs, 423–41. Chico: Scholar, 1986.

Hays, Richard B. *Echoes of Scripture in the Letters of Paul*. New Haven: Yale University Press, 2016.

———. "'Here We Have No Lasting City': New Covenantalism in Hebrews." In *The Epistle to the Hebrews and Christian Theology*, edited by Richard Bauckham et al., 151–73. Grand Rapids: Eerdmans, 2009.

Hayward, Robert. "Shem, Melchizedek, and Concern with Christianity in the Pentateuchal Targumim." In *Targumic and Cognate Studies*, edited by David J. A. Clines and Philip R. Davies, 67–80. Journal for the Study of the Old Testament Supplement Series 230. Sheffield: Sheffield Academic Press, 1996.

Hefele, Karl Joseph Von, et al. *Histoire des conciles d'après les documents originaux*. Paris: Rue des Saints-Peres, 1907.

Bibliography

Hellerman, Joseph. "Purity and Nationalism in Second Temple Literature: *1–2 Maccabees* and *Jubilees.*" *Journal of the Evangelical Theological Society* 46 (2003) 401–21.

Helm, Robert. "Azazel in Early Jewish Tradition." *Andrews University Seminary Studies* 32:3 (1999) 217–26.

Hengel, Martin. *The Son of God: The Origin of Christology and the History of Jewish-Hellenistic Religion*. London: SCM, 1976.

Hengel, Martin, and Daniel P. Bailey. "The Effective History of Isaiah 53 in the Pre-Christian Period." In *The Suffering Servant: Isaiah 53 in Jewish and Christian Sources*, edited by Bernd Janowski and Peter Stuhlmacher, 75–146. Grand Rapids: Eerdmans, 2004.

Henninger, Joseph. *Sanctus Augustinus et doctrina de duplici iustitia*. Mödling: Typus Domus Missionum ad Sanctum Gabrielem, 1935.

Hermann, Johannes. *Die Idee der Sühne im Alten Testament: eine Utersuchung über Gebrauch und Bedeutung des Wortes kipper*. Leipzig: Hinrichs, 1905.

———. "ἱλάσκομαι, ἱλασμός." In *TDNT* 3:301–10.

Hewett, Thomas. *The Epistle to the Hebrews*. London: Tyndale, 1960.

Hiecke, Thomas, and Tobias Nicklas. *The Day of Atonement: Its Interpretation in Early Jewish and Christian Traditions*. Leiden: Brill, 2012.

Hofius, Otfried. *Der Christushymnus Philipper 2.6–11: Untersuchungen zu Gestalt und Aussage eines unchristlichen Psalms*. Tübingen: Mohr, 1976.

———. *KATAPAUSIS: Die Vorstellung vom endzeitlichen Ruheort im Hebräerbrief*. Tübingen: Mohr Siebeck, 1970.

Hoffner, Harry A., Jr. "Hittite-Israelite Cultural Parallels." In *The Context of Scripture, Vol. 3: Archival Documents from the Biblical World*, edited by William Hallo, xxix–xxxiv. Leiden: Brill, 2003.

Holladay, Carl. *Theios Aner in Hellenistic Judaism: A Critique of the Use of this Category in N.T. Christology*. Society of Biblical Literature Dissertation Series 40. Missoula: Scholars, 1977.

Hollander, Harm, and Marinus de Jonge. *Testaments of the Twelve Patriarchs*. Leiden: Brill, 1985.

Hooker, Morna. *Jesus and the Servant: The Influence of the Servant Concept of Deutero-Isaiah in the New Testament*. London: SPCK, 1959.

Horbury, William. *Templum Amicitiae: Essays on the Second Temple Presented to Ernst Bammel*. Sheffield: Sheffield Academic Press, 1991.

Horsley, Richard, ed. *Paul and Politics: Ekklesia, Israel Imperium Interpretation: Essays in Honor of Krister Stendahl*. Harrisburg: Trinity Press International, 2000.

Horton, Fred L., Jr. *The Melchizedek Tradition: A Critical Examination of the Sources to the Fifth Century A.D. and in the Epistle to the Hebrews*. Society for New Testament Studies Monograph. Cambridge: Cambridge University Press, 2011.

Howard, George. "Hebrews and the Old Testament Quotations." *Novum Testamentum* 10 (1968) 208–16.

Hübner, Hans. *The Law in Paul's Thought*. Edinburgh: T. & T. Clark, 1984.

Hughes, Philip Edgcumbe. *A Commentary on the Epistle to the Hebrews*. Grand Rapids: Eerdmans, 1977.

Hurst, L. D. *The Epistle to the Hebrews: Its Background of Thought*. Cambridge: Cambridge University Press, 1990.

———. "How 'Platonic' Are Heb. viii.5 and ix.23f?" *Journal of Theological Studies* 34 (1983) 156–68.

BIBLIOGRAPHY

Instone-Brewer, David. *Traditions of the Rabbis from the Era of the New Testament, Vol. 2A: Feasts and Sabbaths: Passover and Atonement.* Grand Rapids: Eerdmans, 2011.

Isaacs, Marie. *Sacred Space: An Approach to the Theology of the Epistle to the Hebrews.* Sheffield: Sheffield Academic Press, 1992.

Janowski, Bernd. *Sühne als Heilsgeschehen: Studien zur Sühnetheologie der Priesterschrift und zur Wurzel KPR im Alten Testament.* Neukirchen-Vluyn: Neukirchener Verlag, 1982.

Janowski, Bernd, and Peter Stuhlmacher, eds. *The Suffering Servant: Isaiah 53 in Jewish and Christian Sources.* Grand Rapids: Eerdmans, 2004.

Jenson, Robert. *America's Theologian.* New York: Oxford University Press, 1988.

Jeremias, Joachim. *Neotestamentliche Theologie.* Gütersloh: Gütersloher Verlagshaus, 1971.

Johnson, William G. *Defilement and Purgation in the Book of Hebrews.* Ann Arbor: University Microfilms, 1973.

———. "The Pilgrimage Motif in the Book of Hebrews." *Journal of Biblical Literature* 97 (1978) 239–51.

Joslin, Barry C. "Hebrews 7–10 and the Transformation of the Law." In *A Cloud of Witnesses: The Theology of Hebrews in its Ancient Contexts*, edited by Richard Bauckham et al., 100–117. Edinburgh: T. & T. Clark, 2008.

———. *Hebrews, Christ, and the Law: The Theology of the Mosaic Law in Hebrews 7:1–10:18.* Eugene: Wipf & Stock, 2009.

Juel, Donald. *Messianic Exegesis: Christological Interpretation of the Old Testament in Early Christianity.* Philadelphia: Fortress, 1988.

Kaiser, Walter. "Leviticus." In *The New Interpreter's Bible: Genesis to Leviticus, Vol. 1*, 983–1191. Nashville: Abingdon, 1994.

Käsemann, Ernst. *The Wandering People of God: An Investigation of the Letter to the Hebrews.* Minneapolis: Augsburg, 1984.

Kautzsch, E., ed. *Gesenius' Hebrew Grammar.* Translated by A. E. Cowley. Oxford: Clarendon, 1976.

Keck, Leander E. "The Law and 'the Law of Sin and Death' (Rom 8:1–4): Reflection on the Spirit and Ethics in Paul." In *The Divine Helmsman: Studies on God's Control of Human Events, Presented to Lou H. Silberman*, edited by James L. Crenshaw and Samuel Sandmel, 41–58. New York: KTAV, 1980.

Keener, Craig. *Miracles: The Credibility of the New Testament Accounts.* Grand Rapids: Baker, 2011.

Kelber, Werner H. "The Case of the Gospels: Memory's Desire and the Limits of Historical Criticism." *Oral Tradition* 17 (2002) 55–86.

Kendall, R. T. *Calvin and English Calvinism to 1649.* Oxford Theological Monographs. Oxford: Oxford University Press, 1979.

———. *Once Saved, Always Saved.* Chicago: Moody, 1983.

Kennard, Douglas. *Biblical Covenantalism: Engagement with Judaism, Law, Atonement, the New Perspective, and Kingdom Hope: Vol. 1, Biblical Covenantalism in Torah: Judaism, Covenant Nomism, and Atonement.* Eugene: Wipf & Stock, 2015.

———. *Biblical Covenantalism: Engaging the New Perspective and New Covenant Atonement: Vol. 3, Biblical Covenantalism in New Testament Epistles.* Eugene: Wipf & Stock, 2015.

———. *Biblical Covenantalism: In Prophets, Psalms, Early Judaism, Gospels, and Acts: Vol. 2, Judaism, Covenant Nomism, and Kingdom Hope.* Eugene: Wipf & Stock, 2015.

BIBLIOGRAPHY

———. *A Critical Realist's Theological Method: Returning the Bible and Biblical Theology to be the Framer for Theology and Science*. Eugene: Wipf & Stock, 2013.

———. "Epistemology and Logic of the Apostle Paul." In *Epistemology and Logic in the New Testament: Early Jewish Context and Biblical Theology Mechanisms that Fit Within Some Contemporary Ways of Knowing*, 128–62. Eugene: Wipf & Stock, 2016.

———. *The Gospel*. Eugene: Wipf & Stock, 2017.

———. "Hebrews Epistemology of Prophecy as Rhetorical Proclamation that Christ is Supreme." In *Epistemology and Logic in the New Testament: Early Jewish Context and Biblical Theology Mechanisms that Fit Within Some Contemporary Ways of Knowing*, 215–21. Eugene: Wipf & Stock, 2016.

———. *Messiah Jesus: Christology in His Day and Ours*. New York: Lang, 2008.

———. "The Reef of the O.T.: A Method for Doing Biblical Theology that Makes Sense for Wisdom Literature." *Southwestern Journal of Theology* 56.1 (2013) 227–57.

———. "The Two Ways Christian Life View: A Historical Sketch." Paper presented at Evangelical Theological Society meeting , March 1998.

———. "Warnings in the Book of Hebrews: The Two Ways Tradition." Paper presented at ETS meeting, March 1998.

Kent, Homer. *The Epistle to the Hebrews*. Grand Rapids: Baker, 1972.

Kim, Kyong-Shik. *God Will Judge Each One According to Works: Judgment According to Works and Psalm 62 in Early Judaism and the New Testament*. Berlin: De Gruyter, 2011.

Kittel, Gerhard, and Gerhard Friedrich, eds. *Theological Dictionary of the New Testament*. 10 vols. Translated by Geoffrey W. Bromiley. Grand Rapids: Eerdmans, 1964–1976.

Klauck, Hans-Josef. *Ancient Letters and the New Testament: A Guide to Context and Exegesis*. Waco: Baylor University Press, 2006.

Klawans, Jonathan. *Impurity and Sin in Ancient Judaism*. Oxford: Oxford University, 2000.

Klijn, A. F. J. "The Study of Jewish Christianity." *New Testament Studies* 20 (1973–1974) 419–31.

Klijn, A. F. J., and G. J. Reinink. *Patristic Evidence for Jewish-Christian Sects*. Leiden: Brill, 1973.

Kline, Meredith G. *Treaty of the Great King: The Covenant Structure of Deuteronomy*. Grand Rapids: Eerdmans, 1963.

Kobelski, Paul. *Melchizedek and Melchireša'*. The Catholic Biblical Quarterly Monograph 10. Washington, DC: Catholic Biblical Association of America, 1981.

Koester, Craig. *Hebrews*. New York: Doubleday, 2001.

Köster, Helmut. "ὑπόστασις." In *TDNT* 8:572–89.

Kümmel, H. M. "Ersatzkönig und Sündenbock." *Zeitschrift für die alttestamentliche Wissenschaft* 80 (1968) 289–318.

Kurtz, Johann Heinrich. *Sacrificial Worship of the Old Testament*. Edinburgh: T. & T. Clark, 1863.

Laansma, Jon. *"I Will Give You Rest": The Rest Motif in the New Testament with Special Reference to Mt 11 and Heb 3–4*. Tübingen: Siebeck, 1997.

Lane, William. *Hebrews 1–8*. Word Biblical Commentary 47A. Dallas: Word, 1991.

———. *Hebrews 9–13*. Word Biblical Commentary 47B. Dallas: Word, 1991.

Lausberg, H. *Handbook of Literary Rhetoric: A Foundation for Literary Study*. Leiden: Brill, 1998.

Le Déaut, Roger. "Apropos a Definition of Midrash." *Interpretation* 25 (1971) 259–82.

Bibliography

Levine, Baruch A. *In the Presence of the Lord: A Study of Cult and Some Cultic Terms in Ancient Israel.* Leiden: Brill, 1974.

———. *Leviticus.* JPS Torah Commentary. Philadelphia: Jewish Publication Society, 1989.

Liddel, Henry George, et al.. *A Greek-English Lexicon.* Oxford: Clarendon, 1982.

Lim, Timothy. *Pesharim.* London: Sheffield, 2002.

Lincoln, Andrew T. *Paradise Now and Not Yet: Studies in the Role of the Heavenly Dimensions in Paul's Thought with Special Reference to His Eschatology.* Society for New Testament Studies Monograph 43. Cambridge: Cambridge University Press, 1981.

Lindars, Barnabas. *The Theology of the Letter to the Hebrews.* New Testament Theology. Cambridge: Cambridge University Press, 1991.

Linss, Wilhelm. "Logical Terminology in the Epistle to the Hebrews." *Concordia Theological Monthly* 37.6 (1966) 365–69.

Locke, John. "A Discourse of Miracles." In *The Works of John Locke*, 9:256–65. London: C. & J. Rivington, 1824.

———. *An Essay Concerning Human Understanding.* Chicago: Encyclopaedia Britannica, 1952.

———. "The Reasonableness of Christianity." In *The Works of John Locke*, 6. London: C. & J. Rivington, 1824.

———. *The Works of John Locke.* London: C. & J. Rivington, 1824.

Lohse, Eduard. *Märtyrer und Gottesknecht: Untersuchungen zur urchristlichen Verkündigung vom sühntod Jesu Christi.* Forschungen zur Religion und Literature des Alten und Neuen Testaments 49. Göttingen: Vandenhoeck & Ruprecht, 1963.

Longenecker, Richard N. *The Christology of Early Jewish Christianity Studies in Biblical Theology.* London: SCM, 1970.

Lünemann, Gottlieb. *Critical and Exegetical Hand-Book to the Hebrews.* New York: Funk & Wagnalls, 1885.

Luther, Martin. *The Lectures on Hebrews.* St. Louis: Concordia, 1968.

———. *Luther's Works.* Edited by E. Theodore Bachman. Philadelphia: Fortress, 1960.

MacArthur, John. *Hebrews.* Chicago: Moody, 1983.

MacLeod, David. "The Doctrinal Center of the Book of Hebrews." *Bibliotheca Sacra* 146 (1989) 291–300.

———. "The Theology of the Epistle to the Hebrews: Introduction, Prolegomena and Doctrinal Center." ThD diss., Dallas Theological Seminary, 1987.

Manson, William. *The Epistle to the Hebrews: An Historical and Theological Reconstruction.* London: Hodder and Stoughton, 1961.

Markschies, Christoph. "Jesus Christ as a Man before God: Two Interpretive Models for Isaiah 53 in the Patristic Literature and Their Development." In *The Suffering Servant: Isaiah 53 in Jewish and Christian Sources*, edited by Bernd Janowski and Peter Stuhlmacher, 225–320. Grand Rapids: Eerdmans, 2004.

Marmorstein, Arthur. "Les Signes du Messie." *Revue des Études Juives* 52 (1906) 176–86.

Marshall, I. H. *Kept by the Power of God: A Study of Perseverance and Falling Away.* London: Epworth, 1969.

Masterman, J. B. *The First Epistle of St. Peter.* London: Macmillan, 1912.

McFadden, Kevin W. "The Fulfillment of the Law's *Dikaiōma*: Another Look at Romans 8:1–4." *Journal of the Evangelical Theological Society* 52 (2009) 483–97.

McGrath, Alister. *Iustitia Dei: A History of the Christian Doctrine of Justification.* 2nd ed. Cambridge: Cambridge University Press, 1998.

Bibliography

McNamara, Martin. "Some Issues and Recent Writings on Judaism and the New Testament." *Irish Biblical Studies* 9 (1987) 136–49.

Meeks, Wayne A. *The Prophet-King: Moses Traditions and the Johannine Christology.* Leiden: Brill, 1967.

Meeks, Wayne A., and Robert Wilken. *Jews and Christians in Antioch in the First Four Centuries of the Common Era.* Ann Arbor: Scholars, 1978.

Melanchthon, Philip. *The Loci Communes of Philip Melanchthon.* Boston: Meador, 1944.

Menard, Jacques E. "*Pais Theou* as a Messianic Title in the Book of Acts." *Catholic Biblical Quarterly* 19 (1957) 83–92.

Mendenhall, G. E. "Covenant Forms in Israelite Tradition." *Biblical Archaeologist* 17.3 (1954) 50–76.

Milgrom, Jacob. "Israel's Sanctuary: 'The Priestly Picture of Dorian Gray.'" *Revue Biblique* 83 (1976) 390–99.

———. *Leviticus 1–16.* The Anchor Bible. New York: Doubleday, 1991.

———. *Numbers.* The JPS Torah Commentary. Philadelphia: The Jewish Publication Society, 1990.

———. "The Preposition מִן in the חַטָּאת Pericopes." *Journal of Biblical Literature* 126 (2007) 161–63.

———. *Studies in Cultic Theology and Terminology.* Studies in Judaism in Late Antiquity 36. Leiden: Brill, 1983.

———. *Studies in Levitical Terminology: The Encroacher and the Levite: The Term 'Aboda.* Berkeley: University of California, 1970.

Miller, M. P. "Targum, Midrash and the Use of the Old Testament in the New Testament." *Journal for the Study of Judaism in the Persian, Hellenistic, and Roman Period* 2.1 (1971) 29–82.

Milligan, George. *The Theology of the Epistle to the Hebrews.* Edinburgh: T. & T. Clark, 1899.

Mitchel, A. C. "The Use of πρεπειν and Rhetorical Propriety in Hebrews 2:10." *Catholic Biblical Quarterly* 54 (1992) 681–701.

Moffat, James. *An Introduction to the Literature of the New Testament.* Edinburgh: T. & T. Clark, 1961.

Moffitt, David M. "'If Another Priest Arises': Jesus Resurrection and the High Priestly Christology of Hebrews." In *A Cloud of Witnesses: The Theology of Hebrews in its Ancient Contexts*, edited by Richard Bauckham et al., 68–79. Edinburgh: T. & T. Clark, 2008.

Montefiore, H. W. *A Commentary on the Epistle to the Hebrews.* London: Black, 1964.

Moser, Paul, ed. *The Elusive God: Reorienting Religious Epistemology.* Cambridge: Cambridge University Press, 2008.

———. *Jesus and Philosophy.* New York: Cambridge University Press, 2008.

Moulton, James Hope, and George Milligan. *The Vocabulary of the Greek Testament: Illustrated from the Papyri and Other Non-Literary Sources.* Reprint, Peabody: Hendrickson, 1997.

Murray, John. *The Epistle to the Romans.* Grand Rapids: Eerdmans, 1959.

Murray, Robert. *Symbols of Church and Kingdom: A Study in Early Syriac Tradition.* London: Cambridge University Press, 1975.

Mynster, Jacob. "Unsersuchung über den Verfasser des Briefes an die Hebräer." In *Kleine theologische Schriften*, 91–140. Copenhagen: Gyldendal, 1825.

Nairne, Alexander. *The Epistle of Priesthood.* Edinburgh: T. & T. Clark, 1913.

Bibliography

Neusner, Jacob. *The Idea of Purity in Ancient Judaism.* Leiden: Brill, 1973.

Neusner, Jacob, and Ernest Frerichs. *"To See Ourselves as Others See Us": Christian, Jews, "Others" in Late Antiquity.* Chico: Scholar, 1986.

Nickelsburg, George. *Resurrection, Immortality, and Eternal Life in Intertestamrntal Judaism.* Cambridge: Harvard University Press, 1972.

Nicole, Roger. "Some Comments on Hebrews 6:4–6 and the Doctrine of the Perseverance of God with the Saints." *Grace Theological Journal* 3 (1982) 355–64.

Oakes, Peter. *Rome in the Bible and the Early Church.* Grand Rapids: Baker, 2002.

O'Brien, Peter, ed. *The Letter to the Hebrews.* Grand Rapids: Eerdmans, 2010.

―――. "Letters, Letter Forms." In *Dictionary of Paul and His Letters*, edited by Hawthorne et al., 550–53. Downers Grove: InterVarsity, 1993.

Oden, Thomas. *The Justification Reader.* Grand Rapids: Eerdmans, 2002.

Oecaloampadius, Johannes. *In Hieremiam prophetam commentariorum libri tres Ioannis Oecolampadii.* Argentina: Matthiae Apiarii, 1533.

Origen. *Commentary on the Gospel According to John, Books 13–32.* The Fathers of the Church 89. Translated by Ronald E. Heine. Washington, DC: Catholic University of America Press, 1993.

Osborne, Grant R. "A Classical Arminian View." In *Four Views on the Warning Passages in Hebrews*, edited by Herbert W. Bateman IV, 86–128. Grand Rapids: Kregel, 2007.

―――. "Soteriology in the Epistle to the Hebrews." In *Grace Unlimited*, edited by Clark Pinnock, 144–66. Minneapolis: Bethany, 1975.

Oswalt, John. *The Book of Isaiah, Chapters 40–66.* Grand Rapids: Eerdmans, 1988.

Pate, C. Marvin. *Communities of the Last Days: The Dead Sea Scrolls, the New Testament & the Story of Israel.* Downers Grove: InterVarsity, 2000.

Pate, C. Marvin, and Douglas Kennard. *Deliverance Now and Not Yet: The New Testament and the Great Tribulation.* New York, Lang, 2003.

Pearson, Birger A. "The Figure of Melchizedek in Gnostic Literature." In *Gnosticism, Judaism, and Egyptian Christianity*, 108–23. Minneapolis: Fortress, 1990.

Peirce, Charles Sanders. *The Collected Papers of Charles Sanders Peirce, Vol. 5: Pragmatism and Pragmaticism.* Edited by Charles Hartshorne and Paul Weiss. Cambridge: Harvard University Press, 1966.

―――. "The Fixation of Belief." *Popular Science Monthly* 12 (November 1877) 1–15.

―――. "How to Make Our Ideas Clear." *Popular Science Monthly* 12 (January 1878) 286–302.

Pentecost, Dwight. *A Faith That Endures.* Grand Rapids: Discovery, 1992.

Perkins, William. *The Workes of that Famous and Worthy Minister of Christ in the University of Cambridge, Mr. William Perkins.* 3 vols. London: Legat, 1635.

Pool, David de Sola. *The Traditional Prayer Book for Sabbath and Festivals.* New York: Behrman, 1969.

Porten, Bezalel. *Archives from Elephantine.* Berkley: University of California, 1968.

Porton, G. G. "Defining Midrash." In *The Study of Ancient Judaism, Vol. 1: Mishnah, Midrash, Siddur*, edited by J. Neusner, 55–95. New York: KTAV, 1981.

Pritchard, James B., ed. *Ancient Near Eastern Texts Relating to the Old Testament.* 3rd ed. Princeton: Princeton University Press, 1969.

Pucci Ben Zeev, Miriam. *Jewish Rights in the Roman World: The Greek and Roman Documents Quoted by Josephus Flavius.* Texts and Studies in Ancient Judaism 74. Tübingen: Mohr Siebeck, 1998.

BIBLIOGRAPHY

Quell, Gottfried. "B. El and Elohim in the OT." In the *Theological Dictionary of the New Testament*, edited by Gerhard Kittel and Gerhard Friedrich and translated by Geoffrey W. Bromiley, 3:79–89. Grand Rapids: Eerdmans, 1964–1976.

Rainbow, Paul. "Melchizedek as a Messiah at Qumran." *Bulletin for Biblical Research* 7 (1997) 179–94.

Räisänen, Heikii. *Paul and the Law*. Tübingen: Mohr Siebeck, 1983.

Rauer, Max. *Die "Schwachen" in Korinth und Rom nach den Paulusbriefen*. Freiburg: Herder, 1923.

Reiche, Bo. "The New Testament Concept of Reward." In *Aux sources de la tradition chréttiene: Mélanges offerts à M. Maurice Goguel*, edited by P. H. Menoud and Oscar Cullman, 195–206. Paris: Delachaux and Niestlé, 1950.

Reid, Thomas. *Thomas Reid, An Inquiry into the Human Mind on the Principles of Common Mind*. Edited by Derek Brookes. Edinburgh: Edinburgh University Press, 1997.

Ricoeur, Paul. *Memory, History, Forgetting*. Chicago: University of Chicago Press, 2004.

Riesenfeld, Herald. *Jesus Transfiguré, l'arriére-plan récit évangélique de la transfiguration de Notre-Seigneur*. Kobenhaven: Munksgaard, 1947.

Riggenbach, Eduard. "Die Starken und Schwachen in der römischen Gemeinde." *Theologische Studien und Kritiken* 66 (1893) 655–68.

Robinson, H. Wheeler. *The Religious Ideas of the Old Testament*. London: Duckworth, 1956.

Rogers, John. *The Doctrine of Faith*. London: Griffin, 1640.

Rogers, Richard. *Seven Treatises Leading and Guiding to True Happiness*. London: Man, 1610.

Rosenberg, Roy A. "Jesus, Isaac and the Suffering Servant." *Journal of Biblical Literature* 84 (1965) 381–88.

Sabourin, Leopold. "The Biblical Cloud." *Biblical Theology Bulletin* 4 (1974) 290–311.

Sanday, William, and Arthur Headlam. *A Critical and Exegetical Commentary on the Epistle to the Romans*. International Critical Commentary. Edinburgh: T. & T. Clark, 1895.

Sanders, E. P. *Jesus and Judaism*. London: SCM, 2004.

———. *Paul, the Law, and the Jewish People*. Minneapolis: Fortress, 1996.

Sapp, David A. "The LXX, 1QIsa, and MT Versions of Isaiah 53 and the Christian Doctrine of Atonement." In *Jesus and the Suffering Servant: Isaiah 53 and Christian Origins*, edited by William Bellinger and William R. Farmer, 170–92. Atlanta: Trinity, 1998.

Saussure, Ferdinand de. *Cours de linguistique générale*. Paris: Payot, 1969.

Schafer, Peter. *Kehhalot-Studien*. Tübingen: Mohr Siebeck, 1988.

Schaff, Philip, ed. *Creeds of Christendom, with History and Critical Notes: Vol. 3*. New York: Harper & Row, 1919.

Schaff, Philip, and Henry Wace, eds. *Nicene and Post-Nicene Fathers: Series II, Vol. 14*. Peabody: Hendrickson, 1995.

Schenker, Adrian. "*kōper* et expiation." *Biblica* 63 (1982) 32–46.

Schiffman, Lawrence. *Reclaiming the Dead Sea Scrolls: Their True Meaning for Judaism and Christianity*. Philadelphia: Jewish Publication Society, 1994.

Schnabel, Eckhard J. *Law and Wisdom from Ben Sira to Paul: A Tradition Historical Enquiry into the Relation of Law, Wisdom, and Ethics*. Tübingen: Mohr, 1985.

Schniedewind, W. M. "Melchizedek, Traditions of." In *Dictionary of New Testament Background: A Compendium of Contemporary Biblical Scholarship*, edited by Craig A. Evans and Stanley E. Porter, 693–95. Downers Grove: InterVarsity, 2000.

Schoeps, Hans Joachim. *Jewish Christianity: Factual Disputes in the Early Church.* Philadelphia: Fortress, 1969.

———. *Paul: The Theology of the Apostle in the Light of Jewish Religious History.* Translated by Harold Knight. Philadelphia: Westminster, 1961.

———. *Theologie und Geschichte des Judenchristentums.* Tübingen: Mohr, 1949.

Schreiner, Thomas. "Justification Apart from and by Works: at the Final Judgment Works will *Confirm* Justification." In *Four Views on the Role of Works at the Final Judgment,* edited by Alan Stanley and Robert Wilkin, 71–98. Grand Rapids: Zondervan, 2013.

———. *The Law and Its Fulfillment.* Grand Rapids: Baker, 1993.

———. *Romans.* Grand Rapids: Baker, 1998.

Schreiner, Thomas, and Ardel Caneday. *The Race Set before Us: A Biblical Theology of Perseverance & Assurance.* Downer's Grove: InterVarsity, 2001.

Schroeder, H. J., ed. *The Canons and Decrees of the Council of Trent.* St. Louis: Herder, 1941.

Schweitzer, Edward. *Lordship and Discipleship.* Naperville: Allenson, 1960.

Scott, Julius. *Customs and Controversies: Intertestamental Jewish Backgrounds of the New Testament.* Grand Rapids: Baker, 1995.

Seeley, David. *The Noble Death: Greco-Roman Martyrology and Paul's Concept of Salvation.* Journal for the Study of the New Testament Supplement Series 28. Sheffield: JSOT, 1990.

Segal, Alan F. *Two Powers in Heaven: Early Rabbinic Reports About Christianity and Gnosticism.* Leiden: Brill, 1977.

Seifrid, Mark. *Christ, Our Righteousness: Paul's Theology of Justification.* Downers Grove: InterVarsity, 2000.

Shank, Robert. *Life in the Son.* Springfield: Westcott, 1961.

Sholem, Gershom. *Jewish Gnosticism, Merkabah Mysticism, and Talmudic Tradition.* New York: Jewish Publication Society of America, 1960.

Sjöberg, Erik. *Der Menschensohn im äthiopischen Henochbuch.* Lund: Gleerup, 1946.

Skarsaune, Oskar. "Does the Letter to the Hebrews Articulate a Supercessionist Theology? A Response to Richard Hays." In *The Epistle to the Hebrews and Christian Theology,* edited by Richard Bauckham et al., 174–82. Grand Rapids: Eerdmans, 2009.

Skarsaune, Oskar, and Reidar Hvalvik. *Jewish Believers in Jesus: The Early Centuries.* Peabody: Hendrickson, 2007.

Sklar, Jay. "Sin and Atonement: Lessons from the Pentateuch." *Bulletin for Biblical Research* 22 (2012) 472–89.

———. "Sin and Atonement: What the Pentateuch Teaches Us." Paper presented at the Institute for Biblical Research, November 20, 2010.

———. *Sin, Impurity, Sacrifice, Atonement: The Priestly Conceptions.* Sheffield: Sheffield Phoenix, 2005.

Spicq, Ceslus. *L'Epître aux Hébreux.* Paris: Gabalda, 1952.

Stamm, Johann Jakob. *Erlösen und Vergeben im alten Testament: Eine begriffsgeschichtliche Untersuchung.* Bern: Francke, 1940.

Stanley, Alan, and Robert Wilkin. *Four Views on the Role of Works at the Final Judgment.* Grand Rapids: Zondervan, 2013.

Stökl Ben Ezra, Daniel. "Fasting with Jews, Thinking with Scapegoats: Some Remarks on Yom Kippur in Early Judaism and Christianity, in Particular 4Q541, *Barnabus 7,* Matthew 27 and Acts 27." In *The Day of Atonement: Its Interpretation in Early Jewish*

Bibliography

and Christian Traditions, edited by Thomas Hiecke and Tobias Nicklas, 164–88. Leiden: Brill, 2012.

———. *The Impact of Yom Kippur on Early Christianity: the Day of Atonement from Second Temple Judaism to the Fifth Century.* Tübingen: Mohr, 2003.

Strack, Herman L., and Paul Billerbeck. *Kommentar zum Neuen Testament aus Talmud und Midrash.* 5 vols. München: Beck, 1978–1983.

Strathmann, Hermann. *Geschichte der frühchristlichen Askese bis zur Entstehung des Mönchtums im religionsgeschichtlichen Zusammenhange, Vol. 1: Die Askese in der Umgebung des werdenden Christentums.* Leipzig: Leipzig, 1914.

Strecker, Georg. *Das Judenchristentum in den Pseudoklementinen.* Texte und Untersuchungen 70. 2nd ed. Berlin: Akademie-Verlag, 1981.

———. "The Kerygmata Petrou." In *The New Testament Apocrypha, Vol. 2: Writings Relating to the Apostles Apocalypses and Related Subjects*, edited by E. Hennecke and Wilhelm Schneemelcher, 102–27. Louisville: Westminster John Knox, 1991.

———. *Theology of the New Testament.* New York: Walter deGruyter, 2000.

Stuhlmacher, Peter. *Paul's Letter to the Romans.* Louisville: Westminster John Knox, 1994.

Taylor, Joan E. "The Phenomenon of Early Jewish Christianity: Reality or Scholarly Invention." *Vigiliae Christianae* 44 (1990) 313–34.

Tcherikover, Victor, and Alexander Fuks, eds. *Corpus Papyrorum Judaicarum.* 3 vols. Cambridge: Harvard University Press, 1957–64.

Thielman, Frank. *Paul & the Law: A Contextual Approach.* Downers Grove: InterVarsity, 1994.

Thompson, James W. "The Conceptual Background and Purpose of the Midrash in Hebrews VII." *Novum Testamentum* 19 (1977) 209–23.

Thyen, Hartwig. *Der Stil des jüdish-hellenistischen Homile.* Göttingen: Vandenhoeck & Ruprecht, 1955.

Toussaint, Stanley. "The Eschatology of the Warning Passages in the Book of Hebrews." In *Grace Theological Journal* 3 (1982) 67–80.

Turner, Nigel. *A Grammar of New Testament Greek, Vol. 3: Syntax.* Edinburgh: T. & T. Clark, 1963.

van Brock, Nadia. "Substitution Rituelle." *Revue Hittite et Asianique* 17.65 (1959) 117–46.

VanGemeren, Willem, ed. *New International Dictionary of Old Testament Theology & Exegesis.* 5 vols. Grand Rapids: Zondervan, 1997.

Van Voorst, Robert E. *The Ascents of James: History and Theology of a Jewish-Christian Community.* Atlanta: Scholars, 1989.

Vardaman, E. J., and J. L. Garrett. *The Teacher's Yoke.* Waco: Baylor, 1964.

Velasco, Jesus, and Leopold Sabourin. "Jewish Christianity of the First Centuries." *Biblical Theology Bulletin* 6 (1976) 5–26.

Vermes, Geza. *Scripture and Tradition in Judaism: Haggadic Studies in Studia Post-Biblica.* Leiden: Brill, 1961.

Vincent, L. H. "Abraham à Jérusalem." *Revue Biblique* 58 (1951) 360–71.

von Martitz, Peter Wülfing. "υἱός, υἱοθεσια." In *TDNT* 8:334–40.

Volz, Paul. *Die Eschatologie der jüdischen Gemeide im neutestamentlichen Zeitalter, nach den Quellen des rabbinischen, apokalyptischen und apokryphen Literatur.* Tübingen: Mohr, 1934.

Watson, Duane. "Rhetorical Criticism of Hebrews and the Catholic Epistles Since 1978." *Currents in Research Biblical Studies* 5 (1997) 184–87.

Westcott, Brooke. *Epistle to the Hebrews.* Grand Rapids: Eerdmans, 1977.

Bibliography

Westfall, Cynthia Long. *A Discourse Analysis of the Letter to the Hebrews: The Relationship Between Form and Meaning.* London: T. & T. Clark, 2005.

Wikgren, Allen. "Some Greek Idioms in the Epistle to the Hebrews." In *The Teacher's Yoke: Studies in Memory of Henry Trantham*, edited by E. J. Vardaman and J. L. Garrett, 149. Waco: Baylor, 1964.

Wilde, Oscar Fingal O'Flahertie Wills. *The Picture of Dorian Gray.* Philadelphia: Ivers, 1890.

Wiley, Orton. *The Epistle to the Hebrews.* Kansas City: Beacon Hill, 1959.

Willard, Dallas. *The Divine Conspiracy: Rediscovering our Hidden Life in God.* San Francisco: HarperSanFrancisco, 1998.

Williams, Prescott. "The Poems About Incomparable Yahweh's Servant in Isaiah 40–55." *Southwestern Journal of Theology* 11 (Fall 1968) 73–87.

Williamson, Ronald. "Philo and New Testament Christology." In *Studia Biblica 1978, Vol. 3: Papers on Paul and Other New Testament Authors*, edited by E. A. Livingstone, 439–45. Sheffield: JSOT, 1980.

———. *Philo and the Epistle to the Hebrews.* Leiden: Brill, 1970.

Winter, Bruce. "Roman Law and Society in Romans 12–15." In *Rome in the Bible and the Early Church*, edited by Peter Oakes, 67–102. Grand Rapids: Baker, 2002.

Winter, Paul. "Note on Salem-Jerusalem." *Novum Testamentum* 2 (1957) 151–52.

Wood, J. Edwin. "Isaac Typology in the New Testament." *New Testament Studies* 14 (July 1968) 583–89.

Wray, Judith. *Rest as a Theological Metaphor in the Epistle to the Hebrews and the Gospel of Truth: Early Christian Homiletics of Rest.* Atlanta: Scholars, 1998.

Wright, Addison. G. *Midrash: The Literary Genre.* Staten Island: Alba, 1968.

Wright, David P. *The Disposal of Impurity: Elimination Rites in the Bible and in Hittite and Mesopotamian Literature.* Society of Biblical Literature Dissertation Series 101. Atlanta: Scholars, 1987.

Wright, N. T. *The Climax of the Covenant: Christ and the Law in Pauline Theology.* Minneapolis: Fortress, 1992.

———. *Jesus and the Victory of God.* Minneapolis: Fortress, 1996.

———. *Pauline Perspectives: Essays on Paul, 1978–2013.* Minneapolis: Fortress, 2013.

———. "Paul's Gospel and Caesar's Empire." In *Paul and Politics: Ekklesia, Israel Imperium Interpretation: Essays in Honor of Krister Stendahl*, edited by Richard Horsley, 160–83. Harrisburg: Trinity Press International, 2000.

Wuest, Kenneth S. "Hebrews Six in the Greek New Testament." *Bibliotheca Sacra* 119 (1962) 45–53.

Yadin, Yigael. "The Dead Sea Scrolls and the Epistle to the Hebrews." In *Scripta Hierosolymitana, Vol. 4: Aspects of the Dead Sea Scrolls*, edited by Charim Rabin and Yigael Yadin, 36–55. Jerusalem: Magnes, 1958.

Yarnold, E. J. "*Metriopathein apud* Heb. 5, 2." *Verbum Domini* 38 (1960) 149–55.

Yinger, Kent. *Paul, Judaism, and Judgment According to Deeds.* Cambridge: Cambridge University Press, 1999.

Zeitlin, Solomon. "Midrash: A Historical Study." *Jewish Quarterly Review* 44 (1953) 21–36.

Author Index

Aeschylus, 30
Akiva, 25
Albrektson, 116
Allen, 1, 40
Ambroisiater, 34
Ambrose, 32, 53, 71, 108
Anderson, 135
Apollonius, 135
Aquila, 28, 116, 135
Aquinas, 22
Archer, 120
Aristotle, 13, 15–16, 30
Athanasius, 21, 31–32, 52–53, 108
Attridge, 7, 15, 112
Averbeck, 68, 79–80
Augustine, 22, 32, 34, 53, 71, 108

Bailey, 85
Balentine, 67
Baltzer, 32
Barber, 34
Barr, 68, 73
Barthélemy, 79
Bateman, 14
Bauckham, 16
Bauernfeind, 50
Bauer, 41
Behm, 63, 101
Betz, 82–83
Bietenhard, 26
Billerbeck, 82–83
Blaising, 17, 50
Bleek, 1
Bloch, 13, 109
Blum, 121

Bock, 14
Boda, 66–67
Bornkamm, 113
Bray, 34
Bruce, 14
Brueggeman, 16
Buchanan, 13–14, 109, 121
Bunyan, 32, 34, 53, 108

Calvin, 32, 53, 93, 108
Caneday, 34
Cassian, 32, 53, 108
Charlesworth, 39
Chernus, 89, 98
Chilton, 76
Chrysostom, 30, 39, 56–57, 71, 121
Clement Alexandria, 1, 16–18, 31, 52, 98, 108, 112
Clement of Rome, 1–2, 12, 15, 31, 50, 52, 108, 112, 116–17, 139
Climacus, 32, 53, 108
Cockerill, 23, 39, 112, 115–16, 120
Collins, 25, 38
Cody, 17, 98
Commodianus, 31, 52, 108
Conbrink, 21
Cosby, 15
Cragie, 28
Cranfield, 34
Croy, 136
Cullmann, 26, 82–83
Cyprian, 31, 52, 55, 70, 108
Cyril, 32, 53, 71, 108

Dabney, 35

Author Index

Daly, 82–83
D'Angelo, 1
Das, 35
Davidson, 80–81
Dean-Otting, 18, 49, 89, 98
Delcor, 45
Deismann, 2, 26, 138
de Roo, 116
de Silva, 15–16, 99
Dey, 36
Dillow, 121
Dionysius, 31, 44, 52, 108
Domeris, 111
Dunham, 120
Dunn, 16, 21, 26, 32, 35, 39, 44, 53, 101, 108

Eaton, 121
Edwards, 4, 19, 35, 93
Eisenbaum, 15–16, 115
Eliezer, 73
Eliphanius, 25, 42
Elliger, 68
Ellingworth, 107
Elliott, 101
Ellis, 13, 109
Epictetus, 88, 126
Epiphanus, 21, 39, 56
Eusebius, 1, 16, 31, 52, 71, 108, 118
Evans, 59

Fanning, 120
Feder, 68
Filium, 71
Finlan, 70
Fisher, 55
Fitzmyer, 39, 82–84
Ford, 14
Francis, 2, 138
Freedman, 59
Fuks, 60

Gammie, 74
Gane, 67, 74–75, 80
Gaon, 13
Garland, 60
Garuti, 15
Gathercole, 107

Gheorghita, 14, 23, 28, 107, 135
Gieschen, 42, 45
Gleason, 120–21
Godet, 34
Gordon, 18
Gräßer, 114
Greer, 21
Gregory Nazianzus, 21, 32, 53, 108
Gregory Nyssa, 21, 32, 53
Grindheim, 32, 108
Gromacki, 121
Gruenwald, 18, 49, 89, 98
Gubler, 82–83
Gundry, 17, 50
Gurney, 77
Guthrie, 63, 101, 120

Hagen, 3
Harris, 26
Hayman, 56
Hays, 55–56
Hayward, 39
Headlam, 71
Hefele, 57
Hellerman, 63, 101
Helm, 79
Hengel, 26, 85
Henninger, 34
Herodian, 135
Herodotus, 30, 122
Hewett, 120
Hilary, 31–32, 52–53, 108
Hillel, 13–14, 109
Hippolytus, 117
Hofius, 107, 110, 112–13, 121
Hoffner, 77
Hollady, 36
Hooker, 82–83
Horton, 25, 38, 42
Howard, 8, 12, 21–22, 40, 58
Hübner, 35
Hughes, 120
Hurst, 18, 113–14
Hvalvik, 56

Ignatius, 8, 12, 52, 56, 64, 102, 108
Istone-Brewer, 96, 141
Irenaeus, 12, 16, 31, 52, 56, 108

Author Index

Isaacs, 18, 36, 49, 89, 98
Ishmael, 23

Janowski, 68, 70
Jeremias, 82–83
Jerome, 1, 56
Johnson, 15
Johnston, 52, 108
Jose, 25
Josephus, 7–8, 10, 12–13, 18, 22, 30, 34, 38–40, 43–44, 53, 60, 62–63, 73, 79, 98, 101, 107, 109, 115–18, 122, 131, 136, 139
Joslin, 58–59
Juel, 22
Justin, 8, 12, 23, 29, 31, 52, 56–57, 70, 108, 117
Juvenal, 139

Kaiser, 79
Käsemann, 52, 108–10, 121
Kautzsch, 111
Keck, 34
Keener, 17
Kelber, 16
Kendall, 93, 109, 120
Kennard, 3, 12, 14, 17–18, 33, 49–50, 53–56, 58, 61, 81, 87–89, 92, 94–95, 97–99, 111, 122, 131
Kent, 120
Kim, 32, 53, 108
Klauck, 2, 138
Klawans, 72
Klijn, 56
Kline, 32
Kobelski, 41
Koester, 2–3, 13, 15–16, 18, 21–23, 28, 31, 40, 49, 89, 98, 120, 122, 129
Kümmel, 77
Kurtz, 68

Laansma, 112, 121
Lactantius, 31, 52, 108
Lane, 2, 15, 18, 29–30, 39, 62–64, 101–2, 117, 121
Lausberg, 13, 16
Le Déaut, 13, 109
Leo, 32, 71, 108

Levine, 66, 79
Liddell, 11, 21, 39, 110
Lincoln, 18, 49, 89
Lindars, 2, 5, 21
Linss, 17
Locke, 19
Lohse, 83
Longnecker, 82–83
Lucian, 139
Lünemann, 17
Luther, 1, 34

MacArthur, 120
MacLeod, 2–3
Manson, 113
Markschies, 70
Marmorstein, 25
Marshall, 120
Martinez, 42
Masterman, 114
McFadden, 35
McGrath, 34
McNamara, 13, 109
Meeks, 36, 56
Melanchthon, 34
Menard, 82–83
Mendenhall, 32
Methodius, 31, 52, 108
Miano, 59
Milgrom, 67–68, 72–74, 76–80, 95
Milik, 79
Miller, 109
Milligan, 2
Moffat, 114
Moffitt, 58
Montefiore, 120
Moser, 17
Murray, 34
Mynster, 1

Nairne, 31, 52, 108, 121
Nathan, 91
Nazianzen, 71
Neusner, 76, 79, 91
Nickelsburg, 89
Nicole, 120

O'Brien, 2, 14–16, 120, 138

Author Index

Oden, 70–71
Oecolampadius, 34
Olympus, 52
Origen, 1, 8, 12, 17–18, 21, 31, 52, 55, 56, 70–71, 98, 108, 110, 112, 117
Osborne, 120
Oswalt, 87

Pate, 18, 37, 41, 49, 81, 87–89, 98
Pearson, 25, 42
Peirce, 4, 19
Pelagius, 34
Pentecost, 121
Perkins, 93
Philo, 10–13, 15, 17, 21–23, 30–31, 33–34, 36, 38–40, 43, 50, 59–60, 62-3, 73, 79–81, 90–92, 94, 98, 102, 107, 109–10, 112, 116, 118, 130–31, 136, 138–39
Plato, 18
Plotinus, 18
Plutarch, 39, 88
Polybius, 22
Polycarp, 50, 52, 108
Pool, 13–14
Porton, 13, 91, 109
Pritchard, 23
Pucci, 63, 101

Quell, 5
Quintilian, 13, 15–16

Rabad, 76
Rainbow, 42
Räisänen, 35
Rauer, 63, 101
Reiche, 32, 53, 108
Reid, 16
Reinink, 56
Ricoeur, 14, 16
Riesenfeld, 82–83
Riggenbach, 63, 101
Robinson, 80
Rogers, 93, 109
Rosenberg, 82–83

Sabourin, 25, 56
Sanday, 71

Sanders, 35, 56
Sapp, 82–83
Saussure, 68
Schafer, 18, 98
Schaff, 57, 71
Schiffman, 84
Schnabel, 35
Schniedewind, 42, 45
Schoeps, 57, 82–83
Scholasticus, 32
Schreiner, 35, 53, 108
Schafer, 49, 89
Schroeder, 34
Schreiner, 34
Schweitzer, 99
Scott, 10, 110
Seeley, 88
Segal, 6, 24
Seneca, 16, 88
Shank, 120
Sholem, 18, 49, 89
Simeon, 79
Sjöberg, 89
Skarsaune, 56
Sklar, 66–67
Socrates, 108
Sophocles, 30
Spicq, 31, 52, 108
Stamm, 68
Stökl, 59, 79
Strack, 82–83
Strathmann, 63, 101
Strecker, 56–57
Stuhlmacher, 35, 70
Suetonias, 26
Symmachus, 28

Tacitus, 88
Tatian, 21
Taylor, 56
Tcherikover, 60
Tertulian, 1, 55, 57, 117
Theodoret, 71
Theodotion, 28, 135
Theodotus, 13, 109
Thielman, 35
Thomas à Kempis, 32, 53, 108
Thompson, 45

Author Index

Thyen, 2
Toussaint, 120
Turner, 29

Van Brock, 77
Van Dam, 86, 111
VanGemeren, 86
Van Voorst, 57
Velasco, 56
Vermes, 82–83
Vincent, 32, 39, 53, 108
Virgil, 135
Volz, 10
Von Martitz, 26

Wace, 57
Watson, 3
Westcott, 23, 120
Westfall, 16
Wikgren, 29

Wilde, 68
Wiley
Wilken, 56
Willard, 32, 53, 108
Williams, 85
Williamson, 18, 36
Winter, 39, 63, 101
Wood, 83
Wray, 110, 113, 115, 121
Wright, A., 13, 109
Wright, D., 77
Wright, N. T. , 25, 35, 82, 84–85, 135
Wuest, 120

Yadin, 41, 45
Yinger, 32, 53, 108
Yoḥanan 91

Zeitlin, 13, 109

Subject Index

Abraham, 6
Anti-Semitic, 56–57
Apostle Jesus, 4, 29–35
Atonement, 4, 17–19, 48–49, 66–105
Authorship, 1–2

Christ as God, 21–26
Conscience, 8, 19, 58–59, 104–5, 140
Co-sharer, 55

Davidic king, 26–28, 36–40
Divine majesty, 21–22

Ebionite, 21
Epistemology, 12–19
Exodus, 4, 6–7, 10–11, 35, 106–35

Father, 6
Filial knowledge, 19
Firstborn, 22–23
Forgiveness, 19, 99, 103–4

God, 3–8

Healing, 10
Holy Spirit, 8, 12, 34–35, 49, 122, 125–27
Hupostasis, 21–22

Judge, 7–8, 17
Justification, 34

Law, 4, 52–65
Letter form, 2, 136–42
Levitical priests, 46

Love, 139

Moses, 29–35
Melchizedek, 4, 25, 36–51
Merkabah, 3, 17–19
Messiah, 23–28, 54
Midrash, 3–4, 13–14, 19
Miracle, 10, 16–17, 19

New covenant, 4, 8, 19, 49, 52–105
Nicene creed, 21–22

Penal, 70
Perfect, 57–58
Pesher, 12–13
Platonism, 3, 17–19, 48–49
Prayer, 17, 49–51, 139–40
Prophecy, 12–19
Prophet, 9–11
Radiance, 11

Readership, 2–3
Reformed, 35
Restoration eschat., 55–57
Resurrection, 7
Rest, 6, 7, 54–55, 110–13
Rhetorical criticism, 15–16

Shekinah, 21–22, 31
Son, 6–7, 22–25
Spokesman, 9–11
Superior, 3, 13, 19, 53–55, 60, 106
Supercessionism, 55–56

Temptation, 29, 47–48

Subject Index

Testimony, 15–16, 19
Trinity, 6
Two Powers, 4, 6, 24
Two-ways, 4, 31–35, 56, 106–35

Warnings, 15, 120–37
Word, 6

Scripture Index

Genesis

1:6–29	6, 23, 27–28, 115
2:1–3	6, 54, 110–12, 124
4	88, 115
5	115–16
6	20, 116
8	116
9	116
11:6	20
12:1	115
14:18–24	5, 38–42
15:18–21	115
17	111
18	139
19	139
20:8–11	124
21:29–30	69
22	7, 20, 83, 111
23	29
24	7, 111
32:20	69
35:2	67
47	116
49	11, 111, 139
50	116

Exodous

2	106, 117
3:14–15	6
3–4	106
5–15	117
6:7	61
9–12	106
12	106
13	116
14	106
15	67, 106, 123
16	111
17:4–34	67, 123
19	61, 104
20:8–11	110, 112
21	75, 86, 112
24	66, 71, 77, 87, 96, 140
25	7, 78
25–40	8
28:1	43
29:36–37	72
30:12–16	59–60, 69, 75
31	54, 78, 112, 124
32:30–40	69, 123
33	64, 102
34	30, 58, 60, 74, 111
35	78
38	78
39:43	36
40:17–35	36, 111
40:34–38	18, 49, 89, 98

Scripture Index

Leviticus

1–7	70, 91
3	140
4:1–5:26	47, 60, 66–67, 72, 74–78, 80, 88, 95–96, 98
6	67, 74, 76, 118
7	63–64, 76, 78, 101–2, 118–19, 140
8–9	36, 72–73, 78, 95
10	74, 77, 88, 118
11	63, 77, 95, 101
12	71–74, 104–5
13	96, 104–5
14	76–77, 80, 96, 104–5
15:2–33	71, 74, 77, 80, 95–96, 104–5
16	54, 59, 64, 66–67, 69–70, 74, 77–80, 87–88, 91, 95, 102, 104–5
17	69, 75, 77, 88, 91
18	47, 66
19	67, 73, 76
20:2–18	66, 77, 88
23	54, 66, 80
24:10–23	66
25	41, 54, 112
26	54, 86

Numbers

1:55	69
3:10	43
4:15–20	66
5	67, 76–77
6	72, 80
7	78, 111
8	69, 74
9	77, 88
10:4	30
11	67, 86
12	30, 67
13	29, 123
14	20, 67, 77, 88, 107, 123
15	47, 66–67, 73–74, 133
16	67, 75
18	43, 66, 69, 76, 118
19	67, 77–78, 95
20	67, 123
21	67
22	86
24:14	11
25:7–13	69–70, 75
26:12	111
27	123
28	80
29	80
31:50	69, 75
35	69, 75, 86

Deuteronomy

4:30	11
6	123
8	136
9	33, 123
10:16	59
15	112
18:15–22	9
21	22, 69, 74
23:10	71
28	32–33, 55, 77, 86
29	33, 55, 77, 136
30	32–33, 59
31	139
32:3	21
32:7–8	11, 20–21
32:35–36	8, 134
32:43–51	14, 23, 75, 111, 123
33	24, 53, 111, 122, 123

Joshua

1:5	139
2:1–7	107
6:22–25	107
21	124
22	67

Scripture Index

Judges

3	124
5	24, 30, 124
6	24, 139
8	124
9:44	30
11:6–11	30
13	139

1 Samuel

2:35	30
3:14	75
28:8–14	67

2 Samuel

6:13–15	37
7:14	14, 22, 54
12:30	37
21:3–6	69–70, 75

1 Kings

19:10	32

2 Kings

17:23	33

1 Chronicles

5:24	30
8:28	30
17	22, 30, 81
26:26	30

2 Chronicles

21:3–19	23, 67
23:14	30
36:14	67

Nehemiah

2:9	29–30
9:32	33
10:32–33	60

Job

1:6	20
2:1	20
38:7	20

Psalms

1:6	33
2:7	14, 22, 27, 46, 54
4:2	17
6:8–9	17
8:3–6	27–28, 54
10:17	17
11	81, 134
18:1–15	17, 24
19	17, 68
21	134
22:24	17
28:6	17
29:1	20
31:22	17
34:6	17
38:6	21–22
40:1	17
45:6–7	14, 26, 125
49:8–9	69
51:9–10	59, 73, 111
61:5	17
65:3	74
66:19	17

Scripture Index

(Psalms continued)

68:4	24
78	17, 74–75
79	11, 21–22, 67, 74–75, 81, 134
82:6	20
88:48	21–22
89:7	20
89:27	23
95	55, 107, 109–10, 123
95:7–10	4, 13
96:7	23
97:7	14
102:25–27	14
103:12	58, 60, 74
104:3–4	21, 24
104:14–15	63, 101
106	17, 40, 68
107	40
110	13–14, 25, 27, 40–41, 45–46
111	40
118:6	139
119	33, 68
139:24	33
145:3–6	11, 21

Proverbs

3:11–12	135
6:34–35	69
16:6	75
28:6	33

Isaiah

1	86
2:2	11
6:1–8	18, 49, 75, 81, 89
7:14	24
8:8–10	24
9:1–2	33
9:6–7	24, 140
10	24, 86
11:2	24
14	54, 86
16:10	54
17:3	54
19:1	24
21:2	54
22:14	75
24:5	68
26:11	133
27	75, 86
28	24, 75
30	86
37:4–17	5, 78, 95
40:1–11	10, 33, 85
40:28	30
42	9, 82
44:24–45:6	10
45:7	30
47:11	69, 75
49:1–13	10, 82, 85, 94
50:6–11	10, 85
51	87
52	82, 86–87
53	4, 10, 81–85, 87–89, 141
54	87, 140
57:2	140
60:10–17	33, 140
61:1–3	9–10, 41, 112
63:16	24
65	111
66	67, 81, 86, 140

Jeremiah

2:7	68
3:9	68
4:4	134
7:30	67
10:10	5
13:18	37
16:12	124
17:13	5
18:12	124
21:8	32
23:36	5

Scripture Index

31	4, 33, 58–59, 61, 94–95, 103, 105, 111
32–33	33–34, 38, 67, 81, 91, 103
48:33–35	54

Ezekiel

1:4–28	18, 49, 89, 98
5:11	67
9:7–10	32, 67
10:4–20	18
11:22–25	49, 89, 98
19:5	21–22
20:7–31	33, 67
21:3–31	33, 37, 86
22:3–24	67, 86, 133, 134
23:7–38	67
24:13	67
30:10–18	54
36	67, 94
37	67, 94
38	134
40–47	34, 81
43	62, 67, 73, 75, 77–78, 91, 95, 100, 103
44	75, 77, 91, 103
45	75, 91, 103
46	103, 140

Daniel

2:44–45	33
3	20, 117
6	5, 117
7	24–25, 28, 33
9:21	20
9:26	42
10:13–14	11, 20
10:13–21	21
11:1	21
12:1	21

Hosea

1:10	5
3:5	11
5:3	68
6:10	68

Joel

2:28–29	59

Amos

5:21–24	67
9	78

Micah

4:1	11
5:2–5	23, 33
7:18–20	58, 60, 74

Habakkuk

2:3–4	135

Zephaniah

1:18	134
3:8	134

Haggiah

2:1–7	38, 136
2:6–21	8

Scripture Index

Zechariah

4	36, 38
6:9–14	37–38
9:11	96, 140–41
12	86

Malachi

1:11–12	67

Matthew

1:1–17	44
1:19	130
3:14	134
5:23–24	91
7:24–27	33
8:17	10, 88
11:19	33
12:14–37	130
14:14–21	111
15:32–39	111
17:24–27	60
21:11	2, 141
22:41–45	44
25:31–46	34
26:3	44
26:37–44	50
26:57	44
26:64	24–25
27:31	118

Mark

6:34–44	111
7:9	133
7:21–22	139
8:1–9	111
12:35–37	44
14:33–41	50
14:62	24–25
15:20	118
15:43	2, 141

Luke

2:22–24	72
2:69	25
3:2	23–33, 44
4:18	10
7:35	33
9:12–17	110
20:41–44	44
22	24, 50, 88
23:26	118

John

1:1–14	6
1:29	36, 70
1:44	2, 141–42
2:7–10	111
5:28–29	34
5:39–47	9, 30
6:5–13	111
11:43–49	7, 44
18	44
19:20	118
21:2	2

Acts

2	11, 126
4:6	44
6	2, 126, 141–42
7	7, 20, 53–54, 113, 122
8	88, 122, 126
9	126
10	126
13	126
15:3	140
18:18–19	91, 141
19	126
21:23–27	2, 91, 141–42
23:1–4	44, 140
24:1	44
24:16	140
24:18	2, 141–42
28	126

Scripture Index

Romans

3:21	30
3:25	70
4:25	81, 88
8:26–27	50
10:16	88
15:4	140
15:21	88

1 Corinthians

3:13	134
5:1–11	139
6:9–11	139
7:14	139

2 Corinthians

1:3–7	140
3:12–18	30
5:8	34

Galatians

2:20	125
3:19	7, 20, 53–54, 122
4:26	18, 98

Ephesians

1:21	3
5:5	139
6:18–20	139

Philippians

1:23	34
2:7–8	47, 135
2:9–10	3

Colossians

1:15–18	3

1 Thessalonians

5:17	139

1 Timothy

1:3	141
1:10	139
1:19	140
4:14	126
5:22	126

2 Timothy

1:6	126
3:1	11

Philemon

22	140

Hebrews

1	113
1:1	9–11, 53–54, 115
1:1–3:6	125
1:2	11, 16, 22–23, 53–54
1:3	5–6, 18, 21, 23, 31, 48, 53, 129
1:4	3, 18, 53, 100, 109, 114
1:4–2:10	21
1:5	6, 18, 22, 26, 27, 46, 54, 103
1:5–13	22
1:6–7	6–7, 18, 21–23, 27

Scripture Index

(Hebrews continued)

1:8–9	23, 26–27, 54, 61, 105, 125, 127
1:10	6, 27, 105
1:11–13	25, 27, 61, 105
1:13	13, 27–28, 48, 54
1:13–2:1	122
1:14	21, 28, 66, 97, 100, 108–10, 114, 131
2:1–4	15, 28, 121–22, 128–29
2:2	113
2:2–4	2, 6–8, 11–12, 15–16, 20, 53–54, 99, 111, 123, 134
2:2–18	114
2:3	109, 122, 129, 131
2:6–8	14–15, 27–28, 54, 103
2:9	8, 48, 54, 127
2:10	28–29, 31, 48, 52, 58, 110, 122
2:11	114, 125, 131
2:13	7
2:14	48
2:17–18	7, 47
3:1	125
3:1–7	29, 53–56, 123
3:2	106
3:3–4	7, 31, 113
3:5	9, 113
3:6	15, 31, 61, 103, 106, 113–14
3:7	124, 128, 134
3:7–11	8, 12, 46, 53, 55, 110
3:7–4:13	2, 5, 7, 13, 15, 109, 123
3:8	99, 104, 109
3:9	123
3:10	123
3:11–13	99, 104, 107, 109, 124
3:12–16	29, 46, 55, 106, 109, 113
3:14	22, 57, 105, 125–26
3:15	104, 124
3:15–19	7, 55, 99–100, 106, 107, 109
3:19	99, 106
4:1–3	55, 103, 114, 124, 126
4:1–11	105
4:2–4	54, 99, 106, 110, 112–13
4:5–7	99, 109, 113
4:6	107
4:7	29, 46, 55, 124
4:7–9	113, 124
4:10	110, 124
4:11	15, 99, 107
4:14	15, 48
4:15	47
4:16	18, 48
5:1	128
5:1–12	7, 11
5:2–3	46–47, 74, 114
5:4	43
5:5–6	13, 27, 39, 41, 45–46, 104
5:7	17, 47, 50–51, 110, 113
5:8	47–48
5:9	17, 48, 52, 58, 110, 122
5:10	39, 48
5:11	130
5:12–13	127, 130
5:14	58, 130
5:11–6:1	38
5:11–6:20	126–30
5:23–24	11
6	120, 130
6:1	61
6:1–3	130
6:1–20	15
6:4	8, 12, 17, 31, 55, 111, 125, 127–29, 134
6:4–8	130
6:5	129
6:6	109, 129–30
6:7–8	130
6:9	3, 52, 110
6:9–12	19, 66
6:10	7, 131
6:11	57, 131
6:12	100, 108–9, 131
6:13–19	6, 53, 68, 131
6:18–19	15, 129, 131

Scripture Index

6:20–7:17	131	9:9	46, 58, 59, 95, 99, 105, 128, 140
6:26–28	68		
7:1	40, 114	9:10	63
7:1–10	44	9:11	95
7:1–10:31	100, 109	9:11–28	97
7:2	38–40	9:12–13	46, 58, 60, 62, 87, 99–100, 104, 114, 131–32, 134
7:3	39, 45, 57		
7:4	40		
7:4–10	44	9:14	5, 8, 49, 53, 57–59, 61, 93, 100, 103–5, 114, 131–32, 134, 135
7:6	40		
7:7	3, 40		
7:8	44–45	9:15	66, 95, 97, 100, 103, 108–9, 114
7:9	39, 44		
7:11–13	45–46, 58, 61	9:16–17	61, 97, 103
7:14	6, 44	9:18	103
7:15	45	9:18–22	7, 18, 58–59, 71, 74–75, 95–96, 99, 140
7:16	46, 48, 129		
7:17–22	3, 5–7, 13, 27, 39, 45–46, 48, 61, 104	9:20	141
		9:23	3, 62, 100
7:19	58, 104	9:23–24	17, 18–19, 64, 67, 95, 99–100, 102, 113, 131
7:23	43, 45		
7:24–25	11, 40, 49–51, 110	9:25–26	11, 19, 48, 62, 95, 99–100
7:26–27	47, 100, 114		
7:28	48, 58	9:27–28	19, 49, 52, 62, 98–100, 110, 122, 131
8:1–3	5, 18, 48, 128, 131		
8:4	128	10:1	17, 46, 58–60, 91, 105
8:5	7, 17, 62, 100	10:2–3	46, 59–60, 93, 105, 132, 140
8:6	3, 48		
8:6–13	113	10:2–8	57, 60, 91
8:6–10:18	45	10:3–4	19, 129
8:7–9	60–61	10:6–17	132
8:8–10	5–6, 8, 19, 49, 58–59, 61, 66, 94	10:9–10	49, 58–59, 61–62, 91, 99–100, 104, 114, 131–32, 134
8:10	99, 105		
8:11	17, 48, 58–59, 61, 95	10:11–12	8, 11, 48–49, 58, 62, 98, 99–100
8:12–13	49, 58–59, 61, 66, 95, 99, 103	10:14–18	8, 12, 14, 19, 49, 58–62, 66, 95, 100, 104, 128, 131–32, 134
9:1–10	2, 8, 12, 131		
9:1–10:12	17, 66, 70		
9:4–5	60–61, 78	10:16	94, 99, 105
9:6	43	10:17	99, 103, 132
9:7–8	47, 59, 64, 74, 77–78, 95, 99, 102, 114, 128, 131	10:19–22	48, 119, 132
		10:19–39	131–35
		10:22–25	49, 97, 105, 119, 132, 134
9:7–14	132		
9:7–28	118	10:23	15
9:8	131, 134	10:24	140–41

Scripture Index

(Hebrews continued)

10:26–31	2, 5–8, 12, 17, 62, 109, 128, 133–34
10:26–39	15, 19
10:29	130–31
10:30	61, 114, 134
10:31	134
10:32	48, 127, 134
10:32–35	134
10:34	3, 17, 47
10:36	15, 137
10:37	135
10:38	127, 137
10:39	135
11	106, 113–15, 135
11:1–3	16, 22
11:1–12:13	99–100, 139
11:3	6, 23, 115, 129
11:4	115, 127–28
11:5	7, 116
11:6	46, 129
11:7	109, 116, 127
11:7–10	116
11:8	100, 109, 113, 115
11:8–10	113, 115, 118
11:10	10, 29, 113
11:11	15, 129
11:11–12	116
11:13–16	113, 115
11:16	3, 115, 118
11:17	114
11:21	27, 116
11:23	117
11:24–26	117
11:25	7, 117, 139
11:26–29	56, 106, 117
11:30–31	107, 117
11:32	9, 117, 140
11:33–34	117, 127, 129
11:35–40	3, 7, 117, 139
12:1–2	5, 15–16, 18, 58, 113, 115
12:1–13	15, 56
12:3	135
12:3–29	135–36
12:4	135
12:5–6	135
12:7	6
12:7–11	136
12:8	17, 55, 128, 136
12:9	5
12:11	127
12:12–13	136
12:14	136
12:15–16	136
12:16	22, 139
12:17	100, 109, 136
12:18–21	7
12:18–27	136
12:19	129
12:22	5, 7, 18, 89, 98, 107, 115
12:23	7–8, 58, 107, 127
12:24	3, 107, 114
12:24–27	107
12:26	8
12:27–28	17, 21, 136
12:29	7, 107, 136
13:1	114, 138
13:1–24	2, 138
13:2	138
13:3	139
13:4	114, 139
13:5–6	139
13:7–9	101, 118
13:7–17	63–64, 101, 117–18, 139
13:9–10	101–2, 114, 118
13:11	102, 118, 131
13:12	48, 102, 118, 131
13:13	102, 113, 118
13:14–15	7, 29, 101, 103, 113, 115, 118–19
13:16	103, 118–19
13:17	119, 139
13:18	49, 139–40
13:19	139–40
13:20	6, 8, 97, 140–41
13:20–21	138, 140–41
13:22–23	138, 140–41
13:23	1, 138, 141
13:24	138
13:25	138, 141

Scripture Index

James

5:13–18	139

1 Peter

1	11, 87, 96, 114
2:5–3:17	48, 114, 118–19
2:22–25	48, 88–89
3:7	61
3:15–21	49, 119, 132, 140
3:22	3
5:7	139

2 Peter

1:10	93
2	116

1 John

1:1	6
2:1–2	50
5:14–15	17, 50

Jude

25	11, 21

Revelations

3:12	18, 89, 98
12:11	135
16:1–18:6	48
20:9	134
21:2–10	18, 89, 98, 139
22:15	139

www.ingramcontent.com/pod-product-compliance
Lightning Source LLC
Chambersburg PA
CBHW071455150426
43191CB00008B/1348